Communications
in Computer and Information Science   448

Zbigniew Kotulski   Bogdan Księżopolski
Katarzyna Mazur (Eds.)

Cryptography and Security Systems

Third International Conference, CSS 2014
Lublin, Poland, September 22-24, 2014
Proceedings

 Springer

Volume Editors

Zbigniew Kotulski
Warsaw University of Technology, Poland
E-mail: zkotulsk@tele.pw.edu.pl

Bogdan Księżopolski
Maria Curie-Skłodowska University in Lublin, Poland
and
Polish-Japanese Institute of Information Technology
Warsaw, Poland
E-mail: bogdan.ksiezopolski@acm.org

Katarzyna Mazur
Maria Curie-Skłodowska University in Lublin, Poland
E-mail: katarzyna.mazur@umcs.pl

ISSN 1865-0929   e-ISSN 1865-0937
ISBN 978-3-662-44892-2   e-ISBN 978-3-662-44893-9
DOI 10.1007/978-3-662-44893-9
Springer Heidelberg New York Dordrecht London

Library of Congress Control Number: 2014948498

Typesetting: Camera-ready by author, data conversion by Scientific Publishing Services, Chennai, India

Printed on acid-free paper

Springer is part of Springer Science+Business Media (www.springer.com)

Preface

Cryptography and security systems are two fields of security research that strongly interact and complement each other. The series of International Conferences on Cryptography and Security Systems (CSS) is a forum for presentation of theoretical and applied research papers, case studies, implementation experiences, as well as work-in-progress results in these two disciplines. The conference especially invites young researchers and PhD students who have an opportunity to share their results with colleagues, invited keynote lecturers, and the Program Committee members actively participating in conference sessions.

The present volume of the *Communications in Computer and Information Science* series contains 17 papers selected from 43 submissions to the Third International Conferences on Cryptography and Security Systems (CSS 2014) held during September 22–24, 2014, in Lublin, Poland. Seven of these papers concern different areas of cryptography, while the remaining ten deal with recent problems of cryptographic protocols.

The "Numerical Semigroups and Bounds on Impossible Differential Attacks on Generalized Feistel Scheme" by Alexander Toktarev and Maria Pudovkina opens the cryptographic section of this volume. The authors investigate a class of ciphers described as a generalized Feistel scheme. Using the graph theory and the number theory, they provide upper and lower bounds for the maximum number of rounds when an impossible differential technique is applicable. These bounds do not depend on a type of Feistel scheme and a number of nonlinear functions or blocks in the register. In the next paper, entitled "Encrypting Huffman-Encoded Data by Substituting Pairs of Code Words Without Changing the Bit Count of a Pair," Marek Parfieniuk and Piotr Jankowski present a method of combining the Huffman coding with encryption. The encryption is based on replacing the codewords, pair-by-pair, in such a way that the sums of the codeword lengths of an original pair and its substitute are equal. The method preserves the structures and lengths of the bitstreams, which is an advantage if such a bit stream is embedded in a higher-level data container, like a multimedia file. "On Multivariate Cryptosystems Based on Polynomially Compressed Maps with Invertible Decomposition" by Vasyl Ustimenko and Urszula Romańczuk-Polubiec is the third paper in the volume. It presents the concept and the explicit construction of the family of polynomially compressed multivariate maps by relations of degree k with invertible decomposition. Such a construction is based on the edge-transitive family of graphs and uses the equations of a connected component of the graph. The approach introduced by the authors allows one to obtain an effective multivariate public key cryptosystem. An extensively studied problem of pseudo-random number generation is the subject of "Statistical Analysis of the Chaos-Driven Elliptic Curve Pseudo-random Number Generators" by Omar Reyad and Zbigniew Kotulski. The authors propose a method improvement of the well-known Elliptic Curve Pseudo-Random Number Generator by combining it with a Chaotic Pseudo-Random Number Generator. The resultant algorithm has better statistical properties and is computationally more effective than separate component algorithms. Another recent extensively studied problem, which is identity-based cryptography, is discussed in "Identity-Based Cryptography in Credit Card Payments" by Kimmo Halunen and Mirko Sailio. The authors propose a method of how to apply identity-based cryptography to credit card payments, to reduce the possibility of credit card fraud that is prevalent on the Internet. Since the method requires some changes to the functionality of the credit cards standards, it is not an immediate remedy, but rather a recommendation for the future. And finally, the papers concluding the cryptographic track of this volume are devoted to two different applications of graphs. The paper "On a Cipher Based on Pseudo-random Walks on Graphs" by Wit Foryś, Piotr Oprocha, and Łukasz Jęda presents a cryptosystem that uses wandering on a graph in the process of encryption and also exploits some ideas of dynamical systems (symbolic dynamics), while the paper "On LDPC Codes Based on Families of Expanding Graphs of Increasing Girth Without Edge-Transitive Automorphism Groups" by Monika Polak and Vasyl Ustimenko introduces new examples of low-density parity check codes connected with new families of regular graphs of bounded degree and increasing girth.

The second section of this volume represents cryptographic protocols, which dominated the submissions at CSS 2014. It covers both theoretical models of cryptographic protocols, e.g., secure secret sharing schemes or key establishment protocols and protocols in practically used networks (peer-to-peer, wireless sensor networks, real-time transmissions), and Web services, e.g., electronic payments or Bitcoin. Thus, the first paper in this section, prepared by Jakub Muszyński, Sebastien Sébastien, Juan Luis Jiménez Laredo, and Pascal Bouvry, entitled "Analysis of the Data Flow in the Newscast Protocol for Possible Vulnerabilities," deals with a simple, peer-to-peer data exchange protocol. The authors analyze the robustness of the data flow within the Newscast model against a set of vulnerabilities that have not been taken into account in previous analysis. They demonstrate the attack based on a cache content corruption that is able to defeat the protocol by breaking the network connectivity and perform experiments using a framework that implements both the protocol and a corruption model. The next paper, "Efficient Verifiable Multi-secret Sharing Based on Y.C.H Scheme," by Appala Naidu Tentu and Appa Rao Allam, presents an efficient verifiable multi-secret sharing protocol employing an identity based signature scheme, that uses the identities of the participants in this scheme. This scheme does not require the pre-secure communication between dealer and participants or the exponential functions for the verification, and efficiently resists the dealer/participant(s)' cheating behavior. A new lightweight authentication protocol for RFID systems based on non-linear feedback shift register sequences generated by the position digit algebra function is proposed in the paper of Ferucio Laurențiu Țiplea entitled "A Lightweight Authentication Protocol for RFID." The applied function uses only *radix r* additions, which makes the protocol computationally efficient. Aditionally, random sequences generated by this function have a large average period, which results in good privacy and security properties of the protocol. The following "Long-Term Secure Two-Round Group Key Establishment from Pairings," authored by Kashi Neupane, deals with the concept of the long-term security of a protocol, which means resistance against attacks even if later, after completion of the protocol, some security assumptions become invalid. It proposes an authenticated two-round group key establishment protocol, which remains secure if a Computational Bilinear Diffie-Hellman problem is hard, or a server, that shares a symmetric key with each user, is uncorrupted. The paper "Optimizing SHA256 in Bitcoin Mining," written by Nicolas Courtois, Rahuk Naik, and Marek Grajek, revisits the cryptographic process that allows one to make money by producing new bitcoins. It reformulates this problem as a specific sort of constrained input and small output (CISO) hashing problem and reduces it to a pure block cipher problem. The proposed optimizations enable bitcoin miners to save countless millions of dollars per year in electricity bills. Another paper dealing with electronic money is "Protocol for Detection of Counterfeit Transactions in Electronic Currency Exchange" authored by Marek Ogiela and Piotr Sułkowski. The authors present an improvement to Chaum's anonymous currency exchange protocol, and show its vulnerability to serious fraud by both the client and the seller after an electronic coin is spent at least twice. They also propose an improved system based on its original offline version. The next paper by Imed El Fray, Tomasz Hyla, Mirosław Kurkowski, Witold Maćków, and Jerzy Pejaś, "Practical Authentication Protocols for Protecting and Sharing Sensitive Information on Mobile Devices," presents an architecture of the MobInfoSec system for sharing documents with sensitive information using fine-grained access rules described by general access structures. They allow one to establish secure communication channels between different system components, which is exploited in the proposed conference protocol with key transport and key establishment mechanisms. In the paper "Secure Multihop Key Establishment Protocols for Wireless Sensor Networks," Ismail Mansour, Gérard Chalhoub, and Pascal Lafourcade propose four secure multihop key establishment protocols based on elliptic curve cryptography (ECC). For each protocol, they make a formal security proof using the automatic tool Scyther, and, in order to evaluate their performances, present results of implementation on testbeds using TelosB motes and TinyOS. The discussion of protocol' modelling languages is the subject of the paper "Comparison and Assessment of Security Modeling Approaches in Terms of the QoP-ML" by Katarzyna Mazur and Bogdan Ksiezopolski. The authors focus on their capabilities to model relevant information during different phases of the security analysis of protocols. To assess and compare miscellaneous modelling systems, they use a systematic methodology to point out their promiscuous aspects in the context of the QoP-ML language. The last paper in the section on cryptographic protocols is "Context-Aware Secure Routing Protocol for Real-Time Services" by Grzegorz Oryńczak and Zbigniew Kotulski. It proposes a context-aware secure routing protocol suitable for real-time services. The introduced framework systemizes the roles of all actors in establishing optimally

Organization

Third International Conference on Cryptography and Security Systems (CSS 2014) was organized by the Faculty of Mathematics, Physics and Computer Science, Maria Sklodowska-Curie University of Lublin, Poland, and the Faculty of Electronics and Information Technology, Warsaw University of Technology, Poland.

Conference Chair

Zbigniew Kotulski	Warsaw University of Technology, Poland
Bogdan Księżopolski	Maria Sklodowska-Curie University and Polish-Japanese Institute of Information Technology, Poland

Technical Volume Editor

Katarzyna Mazur	Maria Sklodowska-Curie University, Poland

Organizing Committee

Bogdan Księżopolski - Chair	Maria Sklodowska-Curie University and Polish-Japanese Institute of Information Technology, Poland
Zbigniew Kotulski	Warsaw University of Technology, Poland
Damian Rusinek	Maria Sklodowska-Curie University, Poland
Katarzyna Mazur	Maria Sklodowska-Curie University, Poland
Urszula Romańczuk-Polubiec	Maria Sklodowska-Curie University, Poland

Program Committee

Pascal Bouvry	University of Luxembourg, Luxembourg
Nicolas T. Courtois	University College London, UK
Stefan Dziembowski	University of Warsaw, Poland, and University of Rome, Italy
Krzysztof Gaj	George Mason University, USA
Piotr Gajewski	Military University of Technology, Poland
Janusz Górski	Gdańsk University of Technology, Poland
Jaime Gutierrez	University of Cantabria, Spain

Marek Klonowski	Wrocław University of Technology, Poland
Zbigniew Kotulski	Warsaw University of Technology, Poland (Chair)
Mieczysław Kula	University of Silesia, Poland
Pascal Lafourcade	LIMOS, d'Auvergne University, Blaise Pascal University, France
Franck Leprévost	University of Luxembourg, Luxembourg
Marek R. Ogiela	AGH University of Science and Technology, Poland
Björn Ottersten	University of Luxembourg, Luxembourg
Josef Pieprzyk	Macquarie University, Australia
Jacek Pomykała	University of Warsaw, Poland
Peter Ryan	University of Luxembourg, Luxembourg
Franciszek Seredyński	Cardinal Stefan Wyszynski University, Poland
Janusz Stokłosa	Poznań University of Technology, Poland
Vasyl Ustimenko	Maria Sklodowska-Curie University, Poland

Reviewers

Table of Contents

Numerical Semigroups and Bounds on Impossible Differential Attacks on Generalized Feistel Schemes

Marina Pudovkina and Alexander Toktarev

National Nuclear Research University,
Moscow Engineering-Physics Institute,
Moscow, Kashirskoe shosse 31, Russian Federation
maricap@rambler.ru, toktarev@gmail.com

Abstract. In this paper, we investigate a class of ciphers which can be described as a generalized Feistel scheme. Using the graph theory and the number theory, we provide upper and lower bounds for the maximum number of rounds when impossible differential technique is applicable for any cipher from the family. These estimations do not depend on the type of Feistel scheme and the number of non-linear functions.

Keywords: block cipher, generalized Feistel scheme, impossible differential, differential probability.

1 Introduction

Impossible differential technique is one of the most popular cryptanalytic tools for block ciphers. It was firstly proposed by L. Knudsen to analyze DEAL [2] in 1998 and then extended by E. Biham to attack Skipjack [1]. Until now the impossible differential technique has shown its superiority over the differential technique in many block ciphers such as IDEA, Skipjack, CLEFIA and AES. Unlike the traditional differential technique which uses differential characteristics with high probabilities to recover the right key, the impossible differential technique is a sieving method which exploits differentials with probability zero to retrieve the right key filtering out all the wrong keys.

Several factors influence the success of impossible differential technique, including the length of the impossible differentials, specific input/output difference patterns and the strength of one-round encryption/decryption. Among them, the most important factor is the length of an impossible differential. The longer the impossible differential is, the better the attack will be. Another important factor is the input/output difference pattern when two impossible differentials have the same length, because the new impossible differentials may well result in improved attacks. If we find more impossible differentials, we can perform a successful attack to improve the time/data complexities of known attacks with high probabilities.

Z. Kotulski et al. (Eds.): CSS 2014, CCIS 448, pp. 1–11, 2014.
© Springer-Verlag Berlin Heidelberg 2014

In this paper, we introduce an universal mathematical description of generalized Feistel schemes. We have taken into account the results from paper [13] and collected together all types of GFS to one mathematical model. We have also proposed an approach to evaluate the security of GFS against impossible differential technique using an estimation of the upper and lower bounds for the maximal number of rounds when impossible differential technique is applicable for any cipher from the family. Some papers [9,3] contain the estimations of the mentioned maximal number of rounds but these estimations are valid just for special types of GFS. Unlike them we have proposed an approach to get these estimations for an arbitrary GFS.

This paper is organized as follows: In Section 2 we give main mathematical notions and a description of a mathematical model for GFS. In Section 3 we give the detailed mathematical description of the impossible differential technique and its application to GFS. In Section 4 we show a graph-based approach to describe properties of GFS. In Section 5 we present the numerical semigroup based approach to estimate the lower and upper bounds of the maximal number of rounds to apply the impossible differential technique. Finally, we conclude in Section 6.

2   Notations and Descriptions

2.1   Notations

We will use the following notations: $\mathbb{N}$ is the set of all natural numbers; $\mathbb{N}_0 = \mathbb{N} \bigcup \{0\}$; $m, d, c \in \mathbb{N}$; $n = d \cdot m$; $c \in \{1, ..., m\}$; $V_q = \{0, 1\}^q$; $B^\times = B \backslash \{0\}$; $A = (A, A')$ is a partition of the set $\{1, ..., m\}$ into two subsets A, A'; $A^{(m)}$ is the set of all ordered partitions of the set $\{1, ..., m\}$ into two subsets; $P(B)$ is the set of all subsets of B; $S(B)$ is the set of all permutations on B; $k = (k_1, ..., k_c) \in V_d^c$;

$$f_i : V_d^2 \to V_d, f_{i,k_i}(\alpha) = f_i(\alpha, k_i) \tag{1}$$

for all $\alpha \in V_d$, $i = 1, ..., c$;

$$F_d^{(c)} = \left\{ (f_1, ..., f_c) \,|\, f_i : V_d^2 \to V_d, i = 1, ..., c \right\}. \tag{2}$$

$\oplus$ is the bit-wise XOR operation; $\beta_1 \oplus ... \oplus \beta_t = \bigoplus_{i=1}^t \beta_i$, $\beta_i \in V_q$; $\bar{0}$ is the zero vector of V_d.

2.2   Generalized Feistel Schemes Descriptions

Feistel-like schemes come in several flavours beyond the *classical* one used in DES. Speaking of the generalized Feistel schemes, we want to encompass most all of them. There are type-1, type-2, and type-3 Feistel schemes, as described in [6]. Well-known block ciphers that use the generalized Feistel schemes include Skipjack (an unbalanced Feistel scheme), BEAR/LION (alternating). The detailed classifications of 4-cell GFSs are presented in [13] and shown in Figure 1.

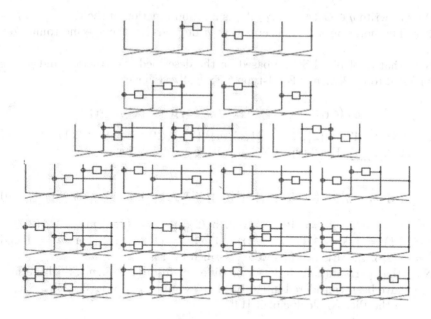

Fig. 1. 4-cell GFS examples

Now we introduce a mathematical model which includes these types of generalization. Consider a family of GFSs defined by: the number c, the partition $A = (A, A') \in A^{(m)}$, the mappings $\chi : A' \to P(A)$, $f \in F_d^{(c)}$, and the bijective mappings $\rho \in S(\{1, ..., m\})$, $\varphi : X(A') \to \{1, ..., c\}$, where $X(A') = \bigcup_{i \in A', j \in \chi(i)} (i, j)$.

Let us also consider the transformations $v_\rho, h_k \in S(V_d^m)$ such that:

$$
\begin{aligned}
v_\rho &: (\alpha_1, ..., \alpha_m) \mapsto \left(\alpha_{\rho^{-1}(1)}, ..., \alpha_{\rho^{-1}(m)} \right), \\
h_k &: (\alpha_1, ..., \alpha_m) \mapsto (\alpha'_1, ..., \alpha'_m),
\end{aligned}
\tag{3}
$$

where

$$
\alpha'_i = \begin{cases} \alpha_i & \text{if } i \in A \\ \alpha_i \oplus \bigoplus_{j \in \chi(i)} f_{\varphi(i,j), k_{\varphi(i,j)}}(\alpha_j), & \text{if } i \in A' . \end{cases}
\tag{4}
$$

GFS is defined by $g_k \in S(V_d^m)$, where $g_k = v_\rho \circ h_k$ is a round function of a block cipher based on the described construction. The l-round encryption function under the key $k = (k^{(1)}, ..., k^{(l)}) \in (V_d^c)^l$ is equal to $g_{k^{(l)}}...g_{k^{(1)}}$.

The family of GFS with a fixed set $(A, \chi, \varphi, \rho)_c$ will be called $(A, \chi, \varphi, \rho)_c$-family. Each specific block cipher from the $(A, \chi, \varphi, \rho)_c$-family is given by fixing $f \in F_d^{(c)}$ and called $(A, \chi, \varphi, \rho, f)_c$-cipher. Let $G_c(A, \chi, \varphi, \rho)$ be the set of all $(A, \chi, \varphi, \rho, f)_c$-ciphers.

We will write $g \in G_c(A, \chi, \varphi, \rho)$ if g is a round function of the $(A, \chi, \varphi, \rho, f)_c$-cipher. The notation $g_{k^{(i)}}$ indicates that g depends on the specific round key $k^{(i)}$.

Note that a lot of GFSs are based on the described construction and ρ^{-1} is often equal to $(1, 2, ..., m)$. For 1-type GFS [5,4], we have:

$$g_k : (\alpha_1, ..., \alpha_m) \mapsto (\alpha_2 \oplus f_{1,k_1}(\alpha_1), \alpha_5, ..., \alpha_m, \alpha_1) , \tag{5}$$

where $c = 1$, $A' = \{2\}$, $A = \{1, ..., m\} \backslash \{2\}$, $\chi(2) = \{1\}$, $\varphi(2, 1) = 1$ and $\rho^{-1} = (1, 2, ..., m)$. For 2-type GFS [6] with even m, we have:

$$g_k : (\alpha_1, ..., \alpha_m) \mapsto (\alpha_2 \oplus f_{1,k_1}(\alpha_1), \alpha_3, \alpha_4 \oplus f_{2,k_2}(\alpha_3), \alpha_3, ..., \alpha_m, \alpha_1) , \tag{6}$$

where $c = m/2$, $A' = \{2i | i \in \{1, ..., m/2\}\}$, $A = \{1, ..., m\} \backslash A'$, $\chi(2i) = \varphi(2i, i - 1) = \{i\}$, $i \in \{1, ..., m/2\}$ and $\rho^{-1} = (1, 2, ..., m)$. For $m = 4$ and $\rho^{-1} = (1, 2, 3, 4)$, various GFSs were classified in [13].

Note that permutations ρ^{-1} can be different from $(1, 2, ..., m)$. Such permutations have been considered in [10,14]. For example, $\rho^{-1} = (1, 3, 5, 7)(2, 8, 6, 4)$ is used in the Piccolo block cipher [14].

3   Impossible Differential Technique

The main idea of impossible differential technique is to specify a differential with zero probability over some rounds of the cipher. Then we can derive the right keys by discarding the wrong keys which lead to impossible differential. The key step of impossible differential technique is to retrieve the longest impossible differential. The main technique is miss-in-middle [15], namely to find two differential characteristics with probability 1 from the encryption and decryption directions and connect them together. When there are some inconsistencies, their combination is the impossible differential that we are looking for.

The existence of the impossible differential for r-round GFS after r rounds implies that impossible differential technique can be applicable for any cipher from the family. To analyze the security of GFS it is important to estimate the maximal number of rounds r for which the impossible differential technique can be applicable for any cipher from the family.

In this section we consider an arbitrary $(A, \chi, \varphi, \rho)_c$-family. Let $\alpha^{(0)}$ be an n-bit plaintext, δ be a nonzero n-bit difference. For $\delta \in V_n^{\times}$ we will estimate upper and lower bounds of the number of rounds $r = r_{A,\chi,\varphi,\rho}(\delta)$ satisfying the following conditions:

1. For any $g \in G_c(A, \chi, \varphi, \rho)$, $(k^{(1)}, ..., k^{(r)}) \in (V_d^c)^r$, $\alpha^{(0)} \in V_n$ and some $\delta' \in V_n^{\times}$ we have:

$$g_{k^{(r)}} ... g_{k^{(1)}}(\alpha^{(0)}) \oplus g_{k^{(r)}} ... g_{k^{(1)}}(\delta \oplus \alpha^{(0)}) \neq \delta' . \tag{7}$$

2. For some $\delta' \in V_n^{\times}$ there exist $\alpha^{(0)} \in V_n$, $g \in G_c(A, \chi, \varphi, \rho)$, $(k^{(1)}, ..., k^{(r+1)}) \in (V_d^c)^{r+1}$, such that:

$$g_{k^{(r+1)}} ... g_{k^{(1)}} \left(\alpha^{(0)} \right) \oplus g_{k^{(r+1)}} ... g_{k^{(1)}} \left(\delta \oplus \alpha^{(0)} \right) = \delta' . \tag{8}$$

Let

$$r_{A,\chi,\varphi,\rho} = \max \left\{ r_{A,\chi,\varphi,\rho}(\delta) | \delta \in V_n^{\times} \right\} \tag{9}$$

and l be an arbitrary number, $l > r_{A,\chi,\varphi,\rho}$. Then $r_{A,\chi,\varphi,\rho}$ is the largest number of rounds such that any l-round $(A, \chi, \varphi, \rho, f)_c$-cipher does not have impossible differentials. So all elements of its differential matrix are nonzero.

Some $(A, \chi, \varphi, \rho)_c$-families have impossible differentials for any number of rounds $l \in \mathbb{N}$. It means that:

$$g_{k^{(r+1)}} ... g_{k^{(1)}} \left(\alpha^{(0)} \right) \oplus g_{k^{(r+1)}} ... g_{k^{(1)}} \left(\delta \oplus \alpha^{(0)} \right) = \delta' \tag{10}$$

for some $g \in G_c(A, \chi, \varphi, \rho)$, $(k^{(1)}, ..., k^{(l)}) \in (V_d^c)^l$, $\alpha^{(0)} \in V_n$, $(\delta, \delta') \in (V_d^{\times})^2$. In that case we suppose $r_{A,\chi,\varphi,\rho} = \infty$. If $r_{A,\chi,\varphi,\rho}$ is finite then after some (finite) number of rounds the $(A, \chi, \varphi, \rho)_c$-family does not have impossible differentials.

There are different estimations of $r_{A,\chi,\varphi,\rho}$ which have been obtained in papers [3,9] for the special type of GFS. In [3], L. Knudsen proved that there always exist 5-round impossible differentials for type-1 Feistel scheme with bijective round functions. In [9], it was proved that the maximal number of rounds for the impossible differential for type-2 4-cell GFS is equal to 6.

To obtain the upper and lower bounds of $r_{A,\chi,\varphi,\rho}$, we consider the additive commutative semigroup $(D, \oplus)$ given on a set $D = \{\gamma, \Delta, \tilde{0}\}$. The similar set with 5 elements has been proposed in [10]. It is defined in the following way:

Table 1. Set of elements defined for $(D, \oplus)$

$\oplus$	γ	Δ	0
γ	Δ	Δ	γ
Δ	Δ	Δ	Δ
0	γ	Δ	0

Note that $\tilde{0}$ means that the difference in the given cell is always zero for any key; γ means that the difference in the given cell is always nonzero for any key; Δ means that the difference in the given cell can take any value for some key.

For arbitrary vectors $\alpha_1 = \left(\alpha_1^{(1)}, ..., \alpha_1^{(m)} \right)$, $\alpha_2 = \left(\alpha_2^{(1)}, ..., \alpha_2^{(m)} \right)$ from V_d^m denote $\alpha_1 \to \alpha_2$ or:

$$\left(\alpha_1^{(1)}, ..., \alpha_1^{(m)} \right) \to \left(\alpha_2^{(1)}, ..., \alpha_2^{(m)} \right) \tag{11}$$

if there exist a round key $k \in V_d^c$ and plaintexts $x_1, x_2 \in V_d^m$ such that:

$$\alpha_1 = x_1 \oplus x_2, \quad \alpha_2 = g_k(x_1) \oplus g_k(x_2) . \tag{12}$$

Let us give an example which describes a differential characteristic based on the introduced semigroup. Consider the following GFS:

$$g_k : (\alpha_1, \alpha_2, \alpha_3, \alpha_4) \mapsto (\alpha_2, \alpha_3 \oplus f_{1,k}(\alpha_4), \alpha_4, \alpha_1) . \tag{13}$$

The differential characteristic is:

$$
\begin{aligned}
(\tilde{0}, \tilde{0}, \gamma, \tilde{0}) &\rightarrow (\tilde{0}, \gamma, \tilde{0}, \tilde{0}) \rightarrow (\gamma, \tilde{0}, \tilde{0}, \tilde{0}) \rightarrow \\
(\tilde{0}, \tilde{0}, \tilde{0}, \gamma) &\rightarrow (\tilde{0}, \Delta, \gamma, \tilde{0}) \rightarrow (\Delta, \gamma, \tilde{0}, \tilde{0}) \rightarrow \\
(\gamma, \tilde{0}, \tilde{0}, \Delta) &\rightarrow (\tilde{0}, \Delta, \Delta, \gamma) \rightarrow (\Delta, \Delta, \gamma, \tilde{0}) \rightarrow \\
(\Delta, \gamma, \tilde{0}, \Delta) &\rightarrow (\Delta, \gamma, \Delta, \Delta) \rightarrow (\gamma, \Delta, \Delta, \Delta) \rightarrow \\
(\Delta, \Delta, \Delta, \gamma) &\rightarrow (\Delta, \Delta, \gamma, \Delta) \rightarrow (\Delta, \Delta, \Delta, \Delta) .
\end{aligned}
\tag{14}
$$

As we can see after 14 rounds there is no impossible differential.

Apparently, the maximal number of rounds for which the impossible differential exists depends on the input differential. We show that the maximal number of rounds can be achieved if just one cell of the input differential is nonzero, the other cells are zero.

Proposition 1. *For an arbitrary* $(A, \chi, \varphi, \rho)_c$- *family,* $i \in \{1, ..., m\}$ *and*

$$\delta = (\bar{0}, ..., \bar{0}, \delta_i, \bar{0}, ..., \bar{0}), \delta' = (\delta_1', \delta_2', ..., \delta_{m-1}', \delta_m') , \tag{15}$$

where $\delta_i, \delta_i', \delta_j'$ *are nonzero d-bit cell's differences for some* $j \in \{1, ...m\}, i \neq j$, *we have:*

$$r_{A, \chi, \varphi, \rho}(\delta') \leq r_{A, \chi, \varphi, \rho}(\delta). \tag{16}$$

Proof. The technical proof of the results is omitted due to the page limit. □

Proposition 2. *For an arbitrary* $(A, \chi, \varphi, \rho)_c$–*family we have:*

$$r_{A, \chi, \varphi, \rho} = r_{A, \chi, \varphi, \rho}(\delta) , \tag{17}$$

where:

$$\delta = \left(\bar{0}, ..., \bar{0}, \underbrace{\alpha}_{i}, \bar{0}, ..., \bar{0} \right) \in V_d^m \tag{18}$$

for some $i \in \{1, ..., m\}, \alpha \in V_d^\times$.

Proof. The proof is obvious. □

Thus, to find the lower bound for $r_{A, \chi, \varphi, \rho}$ we should consider only differentials with one non-zero coordinate.

4 Graph Representation of GFS

For the given $(A, \chi, \varphi, \rho)_c$-family we consider a directed labelled graph $\Gamma_{A,\chi,\varphi,\rho} = (X, Y)$ with the set of vertices X and the set of arcs Y. There is one to one mapping between the vertices of $\Gamma_{A,\chi,\varphi,\rho}$ and cells of GFS. Each vertex has the same number as the corresponding cell. There is an arch between the vertex i and the vertex j if the j-th cell depends on the i-th cell after one round of GFS, in other words if one of the following conditions is true:

1. $\rho(i) = j$,
2. $i \in A$ and $\exists\, l \in A'$ such that $i \in \chi(l)$, $\rho(l) = j$.

If the first condition is true, then the arch does not have a label. Otherwise, if the second condition is true, then the arch is labelled with Φ.

Using the introduced notations, we give an example of a graph corresponding to GFS. Consider the GFS given as:

$$g_k : (\alpha_1, \alpha_2, \alpha_3, \alpha_4) \mapsto (\alpha_2, \alpha_3 \oplus f_{1,k}(\alpha_4), \alpha_4, \alpha_1) \tag{19}$$

this GFS belongs to the $(A, \chi, \varphi, \rho)_c$-family with the parameters:

$$A = (A, A'), (A = \{1, 2, 4\}, A' = \{3\}),$$
$$\chi(3) = \{4\}, \varphi(3,4) = 1, \rho = (1, 4, 3, 2), A = 1. \tag{20}$$

The corresponding graph can be represented on Figure 2.

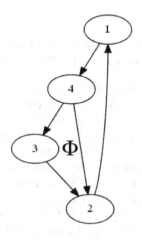

Fig. 2. Graph for GFS

5 Numerical Semigroups with Generators and Estimations

5.1 Some Definitions from the Theory of the Numerical Semigroups

Further in this work, we will use the theory of numerical semigroups. First let us recall the definition of the numerical semigroup.

Definition 1. *Let M be a semigroup from $\mathbb{N}_0$ closed under addition. A numerical semigroup generated by $d_1, \ldots, d_v \in \mathbb{N}$ is defined as:*

$$M = \langle d_1, \ldots, d_v \rangle = \left\{ \sum_{i=1}^{v} n_i d_i \middle| \, n_i \in \mathbb{N}_0 \right\}. \tag{21}$$

Let U be a set of all numerical semigroups. Let $g : U \to \mathbb{N}_0$ be a mapping for the given numerical semigroup which defines the Frobenius number – the biggest non-negative integer which does not belong to this semigroup.

The diameter of an arbitrary graph Γ, denoted by $d(\Gamma)$, is the maximal shortest way between its vertices.

Definition 2. *A primitive graph is a strongly connected graph if GCD of lengths of all its simple cycles is equal to one.*

Definition 3. *A simple cycle is a cycle with no repeated vertices.*

For an arbitrary cycle w of graph denoted as $len(w)$ its length. For any two vertices with the numbers $i, j \in \{1, ..., m\}$ denote as $o(i, j)$ the length of the shortage oriented path from the vertex with the number i to the vertex with the number j.

5.2 Construction of the Set of Generators for the Numerical Semigroup for Each Vertex of the Primitive Graph $\Gamma_{A,\chi,\varphi,\rho}$

Estimations of the maximal number of rounds $r_{A,\chi,\varphi,\rho}$ for which the impossible differential technique can be applicable for any cipher from $(A, \chi, \varphi, \rho)_c$-family will be given using the maximal Frobenius number of the semigroups which are constructed for each vertex of the graph $\Gamma_{A,\chi,\varphi,\rho}$ corresponding to GFS.

In this subsection, for each vertex of the graph $\Gamma_{A,\chi,\varphi,\rho}$ we describe an algorithm to construct a set of generators for the corresponding numerical semigroup. After that we can calculate the Frobenius number for each numerical semigroup constructed for all vertices of the graph $\Gamma_{A,\chi,\varphi,\rho}$.

The algorithm consists of two steps. In the first step, we construct semigroup's generators corresponding to each vertex. In the second step, we find the Frobenius numbers to construct the numerical semigroups. Finally, we output the highest Frobenius number obtained.

Algorithm 1. Finding the maximal Frobenius number

Input: graph $\Gamma_{A,\chi,\varphi,\rho}$
Output: g_{max}

I For each vertex i, do:
  1. Find all simple cycles which contain vertex i and denote this set as C_i.
  2. For each simple cycle w from C_i, do:
    2.1. $s := w$, $C_{i,w} := \emptyset$.
    2.2. For each vertex which belongs to the cycle s (except vertex w) do:
      a Find all simple cycles (except s) which contain vertex j and denote this set as C_j.
      b If the set C_j is not empty then add all its cycles to the set $C_{i,w}$.
      c For each simple cycle s' from C_j define s equal to s' and repeat iterations a,b,c.
    2.3. Compute the set:

$$G\left(i, w\right) = \left\{ len(w) + \sum_{d \in C_{w,i}} m_k d \mid 0 \leq m_k < len(w) \right\}. \qquad (22)$$

II For each vertex i compute the Frobenius number of the semigroup $\left\langle \bigcup_{d \in C_i} G(i,d) \right\rangle$.

III Find the maximal over all Frobenius numbers calculated in step II. Denote it as g_{max}.

Definition 4. *Let p_{max} be the length of the maximal simple cycle of graph $\Gamma_{A,\chi,\varphi,\rho}$.*

Now we will give an example of algorithm application to the GFS defined as:

$$g_k : (\alpha_1, \alpha_2, \alpha_3, \alpha_4) \mapsto (\alpha_2, \alpha_3, \alpha_4, \alpha_1 \oplus f_{1,k}(\alpha_4)), \qquad (23)$$

which belongs to the $(A, \chi, \varphi, \rho)_c$-family with parameters:

$$A = (A, A'), (A = \{2, 3, 4\}, A' = \{1\}),$$
$$\chi(1) = \{4\}, \varphi(1, 4) = 1, \rho = (1, 4, 3, 2), A = 1. \qquad (24)$$

The algorithm consists of the following steps. Note that the graph in Figure 3 contains two simple cycles. The first of them (denoted as w_1) contains all vertices from the set $\{1, 2, 3, 4\}$. The second of them (denoted as w_2) contains one vertex 4. Applying algorithm 1 we get $g_{max} = 3$.

5.3   Estimations of the Maximal Number of Rounds $r_{A,\chi,\varphi,\rho}$

Firstly, we give necessary and sufficient conditions for finiteness of $r_{A,\chi,\varphi,\rho}$ using properties of the graph $\Gamma_{A,\chi,\varphi,\rho}$.

Proposition 3. *For an arbitrary* $(A, \chi, \varphi, \rho)_c$*-family* $r_{A,\chi,\varphi,\rho}$ *is finite iff* $\Gamma_{A,\chi,\varphi,\rho}$ *is primitive.*

Proof. The technical proof of the results is omitted due to the page limit.   □

Note that if $r_{A,\chi,\varphi,\rho}$ is infinite then all ciphers from the $(A, \chi, \varphi, \rho)_c$- family are not secure against impossible differential technique.

Next proposition gives us lower and upper bounds $r_{A,\chi,\varphi,\rho}$ when it is finite. This is the main result of this paper.

Proposition 4. *For any family* $(A, \chi, \varphi, \rho)_c$ *whose graph* $\Gamma_{A,\chi,\varphi,\rho}$ *is primitive, we have:*

$$\max\left(g_{max}, d\left(\Gamma_{A,\chi,\varphi,\rho}\right)\right) \leq r_{A,\chi,\varphi,\rho} \leq g_{\max} + d\left(\Gamma_{A,\chi,\varphi,\rho}\right) + p_{max} . \qquad (25)$$

Proof. The technical proof of the results is omitted due to the page limit.   □

Now using the results of Proposition 4, we give an example how to find upper and lower bounds for the type-1 GFS. Consider the $(A, \chi, \varphi, \rho)_c$- family such that $A = \{i\}$, $A' = \{j\}$ for some $i, j \in \{1, \ldots, m\}$, $\chi(j) = i$ (type-1 GFS). It is clear that the graph $\Gamma_{A,\chi,\varphi,\rho}$ corresponding to the family is combination of two simple cycles with m vertices. It is clear that $d\left(\Gamma_{A,\chi,\varphi,\rho}\right) = m - 1$. The length of the maximal simple cycle is equal to m. Apparently that $g\left(\langle m + o\left(i, j\right), m\rangle\right)$ is the greatest number when $o\left(i, j\right) = m - 1$. From the Sylvester's theorem [11], we have:

$$g_{max} = g\left(\langle 2m - 1, m\rangle\right) = 2m\left(m - 1\right) . \qquad (26)$$

6   Conclusions

In this paper, we have described an approach to calculate bounds of the number of rounds for which the impossible differential cryptanalysis technique is applicable to GFS. This approach is based on an algorithm which calculates the Frobenius numbers. There are lots of known algorithms to calculate the Frobenius number, one of them can be found in [12]. Our approach can be applicable to well-known and widely used GFS type-1 and type-2 to determine its security level against the impossible differential technique.

References

1. Biham, E., Biryukov, A., Shamir, A.: Cryptanalysis of Skipjack reduced to 31 rounds using impossible differentials. In: Stern, J. (ed.) EUROCRYPT 1999. LNCS, vol. 1592, pp. 12–23. Springer, Heidelberg (1999)
2. Knudsen, L.R.: DEAL a 128-bit block cipher. Technical report 151, Department of Informatics, University of Bergen, Norway (February 1998)
3. Knudsen, L.R.: Truncated and High Order Differentials. In: Preneel, B. (ed.) FSE 1994. LNCS, vol. 1008, pp. 196–211. Springer, Heidelberg (1995)
4. Feistel, H., Notz, W., Smith, J.L.: Some cryptographic techniques for machine-to-machine data communications. Proc. IEEE 63(11), 1545–1554 (1975)
5. Schnorr, C.P.: On the construction of a random number generator and random function generators. In: Günther, C.G. (ed.) EUROCRYPT 1988. LNCS, vol. 330, pp. 225–232. Springer, Heidelberg (1988)
6. Zheng, Y., Matsumoto, T., Imai, H.: On the Construction of Block Ciphers Provably Secure and Not Relying on Any Unproved Hypotheses. In: Brassard, G. (ed.) CRYPTO 1989. LNCS, vol. 435, pp. 461–480. Springer, Heidelberg (1990)
7. Nyberg, K.: Generlized Feistel networks. In: Kim, K.-C., Matsumoto, T. (eds.) ASIACRYPT 1996. LNCS, vol. 1163, pp. 91–104. Springer, Heidelberg (1996)
8. Schneier, B., Kelsey, J.: Unbalanced Feistel Networks and Block Cipher Design. In: Gollmann, D. (ed.) FSE 1996. LNCS, vol. 1039, pp. 121–144. Springer, Heidelberg (1996)
9. Zhang, L., Wu, W., Zhang, L.: Proposition of Two Cipher Structures. In: Bao, F., Yung, M., Lin, D., Jing, J. (eds.) Inscrypt 2009. LNCS, vol. 6151, pp. 215–229. Springer, Heidelberg (2010)
10. Suzaki, T., Minematsu, K.: Improving the generalized Feistel. In: Hong, S., Iwata, T. (eds.) FSE 2010. LNCS, vol. 6147, pp. 19–39. Springer, Heidelberg (2010)
11. Sylvester, J.J.: Problem 7382 (and Solution by W. J. Curran Sharp). The Educational Times 37, 26 (1884); reprinted in (a): Mathematical Questions, with their Solutions, from the Educational Times, with Many Papers (. . .) 41, 21 (1884)
12. Bocker, S., Liptak, Z.: The Money Changing Problem revisited: Computing the Frobenius number in time. Technical Report no. 2004-2, Universitat Bielefeld, Technische Fakultat (2004)
13. Bogdanov, A., Shibutani, K.: Generalized Feistel networks revisited. DCC 66, 75–97 (2013)
14. Shibutani, K., Isobe, T., Hiwatari, H., Mitsuda, A., Akishita, T., Shirai, T.: *Piccolo*: An Ultra-Lightweight Blockcipher. In: Preneel, B., Takagi, T. (eds.) CHES 2011. LNCS, vol. 6917, pp. 342–357. Springer, Heidelberg (2011)
15. Biham, E., Biryukov, A., Shamir, A.: Miss in the Middle Attacks on IDEA and Khufu. In: Knudsen, L.R. (ed.) FSE 1999. LNCS, vol. 1636, pp. 124–138. Springer, Heidelberg (1999)
16. Nachef, V., Volte, E., Patarin, J.: Differential Attacks on Generalized Feistel Schemes. In: Abdalla, M., Nita-Rotaru, C., Dahab, R. (eds.) CANS 2013. LNCS, vol. 8257, pp. 1–19. Springer, Heidelberg (2013)

Encrypting Huffman-Encoded Data by Substituting Pairs of Code Words without Changing the Bit Count of a Pair*

Marek Parfieniuk and Piotr Jankowski

Bialystok University of Technology, Faculty of Computer Science,
Department of Digital Media and Computer Graphics,
Wiejska 45A, 15-351 Bialystok, Poland
m.parfieniuk@pb.edu.pl
http://aragorn.pb.bialystok.pl/~marekpk/

Abstract. This paper presents a method for combining the Huffman coding with encryption. The encryption is based on replacing Huffman code words, or symbols, pair-by-pair, in such a way that the sums of the code word lengths of an original pair and its substitute are equal. Thus our method preserves structures and lengths of bit streams that result from the Huffman encoding. This is advantageous if such a bit stream is embedded in a higher-level data container, like a multimedia file. The algorithm has been evaluated using text data and static Huffman dictionaries.

Keywords: encryption, JPEG, image, entropy coding, Huffman.

1 Introduction

The aim of source coding algorithms is to compress data as much as possible. However, the wide-spreading of computer network communications has raised interest in seamlessly combining source coding with other data transformations, which can be used to increase performance, reliability, or confidentiality of data distribution in the Internet or wireless networks.

Such methods were developed especially for distributed multimedia systems that are based on transmission of audio and video. For example, by leaving some redundancy in compressed data, joint source-channel coding (JSCC) allows recipients of encoded streams to detect and correct bit errors caused by a noisy channel of known statistical properties. Multiple description coding (MDC) algorithms produce several data streams, either of which is sufficient to roughly present video or audio, whereas the reception of more streams allows for improving quality. Such streams can be stored on separate servers and sent to a recipient using diverse network paths, so as to make media access immune to server or networks failures. On the other hand, scalable coding produces streams called

---

* This work was supported by the Polish National Science Centre under Decision No. DEC-2012/07/D/ST6/02454.

Z. Kotulski et al. (Eds.): CSS 2014, CCIS 448, pp. 12–22, 2014.

layers, which can be stacked during transmission in order to adapt the quality of multimedia to accessible network bandwidth or to the resolution of the screen of user's terminal.

Another research direction is to combine coding with encryption so as to protect compressed data from unauthorized access. Obviously, a compressed file can always be encrypted using an external cryptographic infrastructure, but this approach is not always optimal. If a file contains not only compressed data but also some metadata, which facilitate organization, indexing and retrieval of information, or owner identification, then encrypting such entire file makes all metadata inaccessible. In such situations, metadata need to be extracted before encryption and stored separately from the file they describe, which makes it difficult to implement some data services. It is usually better to be able to encrypt only the content-related part of a data stream (which is called selective encryption in the literature) without affecting its structure (format-compliant encryption). Reviews of such algorithms, which unify compression and encryption, can be found in [7,11,10]. Most of the approaches are aimed at encrypting compressed images [1,10,8], but general-purpose solutions are also known [9,12,6,7,4].

In the following, we propose a method for combining the Huffman coding [3] with encryption, which is based on substituting Huffman code words pair-by-pair, or, equivalently, on substituting symbol pairs. Two code words are replaced for other two code words in such a way that one original code word can be shorter or longer than its substitute, but the sum of the lengths of two code words must be the same before and after substituting the pairs. Therefore our encryption technique can be viewed as post-processing of Huffman-encoded bit streams, without affecting their lengths, or compression ratios.

In our approach, substituting code words is related neither to modifying or switching Huffman trees nor to simply reordering code words, the fundamental operations in the known methods of encrypting Huffman-encoded data [1,7,9,4,2,13,14,5]. To the best of our knowledge, a similar idea has not been reported in the literature, which would be conceptually simple and easy to implement, but also immune to cryptanalysis.

2   The Principle of Huffman Coding

In the Huffman coding [3], data compression is achieved by assigning binary code words of different lengths to the symbols that form a data stream to be compacted. Shorter code words are assigned to symbols that more frequently occur in the data stream. Such code words are constructed by arranging all symbols into a tree, in which less probable symbols are more distant from its root. After assigning 0 and 1 to siblings in the tree, the code word of a symbol results from concatenating bits assigned to nodes visited when traversing the tree from its root to the leaf with this symbol.

Table 1 shows the representative Huffman dictionary, which has been used as the basis of all experiments described in the remaining part of this paper. The dictionary has been constructed using the text of "The Sign of the Four",

Table 1. A representative Huffman dictionary

Symbol s_k	Percentage of occurrences f_k 100 [%]	Code word length l_k	Huffman code word c_k	Symbol s_k	Percentage of occurrences f_k 100 [%]	Code word length l_k	Huffman code word c_k
A	8.081	4	0001	N	6.420	4	0111
B	1.470	6	001111	O	7.961	4	0010
C	2.608	5	11000	P	1.679	6	001110
D	4.303	5	00000	Q	0.085	10	1101001010
E	12.367	3	100	R	5.826	4	1010
F	2.131	5	11011	S	6.486	4	0110
G	1.783	6	001101	T	8.996	3	111
H	6.636	4	0101	U	3.012	5	10110
I	6.869	4	0100	V	0.975	6	110101
J	0.138	9	110100100	W	2.491	5	11001
K	0.861	7	1101000	X	0.149	8	11010011
L	3.951	5	00001	Y	1.957	6	001100
M	2.721	5	10111	Z	0.044	10	1101001011

a novel by Sir Arthur Conan Doyle featuring Sherlock Holmes. In order to limit the number of symbols, and thus to make experimental results more readable, all non-letter characters have been removed from the text, which has then been converted to upper case. We consider its first 100000 characters, or about 50 pages, assuming 2000 characters per page.

In both Table 1 and the following discussion, s_k, c_k, and l_k are used to denote the k-th symbol, the Huffman code word assigned to the k-th symbol, and the number of bits (the length) of the code word, respectively. The frequency f_k of occurrences of a symbol s_k is defined as the ratio between the number of occurrences of s_k to the number of all symbols in a data stream. The frequency of pair occurrences is calculated in an analogous manner. In order to facilitate comparing the frequencies, which are fractions, they are presented in tables and plots as percentages, after multiplying them by 100%.

3   Encrypting the Huffman Code Words by Substituting Their Pairs

We propose to encrypt Huffman-compressed data by grouping code words into pairs, and by replacing each of the pairs with another pair in such a way that the length of a single code word can change, but the total number of bits of a pair is preserved. That is, the pair (c_k, c_{k+1}) can be replaced with only such a pair $(\underline{c}_k, \underline{c}_{k+1})$ that $l_k + l_{k+1} = \underline{l}_k + \underline{l}_{k+1}$. As the Huffman dictionary is assumed to be static in our approach, such substitution of code words is essentially substitution of symbols with constraint on the sum of the lengths of their code words.

Table 2 shows the results of grouping all possible pairs of the symbols of the Huffman dictionary in Table 1. The pairs have been grouped with respect to the sum of the lengths of the related code words, so each group consists of pairs that can be substituted in accordance with our idea. It is assumed that the groups are ordered, so that they can be identified with fixed arrays.

Table 2. Symbol pairs grouped according to the sum of the lengths of the Huffman code words in a pair

Sum of code word lengths	Number of pairs	Symbol pairs (20 pairs in row)
6	4	EE ET TE TT
7	28	AE AT EA EH EI EN EO ER ES HE HT IE IT NE NT OE OT RE RT SE ST TA TH TI TN TO TR TS
8	77	AA AH AI AN AO AR AS CE CT DE DT EC ED EF EL EM EU EW FE FT HA HH HI HN HO HR HS IA IH II IN IO IR IS LE LT ME MT NA NH NI NN NO NR NS OA OH OI ON OO OR OS RA RH RI RN RO RR RS SA SH SI SN SO SR SS TC TD TF TL TM TU TW UE UT WE WT
9	118	AC AD AF AL AM AU AW BE BT CA CH CI CN CO CR CS DA DH DI DN DO DR DS EB EG EP EV EY FA FH FI FN FO FR FS GE GT HC HD HF HL HM HU HW IC ID IF IL IM IU IW LA LH LI LN LO LR LS MA MH MI MN MO MR MS NC ND NF NL NM NU NW OC OD OF OL OM OU OW PE PT RC RD RF RL RM RU RW SC SD SF SL SM SU SW TB TG TP TV TY UA UH UI UN UO UR US VE VT WA WH WI WN WO WR WS YE YT
10	123	AB AG AP AV AY BA BH BI BN BO BR BS CC CD CF CL CM CU CW DC DD DF DL DM DU DW EK FC FD FF FL FM FU FW GA GH GI GN GO GR GS HB HG HP HV HY IB IG IP IV IY KE KT LC LD LF LL LM LU LW MC MD MF ML MM MU MW NB NG NP NV NY OB OG OP OV OY PA PH PI PN PO PR PS RB RG RP RV RY SB SG SP SV SY TK UC UD UF UL UM UU UW VA VH VI VN VO VR VS WC WD WF WL WM WU WW YA YH YI YN YO YR YS
11	88	AK BC BD BF BL BM BU BW CB CG CP CV CY DB DG DP DV DY EX FB FG FP FV FY GC GD GF GL GM GU GW HK IK KA KH KI KN KO KR KS LB LG LP LV LY MB MG MP MV MY NK OK PC PD PF PL PM PU PW RK SK TX UB UG UP UV UY VC VD VF VL VM VU VW WB WG WP WV WY XE XT YC YD YF YL YM YU YW
12	57	AX BB BG BP BV BY CK DK EJ FK GB GG GP GV GY HX IX JE JT KC KD KF KL KM KU KW LK MK NX OX PB PG PP PV PY RX SX TJ UK VB VG VP VV VY WK XA XH XI XN XO XR XS YB YG YP YV YY
13	46	AJ BK CX DX EQ EZ FX GK HJ IJ JA JH JI JN JO JR JS KB KG KP KV KY LX MX NJ OJ PK QE QT RJ SJ TQ TZ UX VK WX XC XD XF XL XM XU XW YK ZE ZT
14	53	AQ AZ BX CJ DJ FJ GX HQ HZ IQ IZ JC JD JF JL JM JU JW KK LJ MJ NQ NZ OQ OZ PX QA QH QI QN QO QR QS RQ RZ SQ SZ UJ VX WJ XB XG XP XV XY YX ZA ZH ZI ZN ZO ZR ZS
15	40	BJ CQ CZ DQ DZ FQ FZ GJ JB JG JP JV JY KX LQ LZ MQ MZ PJ QC QD QF QL QM QU QW UQ UZ VJ WQ WZ XK YJ ZC ZD ZF ZL ZM ZU ZW
16	23	BQ BZ GQ GZ JK KJ PQ PZ QB QG QP QV QY VQ VZ XX YQ YZ ZB ZG ZP ZV ZY
17	6	JX KQ KZ QK XJ ZK
18	5	JJ QX XQ XZ ZX
19	4	JQ JZ QJ ZJ
20	4	QQ QZ ZQ ZZ

In order to encrypt a pair of symbols, the sum of the lengths of the corresponding code words is calculated and used to select the appropriate array. In this array, the position of the original symbol pair is determined. By adding a pseudo-random offset, determined by the cryptographic key, to this position, modulo the size of the group, the substitute pair is determined which represents the encrypted symbols. The decryption consists in analogously substituting the encrypted symbols using the negated offset.

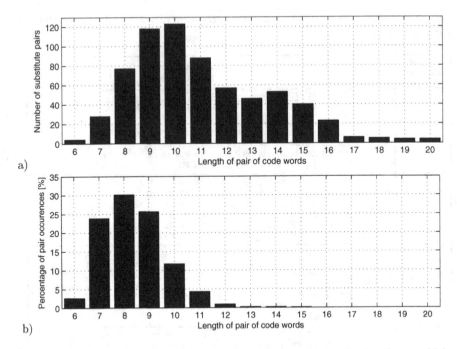

Fig. 1. Numbers of substitutes vs. percentages of occurrences of pairs that could be substituted

The numbers of possible substitutions are depicted in Fig. 1a. In order to verify if the pair substitution is an effective means of encryption, it must be known how often substitutes of each group are used when real messages are encrypted. For our test file, this is shown in Fig. 1b.

The usability of a given group of substitutes is determined by the product of their number and the frequency of occurrences of symbol pairs of the same length. The sum of all such products determines the average number of substitutes per pair of symbols to be encoded. For the data in Fig. 1, the average is $79.36 = 0.027 \cdot 4 + 0.239 \cdot 28 + 0.301 \cdot 77 + 0.256 \cdot 118 + 0.117 \cdot 123 + 0.043 \cdot 88 + \ldots$, which seems to be sufficiently large to make decryption computationally demanding.

Such encryption-by-substitution can be implemented as looping over a Huffman dictionary, comparing symbols or code word lengths, and counting pairs in-the-fly, so as to determine the virtual index of the original pair, and then to seek to the substitute. The complexity of this approach is significant, being determined by $O(N^2)$ comparisons for N symbols. Alternatively, in order to speed up substitutions, pair arrays can be arranged based on the Huffman dictionary, but they would require considerable memory $O(N^2)$. Thus both approaches are resource-demanding, but the first one seems to better suit hardware implementation and to be applicable to adaptive Huffman dictionaries. The complexity issues discouraged us from considering substituting triples, quadruples, etc. of

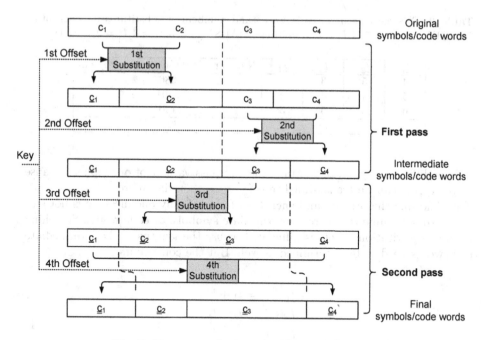

Fig. 2. Two-pass substitution of four code words

code words. In the case of substituting M-tuples, the computational complexity or memory requirements increase to $O(N^M)$, which seems unacceptable.

4   Double-Pass Encryption

Obviously, the simple substitution is vulnerable to plain text attacks. Having both original message and its encrypted version, it is very easy to determine how pairs have been substituted. Then this knowledge can be used to decrypt other texts.

Enhanced encryption can be achieved by allowing the two-pass substitution that is explained in Fig. 2. The k-th encryption unit is formed by four code words $(c_{k+1}, c_{k+2}, c_{k+3}, c_{k+4})$ of original symbols. In the first pass, the pairs (c_{k+1}, c_{k+2}) and (c_{k+3}, c_{k+4}) undergo substitutions, which results in four intermediate code words $(\underline{c}_{k+1}, \underline{c}_{k+2}, \underline{c}_{k+3}, \underline{c}_{k+4})$. Then, in the second pass, the initially encrypted pairs $(\underline{c}_{k+1}, \underline{c}_{k+4})$ and $(\underline{c}_{k+2}, \underline{c}_{k+3})$ are substituted once more, so as to obtain the final encrypted sequence of code words $(\underline{\underline{c}}_{k+1}, \underline{\underline{c}}_{k+2}, \underline{\underline{c}}_{k+3}, \underline{\underline{c}}_{k+4})$. The pair substitutes are determined by four pseudo-random offsets, generated based on the cryptographic key. The algorithm can be identified with bit-count-preserving substitution of quadruplets of symbols. Nevertheless, considering pairs clarifies both analysis and implementation.

Table 3. Possible lengths of code words and numbers of substitutes for encrypting "CODE" ($l_1 = 5, l_2 = 4, l_3 = 5, l_4 = 3$) as "MARS" ($\underline{l}_1 = 5, \underline{l}_2 = 4, \underline{l}_3 = 4, \underline{l}_4 = 4$)

$\underline{l}_1$	$\underline{l}_2$	$\underline{l}_3$	$\underline{l}_4$	Number of substitute quadruplets
4	5	3	5	686
5	4	4	4	2401
6	3	5	3	140
Total				3227

It is difficult to plain-text attack the two-pass variant of our cipher because (c_1, c_2, c_3, c_4) can be transformed into $(\underline{c}_1, \underline{c}_2, \underline{c}_3, \underline{c}_4)$ via different (c_1, c_2, c_3, c_4). Thus knowing the original and encrypted forms of only one message is not sufficient to determine the correct intermediate symbols, or code words. Searching for four substitution offsets is difficult, because the lengths of the intermediate code words need to be determined as well. But the constraints:

$$\underline{l}_1 + \underline{l}_2 = l_1 + l_2 \,,$$
$$\underline{l}_3 + \underline{l}_4 = l_3 + l_4 \,,$$
$$\underline{l}_2 + \underline{l}_3 = \underline{l}_2 + \underline{l}_3 \,,$$
$$\underline{l}_1 + \underline{l}_4 = \underline{l}_1 + \underline{l}_4 \,,$$

$$(1)$$

that must by satisfied by the lengths do not determine them uniquely. Because of this ambiguity, brute-force searching for substitution offsets usually requires testing a lot of possible intermediate symbols, as demonstrated in Table 3. So there could be successful only the attacks that are based on several plain-texts, or even specifically-chosen cipher texts.

The two-pass algorithm can obviously be extended to more code words and to more passes, but ciphers obtainable in these ways seem impractical, because their implementations would be very computationally- or memory-demanding. It seems more advantageous to improve the cipher by making the substitution offsets dependent not only on the cryptographic key, but also on the intermediate symbols of the preceding encryption unit. This would disallow units to be decrypted separately, in parallel, without correctly processing their predecessors.

5   Properties of Encrypted Data

Obviously, the proposed cipher can be interpreted as both substitution and transposition of symbols. Due to space limitations, a detailed study of its properties and possible cryptanalysis techniques is left for future work. In order to only justify the correctness of our novel idea of encryption, it seems sufficient to characterize the solution by investigating statistical properties of encrypted texts.

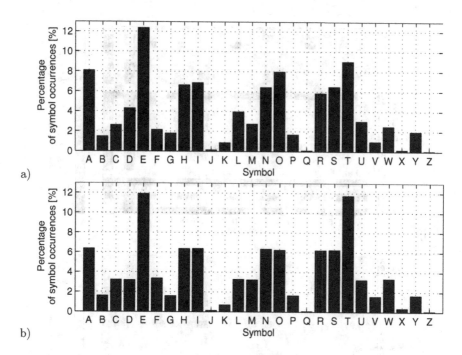

Fig. 3. Percentages of occurrences of symbols in original text (a) and in encrypted text (b)

Figure 3 shows the percentages of symbol occurrences in the texts before and after encryption. It is evident that our cipher equalizes frequencies of occurrences of symbols associated with the Huffman code words of the same length. Symbols described by longer code words still occur more frequently after encryption. The frequency of symbol occurrences depends on the length of code words in a clear way. If code words are 1-bit longer than the others, then the related symbols occur half as much often as those associated with the shorter code words. From another point of view, the frequencies of symbol occurrences in an encrypted file depend on the lengths of code words rather than on the contents of the original file.

After verifying that our method makes it difficult to recognize encrypted symbols, it seems necessary to check if the cipher reorders symbols as well. This can be done by analysing the distributions of symbols pairs before and after encryption, which are illustrated in Fig. 4a and 4b. The encryption evidently causes a complete rearrangement of symbols. It is quite surprising and interesting that pairs of encrypted symbols occur nearly exactly as they should occur taking into account the symbol frequencies of the Huffman dictionary. This can be seen by comparing Fig. 4b with 4c, which shows the theoretical frequencies of pair occurrences determined by the products of the symbol frequencies used for Huffman encoding.

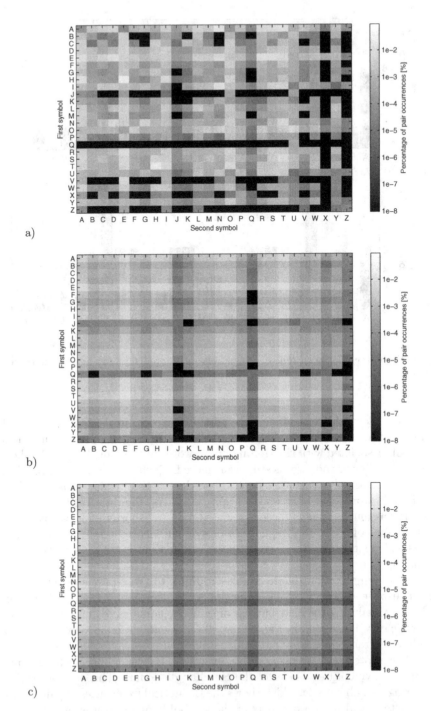

Fig. 4. Percentages of occurrences of symbol pairs: in original text (a), in encrypted text (b), and theoretical, determined by products of symbol frequencies (c)

6   Conclusions

Even though the proposed approach is conceptually simple and easy to implement, it seems interesting and practically useful. Preserving the compression ratio by the encryption comes at the cost of revealing the Huffman dictionary structure, but particular symbols are difficult to decrypt when the two-pass algorithm is used. The two-pass algorithm works poorly only for Huffman dictionaries that contain one dominant symbol which occurs frequently, and whose code word is shorter than all remaining code words. Then, the pairs containing two such symbols, or this symbol and a symbol whose code word is longer by 1 bit, cannot be substituted with the pairs that do not contain the troublesome symbol. Fortunately, Huffman trees of texts usually are balanced so that the above-mentioned disadvantage is not critical.

References

1. Auer, S., Bliem, A., Engel, D., Uhl, A., Unterweger, A.: Bitstream-based JPEG encryption in real-time. Int. J. Digital Crime Forensics 5(3), 1–14 (2013)
2. Hermassi, H., Rhouma, R., Belghith, S.: Joint compression and encryption using chaotically mutated Huffman trees. Commun. Nonlinear. Sci. Numer. Simul. 15(10), 2987–2999 (2010)
3. Huffman, D.: A method for the construction of minimum redundancy codes. Proc. IRE 40, 1098–1101 (1952)
4. Jakimoski, G., Subbalakshmi, K.P.: Cryptanalysis of some multimedia encryption schemes. IEEE Trans. Multimedia 10(3), 330–338 (2008)
5. Kailasananathan, C., Safavi-Naini, R., Ogunbona, P.: Secure compression using adaptive Huffman coding. In: Proc. 1st IEEE Pacific-Rim Conference on Multimedia (IEEE-PCM), Sydney, Australia, pp. 336–339 (2000)
6. Kulekci, M.: A method to ensure the confidentiality of the compressed data. In: Proc. 1st Int. Conf. Data Compression, Communications, Processing (CCP), Palinuro, Italy, pp. 203–209 (2011)
7. Li, S.: On the performance of secret entropy coding: A perspective beyond security. In: Unger, H., Kyamaky, K., Kacprzyk, J. (eds.) Autonomous Systems: Developments and Trends. SCI, vol. 391, pp. 389–402. Springer, Heidelberg (2012)
8. Massoudi, A., Lefebvre, F., De Vleeschouwer, C., Macq, B., Quisquater, J.J.: Overview on selective encryption of image and video: Challenges and perspectives. EURASIP. J. Inf. Secur. 2008, 5:1–5:18 (2008)
9. Tseng, K.K., Jiang, J., Pan, J.-S., Tang, L., Hsu, C.Y., Chen, C.C.: Enhanced Huffman coding with encryption for wireless data broadcasting system. In: Proc. Int. Symp. Computer, Consumer, Control, Taichung, Taiwan, pp. 622–625 (2012)
10. Wu, C.P., Kuo, C.C.J.: Fast encryption methods for audiovisual data confidentiality. In: Multimedia Systems and Applications III. Proc. SPIE, Boston, MA, vol. 4209, pp. 284–295 (2000)
11. Wu, C.P., Kuo, C.C.: Design of integrated multimedia compression and encryption systems. IEEE Trans. Multimedia 7(5), 828–839 (2005)

12. Zhou, J., Au, O., Wong, P.W.: Adaptive chosed-ciphertext attack on secure arithmetic coding. IEEE Trans. Signal Process. 57(5), 1825–1838 (2009)
13. Zhou, J., Liang, Z., Chen, Y., Au, O.: Security analysis of multimedia encryption schemes based on multiple huffman table. IEEE Signal Process. Lett. 14(3), 201–204 (2007)
14. Zhou, Q., Wong, K.W., Liao, X., Hu, Y.: On the security of multiple Huffman table based encryption. J. Vis. Comun. Image Represent. 22(1), 85–92 (2011)

On Multivariate Cryptosystems
Based on Polynomially Compressed Maps
with Invertible Decomposition

Urszula Romańczuk-Polubiec and Vasyl Ustimenko

Institute of Computer Science, Maria Curie-Sklodowska University,
pl. M. Curie-Sklodowskiej 5, 20-031 Lublin, Poland
urszula_romanczuk@yahoo.pl, vasyl@hektor.umcs.lublin.pl

Abstract. Let K be a commutative ring and K^n be an affine space over K of dimension n. We illustrate the concept of a family of polynomially compressed multivariate maps $f(n)$ by relations of degree k with invertible decomposition via presentation of the explicit construction. Such a construction is based on the edge transitive family of graphs $D(n, K)$. It uses the equations of connected component of the graph. The walk on the graph can be given by the sequence of its edges. It induces a cubical bijective transformation $E(n)$ of the flag space isomorphic to K^{n+1}. The transformations related edges of the walk form invertible decomposition of $E(n)$ into simple multipliers. Knowledge of such decomposition allows to find the pre-image of $E(n)(\text{x})$ fast. The map $E(n)$ is not suitable for a public map because its inverse is also cubical. The restriction of the map $\tilde{E}(n)$ on the chosen connected component is a multivariate transformation of unbounded degree (compressed map). The public user has some additional compression rules which allow for fast computation of the value $E(n)$ on a given flag. The key holder (Alice) knows $E(n)$, special decompression rules allow her to decrypt fast. To hide the graph Alice deformates $\tilde{E}(n)$, the compression and decompression rules by two special affine transformations τ_1 and τ_2. The usage of $\tau_1 E(n)\tau_2$ allows to get a more densely compressed map.

Keywords: post quantum cryptography, multivariate cryptography, extremal graph theory, design of cryptographical systems, pseudorandom walks on graphs.

1 Introduction

The formal concepts of the multivariate map with invertible decomposition and polynomially compressed map are presented by one of the authors in Extended Abstracts of Central European Conference on Cryptology 2014. The idea of cryptosystem based on the multivariate map with quadratic compression was formulated in [12]. In our paper we present the generalisation of this cryptosystem in detail with the complexity estimates of encryption and decryption procedures. The construction uses walks on the graphs $D(n, K)$ for the purpose of Multivariate Cryptography. Such walks were used first for the constructions of fast

Z. Kotulski et al. (Eds.): CSS 2014, CCIS 448, pp. 23–37, 2014.
© Springer-Verlag Berlin Heidelberg 2014

stream ciphers. The multivariate maps induced by such walks turns out to be fast cubical transformations of the plainspace variety of vertices or the variety of flags (see [14], [15]). It makes them useful for design of stream ciphers and key exchange protocols. In [22], [24] it was shown that the inverses of encryption maps are also cubical transformations. This fact restricts their use in the public key cryptography. In [16] a more general idea of multivariate map corresponding to *symbolic walk* on the graph was introduced. Paper [17] suggests the deformation of such nonlinear map by two affine transformations and the use of deformated transformation in Multivariate Cryptography but important questions of estimation of degrees, orders, densities are still under investigation. We hope to present the first results on this topic soon. Currently symbolic walks are used for development of stream ciphers with high resistance to plaintext - ciphertext attacks of the adversary.

This paper contains description of algorithms based on ordinary walks on $D(n, K)$ in alternative way. We restrict the transformation induced by walk to the special *symbolic connected component*.

In section 2 we collect preliminaries on Multivariate Cryptography, it contains our definitions of special multivariate maps. Section 4 is devoted to the information about the problems of Extremal Graph Theory which leads to discovery of graphs $D(n, F_q)$. In section 3 the algorithm of deformation of multivariate map with the polynomial compression and decompression rule by affine transformation is presented. The descriptions of graphs $D(n, K)$ and their connected components together with cryptographic applications are given in section 5. The graph based on the explicit construction of the requested multivariate map is given in section 6. It comes together with the decryption of multivariate public key based on the graphs $D(n, K)$. In the last section we conclude and present the complexity estimates.

2   On Multivariate Cryptography and Special Multivariate Transformations

Multivariate cryptography (see [2]-[5], [13]) is one of the directions of Postquantum Cryptography, which concerns the algorithms resistant to hypothetic attacks conducted by Quantum Computer. The encryption tools of Multivariate Cryptography are non-linear multivariate transformations of the affine space K^n, where K is a finite commutative ring. Nowadays this modern direction of research requires new examples of algorithms with theoretical arguments on their resistance to attacks conducted by ordinary computer (Turing machine) and new tasks for cryptanalysts.

Recall that *Cremona group* $C(K^n)$ is a totality of invertible polynomial maps f of affine space K^n over a commutative ring K into itself, such that the inverse map f^{-1} is also a polynomial one.

Let us refer to the sequence of maps $f(n)$ from $C(K^n)$ to $C(K^n)$, $n = 1, 2, \ldots$ as *a family of polynomial degree*, if the degree of each transformation is a parameter s of the size $O(n^t)$. We say that a family $f(n)$ is *a family of linear degree* in the case $t = 1$. We refer to a family $f(n)$ as *a family of bounded degree* if $t = 0$.

Assume that a transformation $f = f(n)$ is written in the form: $\bar{x} \to f_i(\bar{x})$, $i = 1, 2, \ldots, n$, where $\bar{x} = (x_1, x_2, \ldots, x_n)$ and each $f_i \in K^n$ is determined by the list of their monomial terms with respect to some chosen order. We refer to the sequence $f(n) \in C(K^n)$ as a *family of polynomial density* d if total quantity of all monomial expressions within all f_i is given as $O(n^d)$ for an independent constant d.

Let $f(n)$ be a family of polynomial degree s and of polynomial density d. Then the value of $f(n)$ in the point $x \in K^n$ can be computed by $O(n^{s+d})$ elementary steps. We say that the family $f(n) \in C(K^n)$ has an *invertible decomposition of speed* d if $f(n)$ can be written as a composition of elements $f^1(n), f^2(n), \ldots, f^{k(n)}(n)$ and this decomposition will allow us to compute the value of $y = f(x)$ and the re-image of given y in time $k(n)O(n^d)$. In the case $d = 1$ we state that invertible decomposition is of linear speed. The complexity of computation of the value of each $f^i(n)$ in a given point x is $O(n^d)$.

Let us assume that we have a family of polynomial maps of restricted degree. It means that such multivariate maps $f(n)$ in n variables form the family of polynomial density. Let us assume that variables are subdivided into two groups $x_1, x_2, \ldots, x_{m_1}$ and $y_1, y_2, \ldots, y_{m_2}$, where $m_1 = m_1(n)$ and $m_2 = m_2(n)$ are the linear functions in n, $m_1 + m_2 = n$. Let us consider the specialisation:

$$
\begin{aligned}
y_1 &= h_1(x_1, x_2, \ldots, x_{m_1}), \\
y_2 &= h_2(x_1, x_2, \ldots, x_{m_1}, y_1), \\
y_3 &= h_3(x_1, x_2, \ldots, x_{m_1}, y_1, y_2), \\
&\ldots \\
y_{m_2} &= h_{m_2}(x_1, x_2, \ldots, x_{m_1}, y_1, y_2, \ldots, y_{m_2 - 1}),
\end{aligned}
\tag{1}
$$

where h_i are the multivariate functions of restricted degree. It is clear, that compressed map $\tilde{f}(n)$:

$$
\begin{aligned}
\text{x} \to f(n)(\text{x}, &h_1(\text{x}), h_2(\text{x}, h_1(\text{x})), \\
&h_3(\text{x}, h_1(\text{x}), h_2(\text{x}, h_1(\text{x}))), \ldots, \\
&\ldots, h_{m_2}(\text{x}, h_1(\text{x}), h_2(\text{x}, h_1(\text{x})), \ldots, \\
&h_{m_2 - 1}(\text{x}, h_1(\text{x}), h_2(\text{x}, h_1(\text{x})), \ldots))),
\end{aligned}
\tag{2}
$$

where $\text{x} = (x_1, x_2, \ldots, x_{m_1})$, can be neither a polynomial degree nor a polynomial density. In this case we are unable to write it in the standard form. Notice, that it is always possible to use a recurrent rules of the kind as above. If max $\deg(h_i(x_1, x_2, \ldots, x_{m_1}, y_1, y_2, \ldots, y_{i-1})) = d$ and the degree of $f(n)$ is s, then we can compute values of all h_i in a given point in time $m_2 O(m_1{}^d)$ and finish the computation of the value of $\tilde{f}(n)$ for $O(n^s)$.

We refer to such a family as a family with *polynomial compression* by *compression relations* $y_i = h_i(x_1, x_2, \ldots, x_{m_1}, y_1, y_2, \ldots, y_{i-1})$ of degree d.

Let $f(n)$ be given in the decompressed form:

$$
\begin{aligned}
x_1 &\to z_1 = f_1(x_1, x_2, \ldots, x_{m_1}, y_1, y_2, \ldots, y_{m_2}), \\
x_2 &\to z_2 = f_2(x_1, x_2, \ldots, x_{m_1}, y_1, y_2, \ldots, y_{m_2}), \\
&\cdots \\
x_{m_1} &\to z_{m_1} = f_{m_1}(x_1, x_2, \ldots, x_{m_1}, y_1, y_2, \ldots, y_{m_2}), \\
y_1 &\to z_1' = f_1'(x_1, x_2, \ldots, x_{m_1}, y_1, y_2, \ldots, y_{m_2}), \\
y_2 &\to z_2' = f_2'(x_1, x_2, \ldots, x_{m_1}, y_1, y_2, \ldots, y_{m_2}), \\
&\cdots \\
y_{m_2} &\to z_{m_2}' = f_{m_2}'(x_1, x_2, \ldots, x_{m_1}, y_1, y_2, \ldots, y_{m_2}) .
\end{aligned}
\tag{3}
$$

We say that the *map $f(n)$ has decompression rules* if z_i' can be computed alternatively as:

$$
\begin{aligned}
z_1' &= h_1'(z_1, z_2, \ldots, z_{m_1}), \\
z_2' &= h_2'(z_1, z_2, \ldots, z_{m_1}, z_1'), \\
&\cdots \\
z_{m_2}' &= h_{m_2}'(z_1, z_2, \ldots, z_{m_1}, z_1', z_2', \ldots z_{m_2-1}') .
\end{aligned}
\tag{4}
$$

We refer to h_i' as *decompression functions*.

In section 6 we show that families of multivariate maps of finite degree with the polynomial compression and decompression rules, invertible decomposition of finite degree in the decompression form exist.

Now we consider a multivariate cryptosystem corresponding to such a family $f(n) : K^n \to K^n$. Let us assume that Alice can generate this family in the decompression form via the list of monomial terms, compression rules y_i and the decompression functions. Additionally, she can create invertible decomposition of decompressed function.

She sends to Bob the reduced map $K^{m_1} \to K^n$, $n = m_1 + m_2$, in the form of the following public rules:

$$
\begin{aligned}
x_1 &\to z_1 = f_1(x_1, x_2, \ldots, x_{m_1}, y_1, y_2, \ldots, y_{m_2}), \\
x_2 &\to z_2 = f_2(x_1, x_2, \ldots, x_{m_1}, y_1, y_2, \ldots, y_{m_2}), \\
&\cdots \\
x_{m_1} &\to z_{m_1} = f_{m_1}(x_1, x_2, \ldots, x_{m_1}, y_1, y_2, \ldots, y_{m_2}) .
\end{aligned}
\tag{5}
$$

Alice also gives him the compression rules:

$$y_1 = h_1(x_1, x_2, \ldots, x_{m_1}),$$
$$y_2 = h_2(x_1, x_2, \ldots, x_{m_1}, y_1),$$
$$y_3 = h_3(x_1, x_2, \ldots, x_{m_1}, y_1, y_2), \tag{6}$$
$$\ldots$$
$$y_{m_2} = h_{m_2}(x_1, x_2, \ldots, x_{m_1}, y_1, y_2, \ldots, y_{m_2-1}),$$

where h_i are the multivariate functions of restricted degree.

So, Bob writes his plaintext $(x_1, x_2, \ldots, x_{m_1})$, computes its extension $(y_1, y_2, \ldots, y_{m_2})$. He substitutes the parameters x_i, $i = 1, 2, \ldots, m_1$ and y_i, $i = 1, 2, \ldots, m_2$ into available public rules and gets the ciphertext $(z_1, z_2, \ldots, z_{m_1})$. He sends it via open channel to Alice.

Alice uses her decompression rules and gets the decompressed ciphertext as a string $(z_1, z_2, \ldots, z_{m_1}, z'_1, z'_2, \ldots, z'_{m_2})$. So, she has the following equations:

$$z_1 = f_1(x_1, x_2, \ldots, x_{m_1}, y_1, y_2, \ldots, y_{m_2}),$$
$$z_2 = f_2(x_1, x_2, \ldots, x_{m_1}, y_1, y_2, \ldots, y_{m_2}),$$
$$\ldots$$
$$z_{m_1} = f_{m_1}(x_1, x_2, \ldots, x_{m_1}, y_1, y_2, \ldots, y_{m_2}),$$
$$z'_1 = f'_1(x_1, x_2, \ldots, x_{m_1}, y_1, y_2, \ldots, y_{m_2}), \tag{7}$$
$$z'_2 = f'_2(x_1, x_2, \ldots, x_{m_1}, y_1, y_2, \ldots, y_{m_2}),$$
$$\ldots$$
$$z'_{m_2} = f'_{m_2}(x_1, x_2, \ldots, x_{m_1}, y_1, y_2, \ldots, y_{m_2}).$$

Knowledge on invertible decomposition of $F(n) = H_1 H_2 \ldots H_s$ allows her to solve the above system in the polynomial time for $x_1, x_2, \ldots x_{m_1}, y_1, y_2, \ldots, y_{m_2}$. Thus, Alice can read the plaintext.

3   On Affine Deformations of Compressed Function with the Decompression Rules

Let us investigate the compositions of the kind $\tau_1 F(n) \tau_2$, where τ_i, $i = 1, 2$ are the bijective affine transformation of $K^n \to K^n$ such that:

$$(x_1, x_2, \ldots, x_{m_1}, y_1, y_2, \ldots, y_{m_2}) \to (x_1, x_2, \ldots, x_{m_1}, y_1, y_2, \ldots, y_{m_2}) A_i +$$
$$+ (b_1, b_2, \ldots, b_{m_1}, d_1, d_2, \ldots, d_{m_2}). \tag{8}$$

We assume that $F(n)$ is a multivariate map with polynomial compression and decompression rules given by the above functions h_i and h'_i, $i = 1, 2, \ldots, m_2$. Let us $e_1, e_2, \ldots, e_{m_1}, e'_1, e'_2, \ldots e'_{m_2}$ be the basis in which an element of affine space K^n is written as tuple:

$$(x_1, x_2, \ldots, x_{m_1}, y_1, y_2, \ldots, y_{m_2}) \,. \tag{9}$$

Then $W_1 = \langle e_1, e_2, \ldots, e_{m_1} \rangle$ and $W_2 = \langle e_1', e_2', \ldots e_{m_2}' \rangle$ are the invariant subspaces of transformation τ_1 and τ_2. Each representative of W_2 is a fixed point of the second transformation τ_2. We assume that the restriction of τ_1 onto W_2 is given by the rule:

$$\begin{aligned}
(y_1, y_2, \ldots, y_{m_2}) \to (y_1', y_2', \ldots, y_{m_2}') &= (y_1, y_2, \ldots, y_{m_1})B + \\
&\quad (d_1, d_2, \ldots, d_{m_2}) + (r_1(x_1, x_2, \ldots, x_{m_1}), \\
&\quad r_2(x_1, \ldots, x_{m_1}), \ldots, r_{m_2}(x_1, \ldots, x_{m_1})) \,,
\end{aligned} \tag{10}$$

where r_i are the chosen linear forms corresponding to $m_1 \times m_2$ matrix $R = (r_{i,j})$ and B is a triangular nonsingular matrix.

We show that the deformated map $\tau_1 F(n)\tau_2$ is the transformation with polynomial compression and also decompression procedure. Let map τ_1 restricted to the invariant affine space W_1 is written as:

$$\begin{aligned}
x_1 &\to l_1(x_1, x_2, \ldots, x_{m_1}), \\
x_2 &\to l_2(x_1, x_2, \ldots, x_{m_1}), \\
&\quad \ldots \\
x_{m_1} &\to l_{m_1}(x_1, x_2, \ldots, x_{m_1}) \,,
\end{aligned} \tag{11}$$

where $l_i(x_1, x_2, \ldots, x_{m_1})$, $i = 1, 2, \ldots, m_1$ are the multivariate linear functions. The composition of $\tau_1 F(n)$ restricted to the space W_1 can be written as a rule:

$$x_i \to f_1(l_1(\mathbf{x}), l_2(\mathbf{x}), \ldots, l_{m_1}(\mathbf{x}), y_1', y_2', \ldots, y_{m_2}'), \quad i = 1, 2, \ldots, m_1 \,, \tag{12}$$

together with the deformated compression procedure given by:

$$\begin{aligned}
y_1' &= h_1(l_1(\mathbf{x}), l_2(\mathbf{x}), \ldots, l_{m_1}(\mathbf{x})), \\
y_2' &= h_2(l_1(\mathbf{x}), l_2(\mathbf{x}), \ldots, l_{m_1}(\mathbf{x}), y_1'), \\
&\quad \ldots \\
y_{m_2}' &= h_{m_2}(l_1(\mathbf{x}), l_2(\mathbf{x}), \ldots, l_{m_1}(\mathbf{x}), y_1', y_2', \ldots, y_{m_2-1}') \,,
\end{aligned} \tag{13}$$

where $\mathbf{x} = (x_1, x_2, \ldots, x_{m_1})$.

Let map τ_2 restricted to the invariant affine space W_1 be written as:

$$\begin{aligned}
x_1 &\to s_1(x_1, x_2, \ldots, x_{m_1}), \\
x_2 &\to s_2(x_1, x_2, \ldots, x_{m_1}), \\
&\quad \ldots \\
x_{m_1} &\to s_{m_1}(x_1, x_2, \ldots, x_{m_1}) \,,
\end{aligned} \tag{14}$$

where $s_i(x_1, x_2, \ldots, x_{m_1})$, $i = 1, 2, \ldots, m_1$ are the multivariate linear functions, and for the simplicity, let us assume that τ_2 acts on W_2 as identity map. The composition $\tau_1 F(n) \tau_2$ restricted on W_1 can be written as:

$$x_j \to z_j = s_j(f_1(\tilde{x}, y'), f_2(\tilde{x}, y'), \ldots, f_{m_1}(\tilde{x}, y')), \quad j = 1, 2, \ldots, m_1 , \quad (15)$$

where:

$$\tilde{x} = (l_1(x), l_2(x), \ldots, l_{m_1}(x)),$$
$$x = (x_1, x_2, \ldots, x_{m_1}), \quad (16)$$
$$y' = (y'_1, y'_2, \ldots, y'_{m_2}) .$$

The compression rules remain the same:

$$y'_1 = h_1(l_1(x), l_2(x), \ldots, l_{m_1}(x)),$$
$$y'_2 = h_2(l_1(x), l_2(x), \ldots, l_{m_1}(x), y'_1),$$
$$\ldots \quad (17)$$
$$y'_{m_2} = h_{m_2}(l_1(x), l_2(x), \ldots, l_{m_1}(x), y'_1, y'_2, \ldots, y'_{m_2 - 1}) ,$$

where $x = (x_1, x_2, \ldots, x_{m_1})$. We have to rewrite them in terms of $(y_1, y_2, \ldots, y_{m_2})$.
Let τ_2^{-1} be given by the linear function $s'_i(x_1, x_2, \ldots, x_{m_1})$, $i = 1, 2, \ldots, m_1$. Notice that decompression rules for $\tau_1 F(n) \tau_2$ have to be written as:

$$z'_1 = h'_1(s'_1(z), s'_2(z), \ldots, s'_{m_1}(z)),$$
$$z'_2 = h'_2(s'_1(z), s'_2(z), \ldots, s'_{m_1}(z), z'_1),$$
$$\ldots \quad (18)$$
$$z'_{m_2} = h'_{m_2}(s'_1(z), s'_2(z), \ldots, s'_{m_1}(z), z'_1, z'_2, \ldots, z'_{m_2 - 1}) ,$$

where $z = (z_1, z_2, \ldots, z_{m_1})$.

4   Extreme Algebraic Graphs Corresponding to a Special Family of Multivariate Maps

Recall that the girth is the length of minimal cycle in the simple graph. The studies of the maximal size $ex(C_3, C_4, \ldots, C_{2m}, v)$ of the simple graph on v vertices without cycles of length $3, 4, \ldots, 2m$, i. e. graphs of girth $> 2m$, form an important direction of Extremal Graph Theory (see [1]).

As it follows from famous Even Circuit Theorem by P. Erdős, we have inequality:

$$ex(C_3, C_4, \ldots, C_{2m}, v) \leq cv^{1 + 1/m} , \quad (19)$$

where c is a certain constant. The bound is known to be sharp only for $m = 2, 3, 5$. The first general lower bounds of the kind $ex(v, C_3, C_4, \ldots C_{2m}) = \Omega(v^{1+c/m})$, where c is a constant $< 1/2$ were obtained in the 50th by Erdős' via studies of *families of graphs of large girth*, i.e. infinite families of simple regular graphs Γ_i of the degree k_i and the order v_i such that $g(\Gamma_i) \geq c\log_{k_i} v_i$, where c is the constant independent of i. Erdős' proved the existence of such a family with the arbitrary large but bounded degree $k_i = k$ with $c = 1/4$ by his famous probabilistic method.

The following two explicit families of regular simple graphs of large girth with unbounded girth and arbitrarily large k appear first: the family $X(p, q)$ of the Cayley graphs for $PSL_2(p)$, where p and q are the primes, were defined by G. Margulis [1] and investigated by A. Lubotzky, Sarnak [11] and Phillips and the family of algebraic graphs $CD(n, q)$ [8]. The graphs $CD(n, q)$ appear as connected components of the graphs $D(n, q)$ defined via system of quadratic equations [9]. The best known lower bound for $d \neq 2, 3, 5$ was deduced from the existence of the above mentioned families of graphs $ex(v, C_3, C_4, \ldots, C_{2d}) \geq cv^{1+2/(3d-3+e)}$ where $e = 0$ if d is odd, and $e = 1$ if d is even.

Recall that the family of regular graphs Γ_i of degree k_i and increasing order v_i is a *family of graphs of small world* if $\text{diam}(\Gamma_i) \leq c\log_{k_i}(v_i)$ for some independent constant c, $c > 0$, where $\text{diam}(\Gamma_i)$ is a diameter of graph G_i. The graphs $X(p.q)$ form a unique known family of large girth which is a family of small world graphs at the same time. There has been a conjecture known since 1995 that the family of graphs $CD(n, q)$ for odd q is another example of such kind. Currently, it is proved that the diameter of $CD(n, q)$ is bounded from the above by the polynomial function $d(n)$, which does not depend on q. Both families $X(p, q)$ and $CD(n, q)$ consist of edge transitive graphs. The graphs $D(n, q)$ and $CD(n, q)$ have been used in symmetric cryptography together with their natural analogs $D(n, K)$ and $CD(n, K)$ over general finite commutative rings K since 1998 (see [14]). The theory of directed graphs and language of dynamic system were very useful for the studies of public key and private key algorithms based on the graphs $D(n, K)$, $CD(n, K)$ and their quotients (see [10], [19], [7], [21] and further references).

There are several implementations of symmetric algorithms for cases of fields (starting with [15]) and arithmetical rings ([19], in particular). Some comparisons of public keys based on $D(n, K)$ and their quotients are considered in [18].

5   Description of the Graphs $D(n, K)$ and Corresponding Stream Ciphers

We define the family of graphs $D(n, K)$, where $n > 2$ is the positive integer and K is a commutative ring, such graphs have been considered in [9] for the case $K = \mathbb{F}_q$.

Let P_D and L_D be two copies of the Cartesian power $K^{\mathbb{N}}$, where K is the commutative ring and $\mathbb{N}$ is the set of positive integer numbers. The elements of P_D will be called *points* and those of L_D *lines*.

To distinguish points from lines we use parentheses and brackets. If $x \in K^{\mathbb{N}}$, then $(x) \in P_D$ and $[x] \in L_D$. It will be also advantageous to adopt the notation for the co-ordinates of points and lines introduced in [9] for the case of general commutative ring K:

$$(p) = (p_{0,1}, p_{1,1}, p_{1,2}, p_{2,1}, p_{2,2}, p'_{2,2}, p_{2,3}, \ldots, p_{i,i}, p'_{i,i}, p_{i,i+1}, p_{i+1,i}, \ldots),$$
$$[l] = [l_{1,0}, l_{1,1}, l_{1,2}, l_{2,1}, l_{2,2}, l'_{2,2}, l_{2,3}, \ldots, l_{i,i}, l'_{i,i}, l_{i,i+1}, l_{i+1,i}, \ldots].$$
(20)

The elements of P and L can be thought as infinite ordered tuples of elements from K, such that only finite numbers of components are different from zero.

Now we define a linguistic incidence structure (P_D, L_D, I_D) defined by the infinite system of equations as follows. We say that the point (p) is incident with the line $[l]$, and we write $(p)I[l]$, if the following relations between their co-ordinates hold:

$$l_{i,i} - p_{i,i} = l_{1,0}p_{i-1,i}$$
$$l'_{i,i} - p'_{i,i} = l_{i,i-1}p_{0,1}$$
$$l_{i,i+1} - p_{i,i+1} = l_{i,i}p_{0,1}$$
$$l_{i+1,i} - p_{i+1,i} = l_{1,0}p'_{i,i}.$$
(21)

(These four relations are defined for $i \geq 1$, $p'_{1,1} = p_{1,1}$, $l'_{1,1} = l_{1,1}$). We denote structure (P_D, L_D, I_D) as $D(K)$. Now we speak of the *incidence graph* of (P_D, L_D, I_D), which has the vertex set $P_D \cup L_D$ and the edge set consisting of all pairs $\{(p), [l]\}$ for which $(p)I[l]$.

For each positive integer $n \geq 2$ we obtain a quotient $(P_{D,n}, L_{D,n}, I_{D,n})$ as follows. First, $P_{D,n}$ and $L_{D,n}$ are obtained from P_D and L_D, respectively, by simply projecting each vector into its n initial coordinates. The incidence $I_{D,n}$ is then defined by imposing the first $n-1$ incidence relations and ignoring all others. The incidence graph corresponding to the structure $(P_{D,n}, L_{D,n}, I_{D,n})$ is denoted by $D(n, K)$.

To facilitate notation in the future results on "*connectivity invariants*", it will be convenient for us to define $p_{-1,0} = l_{0,-1} = p_{1,0} = l_{0,1} = 0$, $p_{0,0} = l_{0,0} = -1$, $p'_{0,0} = l'_{0,0} = -1$, $p'_{1,1} = p_{1,1}, l'_{1,1} = l_{1,1}$) and to assume that our equations are defined for $i \geq 0$.

Notice, that for $i = 0$, the above written four conditions are satisfied by every point and line, and for $i = 1$ the first two equations coincide and give $l_{1,1} - p_{1,1} = l_{1,0}p_{0,1}$.

Let $n \geq 6$, $t = [(n+2)/4]$, and let $u = (u_\alpha, u_{11}, \cdots, u_{tt}, u'_{tt}, u_{t,t+1}, u_{t+1,t}, \cdots)$ be a vertex of $D(n, K)$ ($\alpha \in \{(1,0), (0,1)\}$, it does not matter whether u is a point or a line). For every r, $2 \leq r \leq t$, let:

$$a_r = a_r(u) = \sum_{i=0,r} (u_{ii}u'_{r-i,r-i} - u_{i,i+1}u_{r-i,r-i-1}),$$
(22)

and $a = a(u) = (a_2, a_3, \cdots, a_t)$. Similarly, we assume $a = a(u) = (a_2, a_3, \cdots, a_t, \ldots)$ for the vertex u of the infinite graph $D(K)$.

Proposition 1. *Let u and v be vertices from the same component of $D(n, K)$. Then $a(u) = a(v)$. Moreover, for any $t - 1$ field elements $x_i \in F_q$, $2 \leq t \leq [(n+2)/4]$, there exists a vertex v of $D(n, K)$ for which $a(v) = (x_2, \ldots, x_t) = (x)$.*

We refer to the first coordinate $x_{1,0} = \rho(\mathrm{x})$ of a point x and the first coordinate $y_{1,0} = \rho(\mathrm{y})$ of a line y as the colour of the vertex (point or line). The following property holds for the graph: there exists a unique neighbour $N_t(v)$ of a given vertex v of a given colour $t \in K$.

A flag of the incidence system $D(n, K)$ (or $D(K)$)is an unordered pair $\{(\mathrm{x}), [\mathrm{y}]\}$ such that $(\mathrm{x})I[\mathrm{y}]$. Obviously, the totality of flags $FD(n, K)$ $(FD(K))$of the bipartite flag $D(n, K)$ $(D(K)$, respectively) is isomorphic to the variety K^{n+1}. So, the flag $\{(\mathrm{x}), [\mathrm{y}]\}$ is defined by the tuple $(x_{10}, x_{11}, \ldots, y_{01})$. Notice, that $N_{y_1}(\{\mathrm{x}\}) = [\mathrm{y}]$.

We consider an operator $NP_\alpha(\{(\mathrm{x}), [\mathrm{y}]\})$, $\alpha \in K$ mapping flag $\{(\mathrm{x}), [\mathrm{y}]\}$ of the incidence structure $D(n, K)$ (or $D(K)$) into its image $\{(\mathrm{x}'), [\mathrm{y}]\}$, where $(\mathrm{x}') = N_{\rho(\mathrm{y})+\alpha}([\mathrm{y}])$. Similarly, an operator $NL_\alpha(\{(\mathrm{x}), [\mathrm{y}]\})$ maps $\{(\mathrm{x}), [\mathrm{y}]\}$ into $\{(\mathrm{x}), N_{\rho(\mathrm{x})+\alpha}(\mathrm{x})\})$.

Let $\alpha_1, \alpha_2, \ldots, \alpha_k$ and $\beta_1, \beta_2, \ldots, \beta_k$ are chosen sequences of elements from the commutative ring K. The composition:

$$E = NP_{\alpha_1} NL_{\beta_1} NP_{\alpha_2} NL_{\beta_2} \ldots NP_{\alpha_k} NL_{\beta_k} \qquad (23)$$

transforms the flag $\{(\mathrm{x}), [\mathrm{y}]\}$ into the new flag $\{(\mathrm{x}'), [\mathrm{y}']\}$. The process of computation of $E(\{(\mathrm{x}), [\mathrm{y}]\} = \{(\mathrm{x}'), [\mathrm{y}']\}$ corresponds to the walk in a graph $D(n, K)$ with the original vertex (x) and the final point (x').

Remark 1. The map E and the combination $\tau_1 E \tau_2$, where τ_i, $i = 1, 2$ are bijective affine transformations, have been used as the symmetric encryption transformation. Flag space isomorphic to K^{n+1} is identified with the plainspace, tuples $(\alpha_1, \alpha_2, \ldots, \alpha_k)$ and $(\beta_1, \beta_2, \ldots, \beta_k)$ together with fixed τ_i, $i = 1, 2$ form a password. In [16] there appears an idea of *symbolic key*, i. e. change constants $\alpha_1, \alpha_2, \ldots, \alpha_k$ and $\beta_1, \beta_2, \ldots, \beta_k$ for different functions from the plaintext F of the kind:

$$f(a_2(F), a_3(F), \ldots, a_t(F)), \qquad (24)$$

where $t = [(n + 2)/2]$, $f(z_1, z_2, \ldots, z_{t-1}) \in K[z_1, z_2, \ldots, z_{t-1}]$. The encryption map corresponding to the symbolic key can be used for public key cryptography under the condition of feasibility of its computation.

As it was shown ([24], [22]) in the case of polynomials of degree 0 the encryption map E is a cubical transformation on the plainspace K^{n+1}. It can be used as the symmetric encryption map, as a base of *symbolic* key exchange protocols. It is not suitable for public keys because of the possibility of linearisation attacks (the inverse map is a cubical one).

It turns out that the scheme of compression described in section 5 is applicable for the map E. The compressed map $\tilde{E}$ has a linear n degree form. It means that straightforward linearisation attacks are not possible. In section 6 we introduce a method of deformation of E by the affine transformation which leads to encryption and decryption procedures of polynomial complexity.

6 On Graph Based Multivariate Map with Polynomial Compression

Let us consider a bipartite induced subgraph D_h of $D(n, K)$ with the vertex set satisfying the solution space of the system of equations $a_2(v) = h_1, a_3(v) = h_2, \ldots, a_t(v) = h_{t-1}$, where $h = (h_1, h_2, \ldots, h_{t-1})$, $t = (n+2)/4$ is a fixed element of K^{t-1}. According to [6] in the case of char$(K) \neq 2$ an induced graph D_h is a connected component of $D(n, K)$. All connected components are isomorphic, each connected component coincides with D_h for an appropriate h. In the case char$(K) = 2$ the induced graph D_h can be a disjoint union of several connected components. We refer to D_h as the generalized connected component of $D(n, K)$.

Each expression $a_i((p))$ can be written as $\pm(p'_{i,i} - p_{i,i}) + \tilde{a}_i((p))$, where the expression $\tilde{a}_i((p))$ does not depend on the parameters $p'_{i,i}$ and $p_{i,i}$. So, the equations:

$$a_2(v) = h_1, \ a_3(v) = h_2, \ \ldots, \ a_t(v) = h_{t-1} , \tag{25}$$

can be written in the form:

$$v'_{i,i} = v_{i,i} \mp \tilde{a}_i(v) \pm h_{i-1}, \quad i = 2, 3, \ldots, t . \tag{26}$$

Notice, that the expression on the right hand side depends only on previous for v'_{ii} coordinates of vector v.

We may assume that v is a flag of $D(n, K)$ because obviously point and line from the flag are in the same connected component. It is convenient for us to change the constant h_{i-1} for the function $H_{i-1}(v_{1,0}, v_{0,1})$, where $H_i(z_1, z_2)$ are bivariate polynomials from $K[z_1, z_2]$.

Finally, we write the equations of a symbolic generalized connected component as:

$$v'_{ii} = v_{ii} \mp \tilde{a}_i(v) \pm H_{i-1}(v_{1,0}, v_{0,1}) , \tag{27}$$

where $i = 2, 3, \ldots, t$.

We can use these equations with the chosen bivariate expressions $H(z_1, z_2)$ As the compression rules for the multivariate map:

$$E = NP_{\alpha_1} NL_{\beta_1} NP_{\alpha_2} NL_{\beta_2} \ldots NP_{\alpha_k} NL_{\beta_k} \tag{28}$$

on the flag space K^{n+1}. So the compressed map $\tilde{E}$ of $K^{n+1-[(n+2)/4]}$ is rather a sophisticated expression. After the deformation by two affine transformations of general kind it becomes much more sophisticated.

Let us find the decompression rule. Let us assume that $\tilde{E}(F) = F'$. The compressed flags $F = \mathrm{x} \in K^{n+1-[(n+2)/4]}$ can be expanded till the string of K^{n+1} by adding the coordinates $x'_{i,i}$ obtained recurrently from the reverse us of compression rules (x'_{ii} are the unknown but the other coordinates are known). Let $\mathrm{y} \in K^{n+1}$ be the vector obtained from x by expansion procedure. Let $\mathrm{z} = E(\mathrm{y})$. The transformation E preserves each generalized connected component. So, both vectors z and y are in the same symbolic generalized connected component. It means that:

$$z'_{i,i} = z_{i,i} \mp a_i(v) \pm H_{i-1}(x_{1,0}, y_{0,1}) , \qquad (29)$$

where $i = 2, 3, \ldots, t$. We can see that $z_{1,0} = x_{1,0} + \alpha_1 + \alpha_2 + \cdots + \alpha_k$ and $z_{0,1} = y_{0,1} + \beta_1 + \beta_2 + \cdots + \beta_k$. Thus, we can write the decompression rules as:

$$z'_{ii} = z_{ii} \mp \tilde{a}_i(v) \pm H_{i-1}(z_{1,0} - \alpha_1 - \alpha_2 - \cdots - \alpha_k, z_{0,1} - \beta_1 - \beta_2 - \cdots - \beta_k) , \quad (30)$$

where $i = 2, 3, \ldots, t$.

6.1   Description of the Cryptosystem Based on the Walk in the Compressed Graph

Let us consider the use of multivariate map with the polynomial compression and decompression rules described in the previous unit.

Alice works with the flag space of the graph $D(n, K)$. She chooses the walk in the graph via strings $\alpha_1, \alpha_2, \ldots, \alpha_k$ and $\beta_1, \beta_2, \ldots, \beta_k$ from the affine space K^k. She generates the cubical map:

$$E = NP_{\alpha_1} NL_{\beta_1} NP_{\alpha_2} NL_{\beta_2} \ldots NP_{\alpha_k} NL_{\beta_k} . \qquad (31)$$

Together with its fast invertible decomposition into transformations corresponding to the edges of the walk.

The inverse map is given as:

$$E' = NL_{-\beta_k} NP_{-\alpha_k} \ldots NL_{-\beta_2} NP_{-\alpha_2} NL_{-\beta_1} NP_{-\alpha_1} . \qquad (32)$$

The existence of invertible decomposition allows computation of E and E' for $kO(n)$ elementary operation.

Let us assume that flag:

$$F = (y_{0,1}, x_{1,0}, x_{1,1}, x_{1,2}, x_{2,1}, x_{2,2}, x'_{2,2}, x_{2,3}, \ldots,$$
$$x_{i,i}, x'_{i,i}, x_{i,i+1}, x_{i+1,i}, \ldots) \qquad (33)$$

is written in the basis:

$$(e_{0,1}, e_{1,1}, e_{1,2}, e_{2,1}, e_{2,2}, e'_{2,2}, e_{2,3}, \ldots, e_{i,i}, e'_{i,i}, e_{i,i+1}, e_{i+1,i}, \ldots) . \tag{34}$$

Alice has two groups of variables:

$$\begin{aligned} U_1 &= \{y_{0,1}, x_{1,0}, x_{1,1}, \ldots, x_{i-1,i}, x_{i,i-1}, x_{i,i}, \ldots\} \\ U_2 &= \{x'_{2,2}, x'_{3,3}, \ldots, x'_{t,t}\} \\ t &= [(n+2)/4] . \end{aligned} \tag{35}$$

They correspond to the subspaces $W_1 = \langle e_{0,1}, e_{1,1}, \ldots, e_{i-1,i}, e_{i,i-1}, e_{i,i}, \ldots \rangle$ and $W_2 = \langle e'_{2,2}, e'_{3,3}, \ldots, e'_{t,t} \rangle$, $t = [(n+2)/4]$. The flag space is a natural direct sum of W_1 and W_2.

Alice writes the restriction of E onto W_1 in the standard form:

$$z_\alpha = f_\alpha(y_{0,1}, x_{1,0}, x_{1,1}, \ldots, x_{i-1,i}, x_{i,i-1}, x_{i,i}, , \ldots, x'_{2,2}, x'_{3,3}, \ldots, x'_{t,t}) , \tag{36}$$

where $\alpha \in \{(0,1), (1,1), (1,2), (2,1), (2,2), \ldots, (i-1,i), (i,i-1), (i,i), \ldots\}$. She has the compression rule:

$$x'_{ii} = x_{ii} \mp \tilde{a}_i(x) \pm H_{i-1}(x_{10}, x_{01}) , \tag{37}$$

where $i = 2, 3, \ldots, t$. She writes for herself the decompression functions.

To hide the graph $D(n, K)$ she chooses special affine transformations τ_1 and τ_2 in a way described in section 5 and makes deformation of the above multivariate map with the polynomial compression rules. Her private key contains two strings $\alpha_1, \alpha_2, \ldots, \alpha_k$ $\beta_1, \beta_2, \ldots, \beta_k$, graphs $D(n, K)$ and affine transformation τ_i, $i = 1, 2$ of special form.

Bob obtains from Alice the deformated compressed encryption function (map from K^{n+1} into K^{n+1-t}, $t = [(n+1)/4]$ and the deformated compression relation. He can encrypt and send the ciphertext from K^{n+1-t} to Alice.

Alice uses the deformated decompressed rules, knowledge on invertible decomposition of E' allows her to compute plaintext fast.

7   Conclusion

We can easily evaluate the complexity of the execution of our public rule. The map $\tau_1 E \tau_2 : K^{n+1} \to K^{n+1}$ is cubical. Its restrictions are publicly presented on W_1 which is a polynomial map from $K^{n+1-[(n+2)/4]}$ into K^{n+1}. It can be computed in given point for $(n+1-[(n+2)/4])n^3$. So, the complexity is $O(n^4)$. The computation has to be done after the expansion of a plaintext by the compression rules. If each bivariate function $\phi(z_1, z_2)$ has the polynomial density $O(n^s)$ and polynomial degree $O(s^t)$. All of them can be computed for time $O(n^{s+t+1})$. If we assume that $s+t \leq 3$, then compression does not increase significantly the complexity of ciphertext computation. It remains $O(n^4)$.

The decryption process consists of two parts. The fist part decompression requires $O(n^4)$ elementary operations, the second part require time $O(n)$ (case of constant k) or $O(n^2)$ (length of the password is $O(n)$). The time of generation of our public rule is investigated in [18] via computer simulations on the symbolic level.

As it was shown in [20] the transformation $\tilde{E}$ is of polynomial density and linear unbounded degree. After the deformation by randomly generated τ_1 and τ_2 the resulting map will be of non polynomial density. So, it is unclear how to write it is truncation $\tau_1 E \tau_2|_{W_1}$ in a standard form and generate Gröbner basis. One can play with idea to invent the decompression rules but it is not clear how to create a pairs of the kind expanded plaintext and its image under $\tau_1 E \tau_2$ which is available only partially. Of course there is room for alternative cryptanalysis. We hope that our cryptosystem will be an interesting object for specialists in Cryptanalysis.

References

1. Bollobás, B.: Extremal Graph Theory. Academic Press, London (1978)
2. Ding, J., Gower, J.E., Schmidt, D.S.: Multivariate Public Key Cryptosystems. Advances in Information Security, vol. 25, p. 260. Springer (2006)
3. Ding, J., Yang, B.-Y.: Multivariate Public-Key Cryptography. In: Post-Quantum Cryptography, pp. 193–241. Springer (2009)
4. Imai, H., Matsumoto, T.: Algebraic methods for constructing asymmetric cryptosystems. In: Calmet, J. (ed.) AAECC 1985. LNCS, vol. 229, pp. 108–119. Springer, Heidelberg (1986)
5. Kipnis, A., Shamir, A.: Cryptanalysis of the oil & vinegar signature scheme. In: Krawczyk, H. (ed.) CRYPTO 1998. LNCS, vol. 1462, pp. 257–266. Springer, Heidelberg (1998)
6. Klisowski, M., Ustimenko, V.: On the Comparison of Cryptographical Properties of Two Different Families of Graphs with Large Cycle Indicator. Mathematics in Computer Science 2, 181–198 (2012)
7. Kotorowicz, J., Ustimenko, V.: On the implementation of cryptoalgorithms based on algebraic graphs over some commutative rings. Special Issue: Proceedings of the International Conferences: Infinite Particle Systems, Complex Systems Theory and its Application, Kazimerz Dolny, Poland (2006), Condenced Matters Physics 11(2(54)), 347–360 (2008)
8. Lubotsky, A., Philips, R., Sarnak, P.: Ramanujan graphs. J. Comb. Theory 115, 62–89 (1989)
9. Lazebnik, F., Ustimenko, V., Woldar, A.J.: A New Series of Dense Graphs of High Girth. J.Bull. Amer. Math. Soc. 32, 73–79 (1995)
10. Lazebnik, F., Ustimenko, V.: Explicit construction of graphs with arbitrary large girth and of large size. Discrete Applied Mathematics 60, 275–284 (1995)
11. Margulis, G.: Explicit group-theoretical constructions of combinatorial schemes and their application to desighn of expanders and concentrators. J. Probl. Peredachi Informatsii. 24(1), 51–60 (1988); English translation publ. Journal of Problems of Information Transmission, 39–46

12. Romańczuk, U., Ustimenko, V.: On regular forests given in terms of algebraic geometry, new families of expanding graphs with large girth and new multivariate cryptographical algorithms. In: Proceedings of International Conference: Applications of Computer Algebra, Malaga, 135–139 (2013)

13. Shamir, A.: Efficient signature schemes based on birational permutations. In: Stinson, D.R. (ed.) CRYPTO 1993. LNCS, vol. 773, pp. 1–12. Springer, Heidelberg (1994)

14. Ustimenko, V.: Coordinatisation of Trees and their Quotients. In: The "Voronoj's Impact on Modern Science". Kiev, Institute of Mathematics, vol. 2, pp. 125–152 (1998)

15. Ustimenko, V.: CRYPTIM: Graphs as Tools for Symmetric Encryption. In: Bozta, S., Sphparlinski, I. (eds.) AAECC 2001. LNCS, vol. 2227, pp. 278–287. Springer, Heidelberg (2001)

16. Ustimenko, V.: Graphs with special arcs and cryptography. Acta Applicandae Mathematicae (Kluwer) 74, 117–153 (2002)

17. Ustimenko, V.: Maximality of affine group and hidden graph cryptosystems. J. Algebra Discrete Math. (1), 133–150 (2005)

18. Ustimenko, V.: On the cryptographical properties of extreme algebraic graphs. In: Algebraic Aspects of Digital Communications. Lectures of Advanced NATO Institute, NATO Science for Peace and Security Series - D: Information and Communication Security, vol. 24, p. 296. IOS Press (2009)

19. Ustimenko, V.: On the extremal graph theory for directed graphs and its cryptographical applications. In: Shaska, T., Huffman, W.C., Joener, D., Ustimenko, V. (eds.) Advances in Coding Theory and Cryptography, Series on Coding and Cryptology, vol. 3, pp. 181–200 (2007)

20. Ustimenko, V.: Algebraic groups an small world graphs of high girth. Albanian Journal of Mathematics 3, 25–33 (2009)

21. Ustimenko, V., Romańczuk, U.: On Dynamical Systems of Large Girth or Cycle Indicator and their applications to Multivariate Cryptography. In: Yang, X.-S. (ed.) Artificial Intelligence, Evolutionary Computing and Metaheuristics. SCI, vol. 427, pp. 231–256. Springer, Heidelberg (2013)

22. Ustimenko, V.: Wróblewska, A.: On some algebraic aspects of data security in cloud computing. In: Proceedings of International Conference: Applications of Computer Algebra, Malaga, pp. 144–147 (2013)

23. Ustimenko V., Wróblewska, A.: On the key exchange encryption with nonlinear multivariate maps of stable degree. Annales UMCS (Informatica) (accepted for publication, 2014)

24. Wróblewska, A.: On some properties of graph based public keys. NATO Advanced Studies Institute: New challenges in digital communications. Albanian Journal of Mathematics 2(3), 229–234 (2008)

Statistical Analysis of the Chaos-Driven Elliptic Curve Pseudo-random Number Generators

Omar Reyad[1,2] and Zbigniew Kotulski[2]

[1] Faculty of Science, Sohag University, Egypt
ormak4@yahoo.com
[2] Faculty of Electronics and Information Technology,
Warsaw University of Technology, Poland
zkotulsk@tele.pw.edu.pl

Abstract. In this paper, after a short survey describing several known constructions recommended for generating sequences of pseudo-random numbers based on elliptic curves over finite fields of prime order, we propose a method of generating such sequences of points with algorithms driven by a chaotic map. Our construction improves randomness of the sequence generated since it combines good statistical properties of an ECPRNG (Elliptic Curve Pseudo-Random Number Generator) and a CPRNG (Chaotic Pseudo-Random Number Generator). Theoretical analysis shows that periods of the proposed constructions are longer than in the case of the ECPRNG without modulation by a chaotic map. In the second part of the paper we present numerical analysis of the proposed construction to obtain optimal parameters of the generator. We also use some tests from the NIST's SP 800-22 *Statistical Test Suite for Random and Pseudorandom Number Generators for Cryptographic Applications* to analyze statistical properties of the proposed constructions for different values of parameters.

Keywords: elliptic curve cryptography, random number generator, chaotic maps, statistical testing of PRNG.

1 Introduction

The security of most known cryptographic systems depends upon generation of unpredictable quantities that must be of sufficient size and randomness. Taking Elliptic Curve Cryptography (ECC) as an example, we need to generate random bits in order to create random curves and the large secret integer [1, 2]. This implies that we usually need to implement a random number generator in a cryptographic system.

However, sources of truly random integers are hard to use in practice. It is therefore common to search for pseudo-random number generators (PRNG). Roughly speaking, a pseudo-random source may not be distinguished from a truly random source by any polynomial time algorithm. Several PRNG have been proposed which are using the form of elliptic curves such as [3]. Since [4] methods, different approaches for extracting pseudo-randomness from elliptic curves have been proposed by [5, 6].

Z. Kotulski et al. (Eds.): CSS 2014, CCIS 448, pp. 38–48, 2014.
© Springer-Verlag Berlin Heidelberg 2014

The great advantage of ECC is operating over small-size finite fields (comparing other public-key cryptosystems, for example RSA). However, in the case of pseudo-random numbers generator small finite fields imply short period of a generator. Therefore, to increase the period of a generator working on an elliptic curve (EC) we propose to combine it with a chaotic dynamical system.

Chaotic dynamical systems are another recent branch of cryptography. Its security is based on high sensitivity of iterations of maps to initial conditions and parameters. The idea of application of discrete dynamical systems for constructing cryptosystems was presented in [7] where the authors proposed using chaotic maps' parameters as a secret key. Their system was instantaneously broken [8] but an improved cryptosystem [9] with an initial condition of the chaotic dynamical system playing the role of a secret key still remains secure. In recent years such cryptosystems have been extensively studied with a large variety of particular algorithms and applications. Among them Chaotic Pseudo-Random Number Generators (CPRNG) initiated in [10] found many effective implementations [11] since their period is (by theory) infinite.

In this paper we propose a new method of generating sequences of pseudorandom points based on elliptic curve operations over finite fields which is driven by a chaotic map. Such a construction increases randomness of the sequence generated and makes its period (theoretically) infinite since it combines positive properties of an ECPRNG and a CPRNG. After transformation of the points into binary digits it can be used for any cryptographic applications.

The organization of the rest of the paper is as follows. In Section 2, the background of EC over finite fields and the ECPRNG construction are discussed in Subsection 2.1. The construction of CPRNG are discussed in Subsection 2.2. In Subsection 2.3 we discuss the Chaos-Driven Elliptic Curve Pseudo-Random Number Generators (C-D ECPRNG) introduced in [12] and describe its C-D ECPRNG construction. The Statistical Analysis of the C-D ECPRNG will be described in Section 3. The test results are reported in Section 4 while the test results for the ECPRNG with chaotic switching are reported in Section 5. In Section 6, discussions and conclusions are made.

2 Background Results

Certainly, any decent sequence of pseudo-random numbers should have a large period. As we have mentioned, the constructions presented here are improved by using chaotic maps to make their period larger. In this paper we assume that the elliptic curve E is defined over a finite field F_p of prime order p which is represented by the elements of the set $0, 1, ..., p - 1$.

2.1 Elliptic Curve Pseudo-random Number Generators

Let E be an elliptic curve over F_p, $p > 3$, given by an affine Weierstrass equation of the form:

$$E : y^2 = x^3 + ax + b \tag{1}$$

with the coefficients $a, b \in F_p$, such that $4a^3 + 27b^2 \neq 0$. We recall that the set $E(F_p)$ of points of any elliptic curve E in the affine F_p-valued coordinates forms an Abelian group (with a point at infinity denoted by O as the neutral element) and the cardinality of this group satisfies the Hasse-Weil bound:

$$|\#E(F_p) - p - 1| \leq 2\sqrt{p} . \tag{2}$$

Points addition and points doubling are the basic EC operations. Number by point multiplication on EC requires a scalar multiplication operation kP, defined for a point $P = (x, y)$ on EC and a positive integer k as k times addition of P to itself. This scalar multiplication can be done by a series of doubling and addition operations of P. Let us start with $P = (x_1, y_1)$ where $P \neq -P$. To determine $2P = (x_3, y_3)$, P is doubled, use the following equation:

$$x_3 = \left(\frac{3x_1^2 + a}{2y_1}\right)^2 - 2x_1 \text{ and } y_3 = \left(\frac{3x_1^2 + a}{2y_1}\right)(x_1 - x_3) - y_1 . \tag{3}$$

To determine $3P$, the addition of points P and $2P$ is used, treating $2P = Q$. Here, P has the coordinates $P = (x_1, y_1)$ and $Q = 2P$ has the coordinates $Q = (x_2, y_2)$, where $P \neq \pm Q$. Then $P + Q = (x_3, y_3)$, where:

$$x_3 = \left(\frac{y_2 - y_1}{x_2 - x_1}\right)^2 - x_1 - x_2 \text{ and } y_3 = \left(\frac{y_2 - y_1}{x_2 - x_1}\right)(x_1 - x_3) - y_1 . \tag{4}$$

Therefore, doubling and addition are applied depending on a sequence of operations determined for k. Every point (x_3, y_3) evaluated by doubling or addition is an affine point (points on the EC). Observe that dividing one element by another is multiplication by the inverse of that element in F_p . For this and some other general properties of elliptic curves see [1, 18–21].

2.2   Chaotic Pseudo-random Number Generators

Consider the following dynamical system defined as a pair (S, Φ), where S is the state space (usually metric space) and $(\Phi : S \rightarrow S)$ is a measurable map which is the generator of the semigroup of iterations [13]. The trajectory starting from the initial state s_0 is the sequence $(s_0)_{i=0}^{\infty}$ of elements of S obtained by iteration:

$$s_{i+1} = \Phi(s_i), i = 0, 1, 2, \ldots . \tag{5}$$

Assume that μ is a normalized invariant measure of the system, equivalent to a Lebesgue measure. The idea of construction of CPRNG is to divide the state space S, $\mu(S) = 1$, into two disjoint parts S_0, S_1 such that $\mu(S_0) = \mu(S_1) = 1/2$. As a seed we shall consider an initial point $s \in S' \subseteq S$, where S' is the set of acceptable seeds (for most systems, $\mu(S') = 1$). To obtain a pseudo-random sequence of bits we observe the iterations of the system governed by the map Φ starting from s, i.e., the sequence $s_i := \Phi^i(s)$. We assume that the i-th bit $b_i(s)$ of the generated pseudo-random sequence is equal to "0" if $s_i \in S_0$, and is equal to "1" otherwise, so as a result of iterations we obtain the infinite sequence of bits $G(s)$. Finally, we obtain the map:

$$G : S' \to \prod_{i=1}^{\infty} \{0, 1\} \, , \tag{6}$$

such that:

$$G(s) = \{b_i(s)\}_{i=1,2,\ldots} = \{b_1(s), b_2(s), \ldots\} \, , \tag{7}$$

and where $\prod_{i=1}^{\infty} \{0, 1\}$ is the Cartesian product of the infinite number of the two-element set $\{0, 1\}$.

In the paper [14] it was proven that if the discrete dynamical system (5) is chaotic, ergodic and it satisfies the mixing property (which is stronger than ergodicity), then the CPRNG defined in (6) and (7) has the fundamental required properties of PRNG:

− unique dependence of the sequence (7) on the seed s,
− equiprobable occurrence of "0" and "1" in the sequence (7),
− asymptotic statistical independence of bits.

Moreover, theoretically the period of such a CPRNG is infinite, since it is iterated over the infinite state space S.

In many practical applications for constructing CPRNG we assume that $S = [0, 1]$ is the interval, $S_0 = [0, 0.5]$, $S_1 = (0.5, 1]$ are two subsets of the measure equal to 0.5 and $\Phi : [0, 1] \to [0, 1]$ is a chaotic map with the positive Lyapunov exponent λ.

Remark In concrete implementations of CPRNG we must carefully check properties of the particular, chosen chaotic map. Since that map can localize iterations in some subregion of the state space (see [9]) we must either prevent this effect by an additional operation of extending actual states space S to its original size or protect the measure μ by adjusting it to be really symmetric over the two sub-intervals S_0 and S_1.

2.3 Chaos-Driven Elliptic Curve Pseudo-random Number Generators

For a given point $G \in E(F_p)$ and an integer $e \geq 2$, we can define the following two sequences:

1. Additive sequence:

$$U_i = i(1 + b_i)G \oplus U_0 = \begin{cases} iG \oplus U_0 & \text{if } b_i = 0 \\ 2iG \oplus U_0 & \text{if } b_i = 1 \end{cases} , i = 1, 2, \ldots , \tag{8}$$

2. Multiplicative sequence:

$$U_i = e^{i(1+b_i)}G = \begin{cases} e^i G & \text{if } b_i = 0 \\ e^{2i}G & \text{if } b_i = 1 \end{cases}, i = 1, 2, \ldots, \tag{9}$$

where $U_0 \in E(F_p)$ is the "initial value" and b_i is the random bits generated by the chaotic map Φ:

$$b_i = \begin{cases} 0 & \text{if } \Phi^i(s) \in S_0 \\ 1 & \text{if } \Phi^i(s) \in S_1 \end{cases}, i = 1, 2, \ldots . \tag{10}$$

Using the EC point sequence U_i and by converting the x, y coordinates of each point $U_i(x, y)$ into the binary format we can obtain the binary sequence B_i by applying the following map:

$$B_i = U_i(x, y) = U_{RHB}(x, y) . \tag{11}$$

This map takes the right-half bits (RHB) from x and y coordinates which is denoted by $U_{RHB}(x, y)$. If the number of bits is odd, we take the small right-half and ignore the infinity points also.

Example Consider the curve $E : y^2 = x^3 + x + 4$ over F_{17} . This curve has order 14 and is cyclic. Here $p = 17$. Let $G = (0, 15)$ be a point on E and choose $U_0 = (4, 2)$ as the initial value. The EC points U, together with the binary sequence B , are listed in Table 1. Note that here the number of $p = 17$ is equal to 5 bits, so we take two different RHB and we ignore the infinity (Inf) points.

Table 1. An example of transforming EC points into binary sequences

i	$U_i(x, y)$	$U_i(x, y)_2$	$B_i(U_i)_{2x2}$
1	$(14, 5)$	$(01110, 00101)$	$(10, 01)$
2	$(16, 11)$	$(10000, 01011)$	$(00, 11)$
3	$(0, 2)$	$(00000, 00010)$	$(00, 10)$
4	(Inf, Inf)	———	——
5	$(0, 15)$	$(00000, 01111)$	$(00, 11)$
6	$(16, 6)$	$(10000, 00110)$	$(00, 10)$
.	......	....	.....

So, the output binary sequence $B = 10010011001000110010\ldots$.

3   Analysis of the C-D ECPRNG

To ensure good statistical properties (which determine the quality of a generator) of the proposed ECPRNG we assume that the used, dynamical systems are also ergodic or preferably mixing. This allows us to use the well-developed theory of dynamical systems to prove the required statistical properties. Traditionally, extensive statistical testing was used to assess or estimate this quality. Test suites developed for this purpose may be found in [15–17]. From these tests we selected 5 tests which taken together verify random properties of the generated sequences. They are:

1. The monobit test (in Tables 2 - 6 named *Frequency Test*), which verifies if the number of "1" bits in the sequence lies within specified limits,
2. The cumulative sums test, which determines whether the cumulative sum of the partial sequences occurring in the tested sequence is too large or too small relative to the expected behavior of that cumulative sum for random sequences. The test has two modes, which are either forward through the sequence or backward through the sequence, named in the Tables *C.Sum (forward)* and *C.Sum (reverse)*, respectively,
3. The runs test (*Runs Test* in the Tables) checking whether the number of runs (the test is carried out for runs of zeros and runs of ones) of length 1, 2, 3, 4 and 5 as well as the number of runs which are longer than 5, each lies within specified limits,
4. The long run test (*Longest Runs Test*) confirming that in the tested sequence there must be no run of length equal to or greater than 34 bits,
5. The discrete Fourier transform test (*DFT*) detecting the periodic features in the tested sequence that would indicate deviation from the assumption of randomness.

Thus, in these 5 tests, the monobit test verifies if globally the binary distribution is symmetric, the cumulative sums tests check if the sequence is symmetrically growing during bits generation, the runs test and the long run test confirm bits independence and the discrete Fourier transform test allows detecting periodic behavior of the generated binary sequences. Additional motivation for such a choice of such a set of 5 tests (from all 15 tests proposed in the document SP800-22b [16]) is that they can be applied for binary sequences of different sizes, also very short ones. In our investigations we used the sequences of 1000, 2000, 5000, 10000, 20000, 40000 bits for the generators constructed on EC over small finite field and additionally, the sequences of 60000, 80000 bits for the generators on EC over a larger finite field.

The statistical tests made in this paper were on the significance level α equal to 0.01, so the tests pass if P-value ≥ 0.01,. Moreover, the larger the P-value is, the better the pseudo-random property the generator is.

To investigate the effect of chaotic modulation of both additive and multiplicative ECPRNG we considered three examples of chaotic dynamical systems and two elliptic curves over different-size finite fields. First, we tested random properties of the binary sequences generated by three discrete dynamical systems governed by the following maps:

the Tent Map [22]:

$$s_{i+1} = \Phi(s_i) = \begin{cases} 2s_i & \text{if } s_i < \frac{1}{2} \\ 2(1 - s_i) & \text{if } s_i \geq \frac{1}{2} \end{cases} \tag{12}$$

the Logistic Map [23]:

$$s_{i+1} = \Phi(s_i) = 4 \cdot s_i (1 - s_i) , \tag{13}$$

both for the state space $S = [0,1]$ and $S_0 = [0, 0.5]$, $S_1 = (0.5, 1]$, and the Chebyshev Map [24]:

$$s_{i+1} = \Phi(s_i) = \cos\left(4 \cos^{-1}(s_i)\right) \tag{14}$$

for the state space $S = [-1, 1]$ and $S_0 = [-1, 0]$, $S_1 = (0, 1]$.

Before engaging a chaotic map into C-D ECPRNG, we test the CPRNG checking its properties for certain initial conditions, later generate the chaotic sequence for the C-D ECPRNG. The statistical tests for the Logistic Map (13), the Tent map (12) and the Chebyshev Map (14) confirmed good randomness of the binary sequences generated.

4   Results of the Statistical Analysis of the Additive and the Multiplicative ECPRNG

In the experiments we used the following equation for the two elliptic curves E_1 and E_2:

$$E : y^2 = x^3 + x + 4 \tag{15}$$

over F_{733} for the curve E_1 and over F_{5477} for E_2.

The results of testing the generated sequences are presented in Tables 2 - 5. Table 2 presents the results for the additive sequence on the curve E_1 without chaotic modulation. As it is expected, the generator works correctly for short binary sequences (5000 bits) due to its periodicity, when is indicated by the DFT Test. Including the C-D ECPRNG enables generating correctly longer sequences (10000 bits) for all the chaotic maps, the tent map example is shown in Table 4.

For the multiplicative sequence on the same curve E_1, the generator works correctly for only very short sequences (2000 bits) without chaotic modulation, see Table 3 and by using C-D ECPRNG we obtain longer sequences (20000 bits) as it can be seen in Table 5. Note that the binary length of $p = 733$ is 10 bits, so we take the five RHB in this case.

Analogous experiments have been performed for the larger elliptic curve E_2 which is over F_{5477}. First, the optimal point-to-bits encoding was fixed as 6 bits for each point coordinate (binary length of $p = 5477$ is 13). Second, the additive and multiplicative sequences in Subsection 2.3 are generated and tested. For the two sequences we found that the non-disturbed ECPRNG gave a correct result up to 10000 bits and by including C-D ECPRNG we get much correct pseudorandom bits up to 40000 bits. For 60000 and more bits the Longest Runs test

Table 2. Additive ECPRNG without chaotic modulation. P-values for the case $EC_{5x5}, p = 733$

Test name	Case 1 1000 bits	Case 2 2000 bits	Case 3 5000 bits	Case 4 10000 bits	Case 5 20000 bits	Case 6 40000 bits
Frequency	0.447884	0.858028	0.820988	0.029257	**0.004475**	**0.000001**
C. Sum (forward)	0.823133	0.790027	0.985938	0.054210	**0.008372**	**0.000001**
C. Sum (reverse)	0.589898	0.932277	0.858353	0.021545	**0.003816**	**0.000001**
Runs	0.556691	0.446663	0.365793	0.526879	0.234892	——
Longest Runs	1.000000	1.000000	1.000000	0.805402	0.417083	0.059569
DFT	0.681519	0.663355	0.783087	**0.000033**	**0.000000**	**0.000000**

Table 3. Multiplicative ECPRNG without chaotic modulation. P-values for the case $EC_{5x5}, p = 733$

Test name	Case 1 1000 bits	Case 2 2000 bits	Case 3 5000 bits	Case 4 10000 bits	Case 5 20000 bits	Case 6 40000 bits
Frequency	0.704336	0.395489	0.322199	0.133614	0.029414	**0.001524**
C. Sum (forward)	0.999758	0.727622	0.538108	0.219194	0.048183	**0.002749**
C. Sum (reverse)	0.922381	0.583328	0.526187	0.223666	0.049984	**0.002609**
Runs	0.413496	0.404359	0.153028	0.045722	**0.007007**	**0.000113**
Longest Runs	1.000000	1.000000	1.000000	0.706404	0.272124	0.019340
DFT	0.100680	0.561658	**0.000000**	**0.000000**	**0.000000**	0.603685

Table 4. Additive ECPRNG modulated with the Tent map. P-values for the case $EC_{5x5}, p = 733$

Test name	Case 1 1000 bits	Case 2 2000 bits	Case 3 5000 bits	Case 4 10000 bits	Case 5 20000 bits	Case 6 40000 bits
Frequency	0.704336	0.720515	0.799064	0.368120	0.223900	0.012774
C. Sum (forward)	0.994708	0.999373	0.930997	0.647610	0.310428	0.013868
C. Sum (reverse)	0.922381	0.885595	0.717597	0.499167	0.327181	0.017845
Runs	0.902935	0.790637	0.235212	0.266142	0.187170	**0.009614**
Longest Runs	1.000000	1.000000	1.000000	0.653236	0.213793	0.194439
DFT	0.681519	0.884636	0.520637	0.845655	**0.000140**	**0.000000**

Table 5. Multiplicative ECPRNG modulated with the Chebyshev map. P-values for the case $EC_{5x5}, p = 733$

Test name	Case 1 1000 bits	Case 2 2000 bits	Case 3 5000 bits	Case 4 10000 bits	Case 5 20000 bits	Case 6 40000 bits
Frequency	0.129041	0.244929	0.820988	0.984043	0.506255	0.026419
C. Sum (forward)	0.258072	0.304777	0.638440	0.897326	0.892023	0.049536
C. Sum (reverse)	0.213590	0.437067	0.846466	0.882140	0.491372	0.020340
Runs	0.758598	0.644070	0.692651	0.041351	0.013443	**0.000509**
Longest Runs	1.000000	1.000000	1.000000	0.706404	0.272124	0.019340
DFT	0.837419	0.884636	0.168669	0.603685	0.679644	0.948263

indicates the generators irregularity in the expected length of the longest run of ones in the random sequence.

5   ECPRNG with Chaotic Switching

To improve the periodicity of small ECs we use the same equation in (15) to get two curves E_3 and E_4 with very small prime numbers 29 and 53 respectively. We take one point from E_3 and one point from E_4 in a staggered manner in order to generate binary sequences from these two curves.

Table 6. Two additive ECPRNG with periodic (rows 1-3) and chaotic (rows 4-6) switching. P-values for the case $EC_{2x3}, p = 29, 53$

Test name	Case 1 100 bits	Case 2 200 bits	Case 3 500 bits	Case 4 1000 bits	Case 5 2000 bits	Case 6 4000 bits
Frequency	1.000000	0.777297	0.371093	0.164104	0.054478	0.020973
Runs	0.045500	0.065056	**0.004908**	**0.001916**	**0.000411**	**0.000001**
DFT	0.745603	0.646355	0.191601	**0.000221**	**0.000000**	**0.000000**
Frequency	1.000000	0.777297	0.371093	0.229493	0.073638	0.020973
Runs	0.071861	0.200911	0.099274	0.051674	0.132312	**0.006677**
DFT	0.745603	0.358795	0.309788	0.837419	0.884636	0.607959

For example, consider that after applying the additive sequence in (8) the resultant E_3 points is A $= (a_1, a_2, ...)$ and E_4 points is D $= (d_1, d_2, ...)$. We take this series of points $(a_1\ d_1\ a_2\ d_2\ ....)$ to generate our sequence. In the case of chaotic switching, we randomly take points on unpredicted series based on a chaotic map to generate pseudo-random sequence as shown in Table 6. In this table we perform only 3 tests to investigate the effect of chaotic switching on selecting points from E_3 and E_4 respectively. As shown in Table 6, the first three tests are without chaotic switching and the next three tests are with it. It is clear that this generates longer sequences with good pseudo-random properties. Note that we take two RHB for E_3 and three RHB for E_4, so called EC_{2x3}.

6   Conclusions and Future Work

In this paper we propose a method for generating sequences of pseudo-random numbers based on elliptic curves over finite fields with algorithms driven by a chaotic map. Our construction improves randomness of the generated sequence since it combines good statistical properties of an ECPRNG and a CPRNG. From our experiments presented in Section 4 and by comparing purely EC-based pseudo-random number generator, our construction has longer period for a fixed size of the finite field F_p where the EC lives. Thus, we can use smaller fields with less computational complexity of arithmetic calculations to obtain a bitstream of a fixed length. Also, as mentioned in Section 5, we can generate longer sequences with good pseudo-random properties by using ECPRNG with the chaotic switching mode and obtain more bits in one iteration: instead 1 bit, as it is in the chaotic case, we can have a large number of bits, which slightly increases the speed of generation.

The experiments presented here confirm that our theoretical assumptions concerning the new construction of C-D ECPRNG are satisfied. However, to optimize the procedures of generation further extensive studies must be performed. One possible extension is generating bits using elliptic curves over binary finite fields, to omit the operation of decoding points of the elliptic curve into binary sequences. Such research will be the subject of our further studies.

References

1. Menezes, A.: Elliptic Curve Public Key Cryptosystems. Kluwer Academic, Dordrecht (1993)
2. Lee, L.P., Wong, K.W.: A random number generator based on elliptic curve operations. Journal of Computers and Mathematics with Applications 47, 217–226 (2004)
3. Jao, D., Jetchev, D., Venkatesan, R.: On the bits of elliptic curve Diffie-Hellman keys. In: Srinathan, K., Rangan, C.P., Yung, M. (eds.) INDOCRYPT 2007. LNCS, vol. 4859, pp. 33–47. Springer, Heidelberg (2007)
4. Kaliski, B.S.: One-way permutations on elliptic curves. Journal of Cryptology 3, 187–199 (1991-1992)
5. Caragiu, M., Johns, R.A., Gieseler, J.: Quasi-random structures from elliptic curves. J. Algebra, Number Theory Appl. 6, 561–571 (2006)
6. Gong, G., Berson, T.A., Stinson, D.R.: Elliptic curve pseudorandom sequence generators. In: Heys, H.M., Adams, C.M. (eds.) SAC 1999. LNCS, vol. 1758, p. 34. Springer, Heidelberg (2000)
7. Habutsu, T., Nishio, Y., Sasase, I., Mori, S.: A secret key cryptosystem by iterating a chaotic map. In: Davies, D.W. (ed.) EUROCRYPT 1991. LNCS, vol. 547, pp. 127–140. Springer, Heidelberg (1991)
8. Biham, E.: Cryptanalysis of the chaotic-map cryptosystem suggested at EUROCRYPT'91. In: Davies, D.W. (ed.) EUROCRYPT 1991. LNCS, vol. 547, pp. 532–534. Springer, Heidelberg (1991)
9. Kotulski, Z., Szczepański, J.: Discrete chaotic cryptography. Annalen der Physik 6(5), 381–394 (1997)
10. Kohda, T., Tsuneda, A.: Statistic of chaotic binary sequences. IEEE Transactions on Information Theory 43(1), 104–112 (1997)
11. Kotulski, Z., Szczepański, J., Górski, K., Paszkiewicz, A., Gorska, A.: On constructive approach to chaotic pseudorandom number generators. In: Proceedings RCMIS 2000, Zegrze, October 4-6, vol. 1, pp. 191–203 (2000)
12. Reyad, O., Kotulski, Z.: On Pseudo-random Number Generators Using Elliptic Curves and Chaotic Systems. Applied Mathematics & Information Sciences 9(1) (2015) (accepted paper)
13. Cornfeld, L.P., Fomin, S.V., Sinai, Y.G.: Ergodic Theory. Springer, Berlin (1982)
14. Kotulski, Z., Szczepański, J.: Pseudorandom number generators based on chaotic dynamical systems. Open Systems & Information Dynamics 8(2), 137–146 (2001)

15. FIPS 140-2: Security Requirements for Cryptographic Modules, NIST (2000)
16. Rukhin, A., Soto, J., Nechvatal, J., et al.: A Statistical Test Suite for Random and Pseudorandom Number Generators for Cryptographic Applications. NIST Special Publication 800-22 with revisions (May 15, 2001)
17. Knuth, D.E.: The Art of Computer Programming - Seminumerical Algorithms, vol. 2. Addison-Wesley, Reading (1981)
18. Blake, I., Seroussi, G., Smart, N.: Elliptic curves in cryptography. London Math. Soc., Lecture Note Series, vol. 265. Cambridge Univ. Press (1999)
19. Silverman, J.H.: The arithmetic of elliptic curves. Springer, Berlin (1995)
20. Hallgren, S.: Linear congruential generators over elliptic curves. Preprint CS-94-143, Dept. of Comp. Sci., Cornegie Mellon Univ., 1–10 (1994)
21. Shparlinski, I.E.: Pseudorandom number generators from elliptic curves. In: Affine Algebraic Geometry, pp. 121–142. Amer. Math. Soc. (2009)
22. Amigo, J.M., Kocarev, L., Szczepański, J.: Theory and Practice of Chaotic Cryptography. Physics Letters A 366(3), 211–216 (2007)
23. Phatak, S.C., Rao, S.S.: Logistic map: A possible random-number generator. Physical Review E 51(4), 3670–3678 (1995)
24. Liao, X.F., Li, X.M., Peng, J., et al.: A digital secure image communication scheme based on the chaotic Chebyshev map. Int. J. Commun. Syst. 17(5), 437–445 (2004)

Identity-Based Cryptography
in Credit Card Payments

Kimmo Halunen and Mirko Sailio

VTT Technical Research Centre of Finland,
Oulu, Finland
{kimmo.halunen,mirko.sailio}@vtt.fi

Abstract. In this paper we describe how to apply identity based cryptography to credit card payments. This would help with reducing the possibility of credit card fraud that is prevalent on the Internet. Our method is founded on the identity-based cryptography and it secures the credit card transactions in such a way that many types of credit card fraud become either impossible or much more difficult for the attacker to perform simply by stealing the credit card number and some related information. Our method would require some changes to the functionality of the credit cards and thus it is not an immediate remedy. However, the decreasing costs of more advanced hardware and the fairly fast cycle of reissuing new credit cards make it possible to include identity-based cryptography methods to credit cards in the near future.

1 Introduction

Modern networked society has made it possible to conduct credit card transactions over the Internet and this has had a huge impact on the trade of goods and services across the world. It is now fairly easy to purchase almost anything from anywhere in the world with your laptop or even mobile phone. The payments are usually made using credit cards, although in recent years different online systems such as PayPal and even digital currencies (e.g. Bitcoin [14]) have emerged.

Credit card fraud is a global problem that costs billions of dollars to different actors annually. As the credit cards had emerged already before the explosive growth of online commerce, there were few security measures against novel attacks on payments. New security methods and procedures, e.g., security codes on the back of the card, chip and PIN authentication and the opt-in use of online transactions on the cards provided by some banks, have been deployed as new forms of attacks and fraud have been discovered. Still, the amount of credit card fraud worldwide was over 5 billion dollars in 2012.[1]

The new countermeasures have not been able to stop the growth of credit card fraud especially in the e-commerce. One of the key problems is that the credit card number itself is used partially as a secret that then enables transactions on that card's account. However, this credit card number is stored by many

---

[1] See http://www.statisticbrain.com/credit-card-fraud-statistics/

Z. Kotulski et al. (Eds.): CSS 2014, CCIS 448, pp. 49–58, 2014.

vendors in order to make the purchasing of goods and services online as easy as possible and can not be considered a secret known only to the credit card holder. This has led to a situation, where attackers can get into their hands sometimes enormously large databases containing credit card numbers. Even though there are standards such as PCI DSS [17] and EMV [6] for processing payments and handling this data and these have helped against fraud, these attacks continue to be successful. In 2013 there were 84 reported hacking attacks with lost credit card numbers with over 250 million credentials lost. The majority of incidents (57) had unknown amount of credentials lost and thus the total tally may be even greater.[2] Also there are some results that show that even the EMV protocols contain weaknesses that can be exploited [2]. Thus, there is a need to enhance the security of credit card payments.

Modern cryptography has provided our society with a wide variety of tools for conducting secure actions over the Internet. Public key cryptography (PKC) in general has made it possible for example to exchange keys between two previously unacquainted entities [4]. More recent developments have provided systems for electronic voting [18], digital signatures [8] etc. One particular special case of public key cryptography is identity-based cryptography (IBC), which was first introduced in [19]. Later on practical constructions realising both identity-based encryption (IBE) [3] and signatures (IBS) [9] have been proposed. With the help of these techniques, new countermeasures against credit card fraud can be devised.

1.1   Our Contributions

In this paper, we introduce a method for applying IBC in credit card payments. In our method, the credit card number, together with some other identifying information, acts as the identity of the person conducting the payments and thus is also the public key in the underlying IBC system. The secret key related to that public key is stored on the card and then used to sign the transactions. This means that the credit card number itself cannot be utilised by an attacker to make fraudulent transactions. The attacker needs to obtain the secret key by some manner and the security proofs of the IBC systems show that this is infeasible by merely knowing the credit card number, i.e., the public key. Our method for credit card payments requires some changes to the payment infrastructure, but provides better security against the theft of the credit card number. We also present an idea of a partial solution that could be used with existing systems, but does not offer all the benefits of our IBC based system and has also some other weaknesses.

This paper is organised as follows. The next section presents the most relevant previous work on IBC systems and some basic information on e-commerce, online payments and credit card fraud. The third section describes the basic theoretical foundations of the IBC systems that can be utilised in our methods. The fourth section contains our proposal for payment system with the help of IBC. Finally, we discuss our findings and their implications and give some conclusions of our work.

---

[2] http://datalossdb.org/

2   Previous Work

As mentioned above, the identity-based cryptography was already proposed in [19]. The first proposal lacked a concrete system over which the IBC could be realised. Fortunately, later on there have been several proposals that provide both IBE and IBS. For example, the scheme in [3] provides identity-based encryption in a fairly efficient manner. An example of an identity-based signature system can be found in [9].

E-commerce is nowadays an integral part of the global economy. When global transactions are concerned, credit cards are one of the most used methods of payment and thus also a very attractive target for criminals. For example, in [16] the trends show that there is a growing amount of malicious software that attacks banking and credit card information. Furthermore, the Internet provides a lot of opportunities to monetise the stolen credit card numbers. The price of a credit card number can vary greatly from a few dollars to hundred dollars or more depending on the known qualities of the card [16].

Today, a lot of research on securing the transactions of the networked world is directed at so-called *cryptocurrencies*. The most famous form of such a digital currency is Bitcoin [14], which has gathered a fairly large (and somewhat underground) economy around it.[3] These new ideas have not yet been adopted as widely as the credit card system and are thus not so vital to the functioning of our e-commerce. There are also many new security issues raised by the new cryptocurrencies.

As the research on cryptocurrencies is getting more and more traction, there have not been very many proposals to improve the security of the credit card payment system. Especially, there has not been research on radical improvements in the system and some of the implemented improvements towards security, such as the '3-D Secure' protocol, have been critiqued [13]. On the other hand, the security of the credit card system has been proven vulnerable by the amount of fraud and the large scale database leaks of large vendors. Furthermore, there has been some critique on the forensic capabilities of the modern credit card payment system, although many other alternatives such as Bitcoin fall short of the required forensic properties [12].

3   Identity-Based Cryptography

IBC systems are usually based on *pairings*. In cryptography, a pairing is defined as a mapping $e : G_1 \times G_2 \to G_3$, where G_1, G_2 and G_3 are the groups of prime order p with the generators g_1, g_2 and g_3 respectively. Furthermore, the pairing needs to satisfy two conditions: For all $a, b \in \{0, 1, \ldots, p-1\}, e(g_1^a, g_2^b) = e(g_1, g_2)^{ab}$ and $e(g_1, g_2) \neq 1 \in G_3$. Also these pairings need to be efficiently computable in order to be useful. The Weil pairing and the Tate pairing over elliptic curves have been popular choices to build IBC systems on. An interested

---

[3] See for example https://coinmarketcap.com/ for recent trading volumes.

reader can find more on the basic properties of pairings and a survey of IBC systems in [5].

Pairings have also been used in the attribute-based cryptography, which offers a more granular approach to user identities (see for example [11,15] for concrete proposals). In the attribute-based cryptography, there is no single identity, but a set of attributes that are verified by some attribute authorities. Then different predicates over these attributes can be formed and for example signatures attesting to having a certain set of attributes can be computed. Thus, in contrast to IBC, the "complete" identity of a user does not need to be revealed.

One important thing to note about IBC is that the identities in this respect do not need to be identities as we usually understand them. The identity information can be some string of information related to identity, e.g., an email address, name or even social security number. The methods of IBC map this information to a public key of a cryptosystem and also generate the corresponding secret key to form a public/private key pair. Usually, this is done with the help of cryptographic hash functions, which can map arbitrary strings of information into values of a fixed length. Furthermore, hash functions ensure that the likelihood of a collision, i.e., two-identities mapping to same hash value, is negligible.

4   Applying IBC to Credit Cards

In this section we present our method for applying IBC to credit cards. We also discuss the effect of our system to the overall credit card payment ecosystem.

4.1   Our Method

The standard four-party payment card scheme is described in Figure 1. Our proposal would be a new specification on the Payment card scheme that is utilised in the transactions between the different parties and is presented in the center of Fig. 1. The Cardholder is making an (online) purchase from the merchant that wants to receive payment from the Cardholder. The Issuer has granted the Cardholder a credit card and generates a public/private key pair for that card. The private key is stored on the credit card and is awarded to be used by the Cardholder. In addition, the card could also have separate functionality to identify or authenticate the Cardholder. The purpose of the card is to conduct signature operations on the chip in order to facilitate payment.

The public key, i.e. the identity, would be the credit card number of the Cardholder's card together with the expiry date. This would be signed with the credit card Issuer's private key. Also other identifying information such as the Cardholder's name may be included to the public key. However, adding too much identity information on the public key makes the system more cumbersome and may lead to situations, where the card needs to be replaced too often. The credit card number and expiry date at least are usually required by the vendors and thus should be considered public information in any case. Name, address and other identifying information are also many times required for purchases,

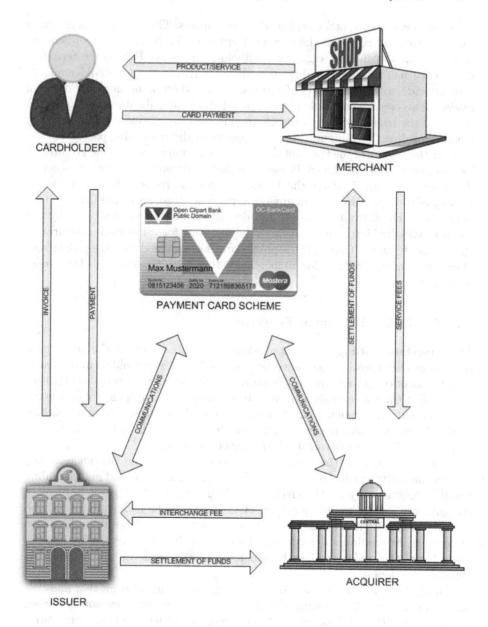

Fig. 1. Standard Four-Party Payment Card Scheme

but may be a subject to changes during the validity period of the card and thus be limiting factors in the use of the credit card.

If the card provided to the Cardholder does not contain methods for identifying or authenticating the Cardholder and communicating the results of the signature computation to the payment framework, it can only be used with point of sale systems or with other card reader mechanisms. Then the system interacts with the card and conducts the signing after the reader has received authentication from the Cardholder, e.g., the Cardholder enters her PIN to the terminal. If the card has the functionality to both authenticate the Cardholder and to communicate with other parts of the framework, there is no need for external readers. This could be a simple numerical pad and a small display for showing the results of the computations to the Cardholder or some wireless communication method for directly communicating the results to the requesting party.

After the signing of the transaction, an authorisation request would go through its designated route in the credit card payment ecosystem to the card issuer as described in Figure 1. After the Issuer receives the request, it can check the validity of the signature (as can any other party with access to the Cardholder's public key), check available funds and decide whether to approve or deny the request. Also the Merchant could check the signature for validity after confirming the certificate on the Cardholder's public key. It is assumed that the public keys of card issuers are available for all merchants that accept credit cards from these issuers.

4.2   Credit Card Payment Ecosystem

The presentation of Figure 1 is somewhat a simplified view of the credit card ecosystem and in reality there are a few more different stakeholders in the credit card payment ecosystem and it is important to know how our proposed changes would affect their view of the system. The most evident players are of course the customer and the merchant. In addition to them, there are several other entities involved.[4] In the following, we briefly mention some of the other stakeholders and the possible effect of our method on their position.

First of all, there is the bank or credit card issuer of the customer. In our system this party would be responsible for issuing the credit card and providing the IBC functionality on the credit card. Thus, one of the biggest burdens of changing the system would be carried by the issuers. The merchants would also need to update their systems to accept these new types of credit cards. These updates might require new readers that can be prohibitively expensive. On the other hand, the updates might be possible at software level and not be that expensive to deploy.

Usually, the online payment is processed via a payment gateway, that finds the correct processors for payments. Furthermore, the payment processor authorises payments for different businesses and communicates with the credit card interchange that either acts on behalf of the credit card issuer (in the case of many large credit card companies) or furthers the request to the issuing bank. The merchant's bank handles the transaction from the merchant's side, i.e., accepts the money from the credit card interchange or the card issuing bank. These parties would not necessarily need to make much adoptions as most of these

---

[4] See for example http://www.practicalecommerce.com/articles/ 168-Credit-Card-Processing-How-It-All-Works

could adopt the new IBC infrastructure and make their respective checks on the signatures with the IBC. Also, the system as a whole would not need to be overhauled and it would be possible to forward the requests based only on the certificate on the public key of the customer's credit card. There is no need to new trust relationships as the card issuers can be the facilitators of the new IBC infrastructure.

4.3 Partial Solution Without IBC

As the merchant databases have been a popular source of credit card information for the attackers, there is an incentive to try to keep the merchant from storing the sensitive credit card number in its database. The above IBC based method solves this problem, but with the introduction of new public key infrastructure. Below we detail another possible solution to this problem that has the benefit of being usable without any new public key cryptography infrastructure for the credit card issuer and the merchant.

Our solution would be to treat the credit card number and expiry date (and possibly other identity information) as a (single) password that is used to authenticate the transaction. With this method, the expiry date could be public and available in the clear for the merchant. The credit card number, expiry date and other data would be hashed with a secure password hashing method and this value would be stored by the merchant. Thus the merchant would not have the real credit card number stored. The authorisation of the transaction could be conducted by a well-established password based authentication protocol, e.g. [1] and should also include unique transaction numbers to prevent replay attacks. By using tag-based methods (see [7,10] for more details), the transaction number and other relevant information can be linked to the password-based authentication.

One downside of the above method is that the guessing of a credit card number from such a hash value could be fairly easy. There is fairly little entropy in the credit card numbers as they convey a fairly large amount of information about the issuing bank etc. and thus are not even close to random strings of digits. Any attacker obtaining the hashes could use this information to speed up their guessing activities and even if the numbers were completely random, 16 decimal digits is not enough to withstand brute force attacks. Thus, it is our opinion that the IBC based method presented earlier is far superior to this partial solution, even though it requires completely new infrastructure to operate and is not applicable online without new capabilities on the credit cards.

5   Discussion

Our proposal presents a novel way to apply IBC systems to a practical and global problem. However, some of the benefits that can be gained with our methods require changes in the credit card payment infrastructure. As the industry is both global and somewhat slow to adopt changes, it is possible that new systems implementing our method cannot be delivered to all customers in a timely manner. In any case, it is important to provide new options to increase security in credit card payments.

The most evident limitation of our proposed method is that it cannot be used without utilising the secret within the credit card. Thus, for backwards compatibility with legacy systems, the old way of payments may be needed in parallel to the new one. This could be overcome in a fairly short amount of time as the processing power and capabilities of the credit cards could increase and provide a way to interact with the payment ecosystem without a special reader. This could be done for example with integrated numerical pads or other means of input as well as some small displays on the credit cards. Then a standard challenge-response protocol could be utilised even in online transactions made from computers, handheld devices and other personal devices. However, credit cards are replaced in a fairly fast cycle of a few years and thus this new technology could reach customers in a few years.

The other part of the problem is in the point of sale terminals which are not replaced that often. Furthermore, there is a disparity between different regions in the world and many old systems are still in use in the developing countries and other parts of the world that have not yet been able to adopt for example the chip and PIN systems. This could be a more complicated problem, especially if there is no possibilty to update the terminals with only a software update. When parallel systems for payments exist, the attackers will choose the weakest one for their purposes.

Also at the moment it seems that the most advanced proposals of IBC systems are not yet optimised for the efficient use in resource constrained devices such as credit cards. Thus, the credit card itself could only be used as a storage device for the secret key at first. However, as already mentioned above, the capabilities of the credit cards and the chips used on them become more powerful and will soon enable the full-fledged use of IBC in consumer settings.

In any case, our proposal would make it more secure for the merchant to store the credit card numbers of their customers or not to store them at all. The very idea of public key systems is that the public key information cannot be used to conduct actions that require the knowledge of the secret key, nor can any information about the secret key be inferred from the public key. Thus, an attacker does not stand to gain anything from the knowledge of the credit card number or any other property used as the public identity.

As with almost all public key infrastructures, there is the question of reliability of the public identities. This should be addressed by the card issuers and it is their responsibility to make checks on the customer as it is also their incentive not to give credit to unreliable customers. The issued credit card should also include a digital certificate for the public key of that card. This certificate should be provided to the merchant that the card holder makes purchases from. The certificate would be signed by the card issuer and the merchant would have the card issuers public key for checking the certificate for validity.

6 Conclusion

In this paper we described one possible application of identity based cryptography in protecting credit card transactions. Our method would require new public key infrastructure to be established on the credit card ecosystem, but it would effectively make stealing the credit card numbers en masse from different e-commerce vendors ineffective for the attackers. The attackers would need to steal the private keys from the individual credit cards in order to do similar damage as with mere credit card numbers in the current system. This should be much harder as there would not necessarily be any large databases, where the lucrative information is stored.

Our proposed system would also require the credit card to sign the transactions (as the card contains the necessary secret keys) and thus it could be difficult to apply it to online purchases at first, if for example special readers are required. As the capabilities of the credit cards increase in the future, the system could be used also online with a challenge-response type of protocol, where the responses are computed on the credit card with the help of user input. If these results can be easily communicated to the computer or other device on which the service is provided, this system could offer usability comparable with the current system. In any case, we think that there should be new security measures developed to tackle the credit card fraud problem. In a very extreme scenario, if no new measures can be found and adopted, credit cards may become outdated by the rapidly developing cryptocurrencies and other alternative online payment systems, even though these are not immune to fraud either.

References

1. Bellare, M., Pointcheval, D., Rogaway, P.: Authenticated key exchange secure against dictionary attacks. In: Preneel, B. (ed.) EUROCRYPT 2000. LNCS, vol. 1807, pp. 139–155. Springer, Heidelberg (2000)
2. Bond, M., Choudary, O., Murdoch, S.J., Skorobogatov, S., Anderson, R.: Chip and skim: cloning emv cards with the pre-play attack. IEEE Symposium on Security and Privacy (2014),
   http://www.cl.cam.ac.uk/~sjm217/papers/oakland14chipandskim.pdf
3. Boneh, D., Franklin, M.: Identity-based encryption from the weil pairing. SIAM Journal on Computing 32(3), 586–615 (2003)
4. Diffie, W., Hellman, M.E.: New directions in cryptography. IEEE Transactions on Information Theory 22(6), 644–654 (1976)
5. Dutta, R., Barua, R., Sarkar, P.: Pairing-based cryptographic protocols: A survey. Cryptology ePrint Archive, Report 2004/064 (2004), http://eprint.iacr.org/
6. EMV co.: The EMV 4.3 standard specifications (November 2011),
   http://www.emvco.com/specifications.aspx?id=223
7. Fleischhacker, N., Manulis, M., Sadr-Azodi, A.: Modular design and analysis framework for multi-factor authentication and key exchange. Cryptology ePrint Archive, Report 2012/181 (2012), http://eprint.iacr.org/
8. Goldwasser, S., Micali, S., Rivest, R.L.: A digital signature scheme secure against adaptive chosen-message attacks. SIAM Journal on Computing 17(2), 281–308 (1988)

9. Hess, F.: Efficient identity based signature schemes based on pairings. In: Nyberg, K., Heys, H.M. (eds.) SAC 2002. LNCS, vol. 2595, pp. 310–324. Springer, Heidelberg (2003)

10. Jager, T., Kohlar, F., Schäge, S., Schwenk, J.: Generic compilers for authenticated key exchange. In: Abe, M. (ed.) ASIACRYPT 2010. LNCS, vol. 6477, pp. 232–249. Springer, Heidelberg (2010)

11. Maji, H.K., Prabhakaran, M., Rosulek, M.: Attribute-based signatures. In: Kiayias, A. (ed.) CT-RSA 2011. LNCS, vol. 6558, pp. 376–392. Springer, Heidelberg (2011)

12. Murdoch, S.J., Anderson, R.: Security protocols and evidence: Where many payment systems fail (2014),
http://www.ifca.ai/fc14/papers/fc14_submission_124.pdf

13. Murdoch, S.J., Anderson, R.: Verified by visa and mastercard securecode: Or, how not to design authentication. In: Sion, R. (ed.) FC 2010. LNCS, vol. 6052, pp. 336–342. Springer, Heidelberg (2010),
http://dx.doi.org/10.1007/978-3-642-14577-3_27

14. Nakamoto, S.: Bitcoin: A peer-to-peer electronic cash system (2008),
https://bitcointalk.org/bitcoin.pdf

15. Okamoto, T., Takashima, K.: Decentralized attribute-based signatures. In: Kurosawa, K., Hanaoka, G. (eds.) PKC 2013. LNCS, vol. 7778, pp. 125–142. Springer, Heidelberg (2013)

16. Panda Security: The cyber crime black market (2011),
http://press.pandasecurity.com/wp-content/
uploads/2011/01/The-Cyber-Crime-Black-Market.pdf

17. PCI Security Standards Council: Payment card industry data security standard v3.0 (2013),
https://www.pcisecuritystandards.org/security_standards/documents.php

18. Schoenmakers, B.: A simple publicly verifiable secret sharing scheme and its application to electronic voting. In: Wiener, M. (ed.) CRYPTO 1999. LNCS, vol. 1666, pp. 148–164. Springer, Heidelberg (1999)

19. Shamir, A.: Identity-based cryptosystems and signature schemes. In: Blakley, G., Chaum, D. (eds.) CRYPTO 1984. LNCS, vol. 196, pp. 47–53. Springer, Heidelberg (1985), http://dx.doi.org/10.1007/3-540-39568-7_5

On a Cipher Based on Pseudo-random Walks on Graphs

Wit Foryś[1], Łukasz Jęda[2], and Piotr Oprocha[2]

[1] Institute of Computer Science, Jagiellonian University,
Łojasiewicza 6, 30-348 Kraków, Poland
forysw@ii.uj.edu.pl
[2] AGH University of Science and Technology, Faculty of Applied Mathematics,
al. A. Mickiewicza 30, 30-059 Kraków, Poland
{ljeda,oprocha}@agh.edu.pl

Abstract. In the paper a cipher which uses transition graph in the encryption and decryption processes is presented. It is created based on some ideas of dynamic systems (symbolic dynamics). The introduced cipher is tested according to the suggestions of FIPS 140-2 standard and the results are presented in the paper.

1 Introduction

Some ideas of how to apply dynamic systems to define a cipher were given in [2,3,6]. However, the presented systems are largely dependent on an implementation method and an operational system (arithmetical functions delivered by the system). Furthermore, the encryption operations obtained in this way require many iterations of mappings which define them to obtain a kind of numerically unpredictable behavior. From the dynamic systems theory or more exactly from the symbolic dynamics it is known fact that a subclass of dynamic systems, called irreducible sofic shifts, which are presented by strongly connected graphs with at least two cycles are expansive, chaotic in the sense of Devaney and have a positive topological entropy - for all undefined here notions from the dynamic system theory see [4]. These properties made sofic systems a good base for a cipher design. This idea is confirmed by the research on ciphers based on the graph theory. See, for example, [5,8].

In this article we will present a cipher which uses wandering on a graph in the process of encryption. To ensure the sufficient security level of our design, the introduced cipher was tested according to the suggestions of FIPS 140-2 standard (published by the National Institute of Standards and Technology, US), see also [12]. The results of these tests are presented in the last part of the paper.

2 Transducers and Encryption

There are two possible approaches to a cipher which we are presented now. The first, based on a transition graph of a rational transducer and the second on

Z. Kotulski et al. (Eds.): CSS 2014, CCIS 448, pp. 59–73, 2014.

a transition graph of a sofic shift. The first approach leads to a comparatively simple construction of a cipher and we choose it in this paper. The second enables application of the shift theory that concerns chaotic behaviour and positive entropy of such systems.

The presented cipher is a symmetric stream cipher. Encryption and decryption operations are defined using a transition graph and two keys. One of them is important for encryption, another is used to make the results more mixed. It also makes changes of the first key harder to track.

First, let us introduce some notions used in the formal definition of our cipher. We call a set $\mathcal{A} = \{0, \ldots, l\}$ an alphabet. An element $e \in \mathcal{A} \times \mathcal{A}$ is said to be an *edge*. Monoids $\mathcal{A}^*$ and $\Sigma = \{0, 1\}^*$ will be called *a plaintext space* and *a key space*, respectively. The plaintext space $\mathcal{A}^*$ is also *a cryptotext space*.

Below we present a restricted version of the definition of transducer.

Definition 1. *A transducer* $T = (X, Y \times Z, Q, t_Q, t_Y, t_Z)$ *is composed of an input alphabet* X, *an output alphabet* $Y \times Z$, *a finite set of states* Q *and functions* $t_Q : Q \times X \mapsto Q$, $t_Y : Q \times X \mapsto Y$ *and* $t_Z : Q \times X \mapsto Z$.

Definition 2. *A quadruple* $(q, x, (y, z), p)$ *such that* $t_Q(q, x) = p$, $t_Y(q, x) = y$ *and* $t_Z(q, x) = z$ *is said to be a* move *or a* transition *of a transducer from the state* q *to the state* p *according to the input letter* x *which gives the output* (y, z).

Fixing the first argument $q \in Q$, for the functions t_Q, t_Y and t_Z, denote the resulted functions by t_Q^q, t_Y^q and t_Z^q, respectively.

Let us fix now a set $\mathcal{A} = \{0, \ldots, l\}$. We assume in the sequel that:

1. $Q = X = Y = Z = \mathcal{A}$,
2. functions t_Q^q, t_Y^q and t_Z^q are bijections for any $q \in A$,
3. condition $t_Y(q, w) \neq t_Z(q, w)$ holds for any $q, w \in A$,
4. if $q, p, w \in A$ are such that $t_Q(q, w) = t_Q(p, w)$, then $q = p$.

Any transducer T fulfilling the above conditions defines the four-tuple $G_T = \{\mathcal{A}, t_Q, t_Y, t_Z\}$ which is called a labelled transition graph (abbrev. lt-graph) of the transducer. Each transition $(q_1, x, (y, z), q_2)$ defines two nodes q_1, x and an arrow from q_1 to x is labelled $q_1 / (y, z)$. In other words, arguments of functions t_Q, t_Y, t_Z define edges; labels are assigned via their values.

Notice that an lt-graph of a transducer is a full graph with the labels assigned to each edge. The set of vertices (states) and all three alphabets of a transducer coincide. Thus an arrow in this graph is labelled by $u / (v, w)$ where $u, v, w \in \mathcal{A}$.

Remark 1. Observe that a class of all lt-graphs is quite large. It is easy to notice that there is at least $|\mathcal{A}|!$ possibilities of different lt-graphs, however this number is a very weak low boundary. However, the memory needed to keep a fixed representation of such a graph is $\mathcal{O}(|\mathcal{A}|^2 \log |\mathcal{A}|)$.

Definition 3. *Let* $G_T = \{\mathcal{A}, t_Q, t_Y, t_Z\}$ *be an lt-graph of a transducer* T. *For any* $v, a \in \mathcal{A}$ *and* $s, p \in \{0, 1\}$ *we define:*

$$N(v, a, p) = (t_Q^v)^{-1}(a + p \mod |\mathcal{A}|), \qquad (1)$$

$$L(v, a, s, p) = \begin{cases} (t_Y^v \circ N)(v, a, p), & s = 0 \\ (t_Z^v \circ N)(v, a, p), & s = 1 \end{cases}. \tag{2}$$

Now we start to define an encryption operation.

Definition 4. *Let* $G_T = \{\mathcal{A}, t_Q, t_Y, t_Z\}$ *be an lt-graph of a transducer* T. *Let* $k, r \in \Sigma$ *and* $u = u_0.....u_s \in \mathcal{A}^+$. *We define a word* $\overrightarrow{enc_{k,r}}(u) \in \mathcal{A}^*$ *inductively. For* $j = 0$ *let* $v_0 = N(0, u_0, r_0)$ *and* $c_0 = L(0, u_0, k_0, r_0)$. *Assuming that the letters* v_j, c_j *are defined for* $0 \leq j \leq i$ *we define* v_{i+1}, c_{i+1} *putting:*

$$\begin{aligned} v_{i+1} &= N(v_i, u_{i+1}, r_{i+1 \mod |r|}), \\ c_{i+1} &= L(v_i, u_{i+1}, k_{i+1 \mod |k|}, r_{i+1 \mod |r|}). \end{aligned} \tag{3}$$

After $s + 1$ *steps we obtain a sequence* $c_0, \ldots, c_s$ *and finally we put:*

$$\overrightarrow{enc_{k,r}}(u) = c_0.....c_s \in \mathcal{A}^*. \tag{4}$$

Denoting a mirror image of a word u *by* $inv(u) = u_s u_{s-1} \ldots u_0$ *we define:*

$$\overleftarrow{enc_{k,r}}(u) = inv(\overrightarrow{enc_{k,r}}(inv(u))). \tag{5}$$

Words $\overrightarrow{enc_{k,r}}(u)$, $\overleftarrow{enc_{k,r}}(u)$ defined by the above operation are strongly related with the choice of transducer (equivalently, its transition graph). To compute $\overrightarrow{enc_{k,r}}(u)$ for a word u we start in the vertex 0 of the transition graph and then the function t_Q points out the subsequent vertex in the path we are going to walk through. More exactly, this path is determined by the word u and the choice of key r. By the definition we associated a pair of labels to each edge. The second key k decides which of these labels will be used as the value of our computation.

Computing $\overrightarrow{enc_{k,r}}$ for two words u, v which have a common prefix and differ only in one letter leads to two different paths on lt-graph. These two paths branch out exactly after the walk determined by the end of the longest common prefix. Up to this point both computed words are the same and have different remaining parts. It is not exactly the diffusion property which is expected from the encryption operation. To assure diffusion we extend the above procedure to the encryption operation in the following way.

Definition 5. *Let* G *be a transition graph and let* $n \in \mathbb{N}$. *We define* n-*runs encryption operation* Enc_n *putting:*

$$Enc_n : \mathcal{A}^* \times \Sigma^2 \to \mathcal{A}^*, \ Enc_n(u, k, r) = \overrightarrow{enc_{k,r}}(\overleftarrow{enc_{k,r}} \circ \overrightarrow{enc_{k,r}})^n(u), \tag{6}$$

where $k, r \in \Sigma$ *and* $u \in \mathcal{A}^*$.

Notice that the defined encryption operation executes $2n + 1$ steps (i.e. walks of length $|u|$ on the associated lt-graph) to compute a cryptotext for a plaintext u. The first one coincides with the calculation of the function $\overrightarrow{enc_{k,r}}$ which was described above. Hence, during the first step applied to two words u, v which have a common prefix and differ only in one letter we obtain almost the same words. But mirror images of the obtained words have the completely different first symbol, hence the continuation of computation of the first step, as well as the second, third and subsequent steps uses essentially different paths and therefore produces essentially different cryptotexts. This observation, supported by the statistical tests presented in the last section of the paper, implies the conclusion that the diffusion property holds for Enc_n. The similar effect could be observed for two close keys r_1, r_2 which assures the confusion property of the encryption operation.

Now we describe the decryption operation.

Definition 6. *Let* $G_T = \{\mathcal{A}, t_Q, t_Y, t_Z\}$ *be a transition graph. For any* $v, a \in \mathcal{A}$ *and* $s, p \in \{0, 1\}$ *we define:*

$$P(v, b, s) = \begin{cases} (t_Y^v)^{-1}(b), s = 0 \\ (t_Z^v)^{-1}(b), s = 1 \end{cases} , \quad D(v, b, p) = (t_Q^v(b) - p) \mod |\mathcal{A}| . \quad (7)$$

Theorem 1. *Let* $G_T = \{\mathcal{A}, t_Q, t_Y, t_Z\}$ *be a transition graph. If* $v, a \in \mathcal{A}$ *and* $s, p \in \{0, 1\}$, *then:*

$$P(v, L(v, a, s, p), s) = N(v, a, p), \quad D(v, N(v, a, p), p) = a . \quad (8)$$

□

Proof. Let us assume that $s = 0$ (for $s = 1$ proof is identical). In this case:

$$\begin{aligned} P(v, L(v, a, s, p), s) &= (t_Y^v)^{-1}(L(v, a, 0, p)) = (t_Y^v)^{-1}(t_Y^v(N(v, a, p))) \\ &= ((t_Y^v)^{-1} \circ t_Y^v)(N(v, a, p)) \\ &= N(v, a, p) . \end{aligned}$$

Next, observe that:

$$\begin{aligned} D(v, N(v, a, p), p) &= (t_Q^v(N(v, a, p)) - p) \mod |\mathcal{A}| \\ &= (t_Q^v((t_Q^v)^{-1}(a + p \mod |\mathcal{A}|)) - p) \mod |\mathcal{A}| \\ &= (t_Q^v \circ (t_Q^v)^{-1})(a + p \mod |\mathcal{A}|)) - p) \mod |\mathcal{A}| \\ &= a + p - p \mod |\mathcal{A}| = a . \end{aligned}$$

□

Definition 7. *Let* $G_T = \{\mathcal{A}, t_Q, t_Y, t_Z\}$ *be a transition graph,* $k, r \in \Sigma$ *and* $w = w_0.....w_s \in \mathcal{A}^*$. *We define a word* $\overrightarrow{dec_{k,r}}(w) \in \mathcal{A}^*$ *inductively. For* $j = 0$ *let* $v_0 = P(0, w_0, k_0)$ *and* $d_0 = D(0, v_0, r_0)$. *Assuming that letters* v_j, d_j *are defined for* $0 \leq j \leq i$ *we define* v_{i+1}, d_{i+1} *putting:*

$$v_{i+1} = P(v_i, w_{i+1}, k_{i+1 \mod |k|}), \ d_{i+1} = D(v_i, v_{i+1}, r_{i+1 \mod |r|}) . \qquad (9)$$

After $s+1$ steps we obtain a sequence $d_0, \ldots, d_s$ and finally we put:

$$\overleftarrow{dec_{k,r}}(w) = d_0 ..... d_s \in \mathcal{A}^* . \qquad (10)$$

We also define:

$$\overrightarrow{dec_{k,r}}(w) = \mathrm{inv}(\overleftarrow{dec_{k,r}}(\mathrm{inv}(w))) . \qquad (11)$$

Theorem 2. Let $G_T = \{\mathcal{A}, t_Q, t_Y, t_Z\}$ be a transition graph. For any $k, p \in \Sigma$ and $u \in \mathcal{A}^*$ the following equalities are true:

$$\overleftarrow{dec_{k,r}}(\overleftarrow{enc_{k,r}}(u)) = u, \ \overrightarrow{dec_{k,r}}(\overrightarrow{enc_{k,r}}(u)) = u . \qquad (12)$$

$\square$

Proof. Let u be a word in $\mathcal{A}^*$, let $\overleftarrow{enc_{k,r}}(u) = c_0 \ldots c_s$ and let $\{v_1, \ldots, v_s\}$ be a sequence which supports calculation of $\overleftarrow{enc_{k,r}}(u)$. Next, let $\overleftarrow{dec_{k,r}}(c_0 \ldots c_s) = d_0 \ldots d_s$ and $\{v'_1, \ldots, v'_s\}$ be a sequence which supports calculation of d_i for $i = 1, \ldots, s$.

We claim that $v_i = v'_i$ and $d_i = u_i$ for $i = 1, \ldots, s$. Just from Theorem 1 we have the equalities $v_0 = v'_0$ and $d_0 = u_0$. Next, let us assume that $v_j = v'_j$ and $d_j = u_j$ for $0 \leq j \leq i < s$. Then we have:

$$v_{i+1} = N(v_i, u_{i+1}, r_{i+1 \mod |r|}) \qquad (13)$$

$$c_{i+1} = L(v_i, u_{i+1}, k_{i+1 \mod |k|}, r_{i+1 \mod |r|}) \qquad (14)$$

$$v'_{i+1} = P(v_i, c_{i+1}, k_{i+1 \mod |k|}), \ d_{i+1} = D(v_i, v'_{i+1}, r_{i+1 \mod |r|}) \qquad (15)$$

and therefore using once again Theorem 1 we conclude that:

$$\begin{aligned}
v'_{i+1} &= P(v_i, c_{i+1}, k_{i+1 \mod |k|}) \\
&= P(v_i, L(v_i, u_i, k_{i+1 \mod |k|}, r_{i+1 \mod |r|}), \\
&\quad k_{i+1 \mod |k|}) \\
&= N(v_i, u_{i+1}, r_{i+1 \mod |r|}) = v_{i+1},
\end{aligned} \qquad (16)$$

$$d_{i+1} = D\left(v_i, N(v_i, u_{i+1}, r_{i+1 \mod |r|}), r_{i+1 \mod |r|}\right) = u_{i+1}.$$

This ends the proof of the claim, hence $\overleftarrow{dec_{k,r}}(\overleftarrow{enc_{k,r}}(u)) = u$. Directly from this fact combined with the equality $\mathrm{inv}(\mathrm{inv}(x)) = x$ we immediately obtain that:

$$\overrightarrow{dec_{k,r}}(\overrightarrow{enc_{k,r}}(u)) = \mathrm{inv}(\overleftarrow{dec_{k,r}}(\mathrm{inv}(\overleftarrow{enc_{k,r}}(u))))$$
$$= \mathrm{inv}(\overleftarrow{dec_{k,r}}(\mathrm{inv}(\mathrm{inv}(\overleftarrow{enc_{k,r}}(\mathrm{inv}(u))))))$$
$$= \mathrm{inv}(\overleftarrow{dec_{k,r}}(\overleftarrow{enc_{k,r}}(\mathrm{inv}(u)))) = \mathrm{inv}(\mathrm{inv}(u))$$
$$= u.$$

The proof is completed.   □

Definition 8. *Let G_T be an lt-graph and let $n \in \mathbb{N}$. We define n-runs decryption operation Dec_n putting:*

$$\mathrm{Dec}_n \colon A^* \times \Sigma^2 \to A^*, \ \mathrm{Dec}_n(u,k,r) = (\overrightarrow{dec_{k,r}} \circ \overleftarrow{dec_{k,r}})^n(\overrightarrow{dec_{k,r}}(u)) \qquad (17)$$

where $k, r \in \Sigma$ and $u \in A^*$.

Corollary 1. *If $k, r \in \Sigma$ and $u \in A^*$, then:*

$$\mathrm{Dec}_n(\mathrm{Enc}_n(u,k,r),k,r) = u . \qquad (18)$$

                                                                    □

Combining all the introduced operations and their properties we obtain the following well defined cipher.

Definition 9. *Let G_T be an lt-graph and let $n \in \mathbb{N}$. An lt-graph cipher is the tuple $(A, \mathrm{Enc}_n, \mathrm{Dec}_n)$.*

Example 1. Let us consider an lt-graph cipher:

$$(A^* = \{0,1,2,3\}^* , \Sigma = \{0,1\}^* , \mathrm{Enc}_1, \mathrm{Dec}_1) , \qquad (19)$$

with lt-graph G_T presented in Fig. 1, where the graph G_T is decomposed into four subgraphs for better presentation of labels of outgoing edges for each vertex.

Let $k = 011001, r = 10011010$ and let $u = 1230123012301230$. Table 1 presents step by step computations of the resulting word $\overleftarrow{enc_{k,r}}(u)$. Notice that it is not a cryptogram of u.

Table 1. Computation of cryptotext via lt-graph from Fig. 1

word u	1	2	3	0	1	2	3	0	1	2	3	0	1	2	3	0
key r	1	0	0	1	1	0	1	0	1	0	0	1	1	0	1	0
$u_i + r_i \ \mathrm{mod}\ 4$	2	2	3	1	2	2	0	0	2	2	3	1	2	2	0	0
vertex v_i	0	2	1	2	3	3	3	0	1	0	2	0	0	2	1	3
vertex $N(v_i, u_i, r_i)$	2	1	2	3	3	3	0	1	0	2	0	0	2	1	3	0
key k	0	1	1	0	0	1	0	1	1	0	0	1	0	1	1	0
output $\overleftarrow{enc_{k,r}}(u)$	3	1	3	3	3	2	0	3	1	3	0	2	3	1	0	0

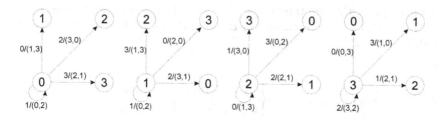

Fig. 1. Lt-graph for the transducer over four letters alphabet

Table 2. Intermediate steps of encryption operation

u	1230123012301230
$\overrightarrow{enc_{k,r}}(u)$	3133320313023100
$\overleftarrow{enc_{k,r}} \circ \overrightarrow{enc_{k,r}}(u)$	1131332320012230
$Enc_1(u)$	3003130102000031

Encryption of u using the considered cipher gives the following cryptogram:

$$Enc_1(1230123012301230, 011001, 10011010) = 3003130102000031.$$

Intermediate steps of the computation are given in Table 2.

Now let us consider the complexity of cipher $(\mathcal{A}^*, \Sigma, Enc_n, Dec_n)$. Assuming implementation of lt-graph using the adjacency matrices (one for each of the functions t_Q, t_Y, t_Z), for every $a \in \mathcal{A}$ computing value $t_Q^v(a), t_Y^v(a), t_Z^v(a)$ costs $\mathcal{O}(1)$, since it involves only reading one element of matrix. On the other hand, for every $a \in \mathcal{A}$ computing value $(t_Q^v)^{-1}(a), (t_Y^v)^{-1}(a), (t_Z^v)^{-1}(a)$ costs $\mathcal{O}(|\mathcal{A}|)$, since it requires finding element a in the row corresponding to the letter v. Computing the inverse of word $u \in \mathcal{A}^*$ costs $\mathcal{O}(|u|)$.

Having the above, we can estimate the bit complexity of encryption and decryption operations. To encrypt the word $u = u_0 \dots u_s \in \mathcal{A}^*$ using the keys $r, k \in \Sigma$ there need to be performed $2n + 1$ computations of Enc_n functions, each computing (compare with Definition 4):

$$v_i = N(v_{i-1}, u_i, r_{i \mod |r|}) = (t_Q^{v_{i-1}})^{-1}(u_i + r_{i \mod |r|} \mod |\mathcal{A}|), \qquad (20)$$

$$c_i = L(v_{i-1}, u_i, k_{i \mod |k|}, r_{i \mod |r|}) = \begin{cases} t_Y^v(v_i), & k_{i \mod |k|} = 0 \\ t_Z^v(v_i), & k_{i \mod |k|} = 1 \end{cases} \qquad (21)$$

for every $i \in \{0, \dots, s\}$ (assuming $v_{-1} = 0$). Hence complexity of computing v_i is $\mathcal{O}(|\mathcal{A}|)$ and the value c_i is $\mathcal{O}(1)$ (since it uses the obtained value v_i). Each two consecutive runs of $\overrightarrow{enc_{k,r}}$ function are separated by computation of inv function, whose complexity is $\mathcal{O}(s)$. Summarising, the complexity of computation $Enc_n(u, k, r)$ is $\mathcal{O}(|\mathcal{A}|sn)$.

When decrypting the cryptotext $w = w_0 \ldots w_s \in \mathcal{A}^*$, there need to be performed similarly $2n + 1$ computations of Dec_n functions, each computing (compare with Definition 7):

$$v_i = P(v_{i-1}, w_i, k_{i \mod |k|}) = \begin{cases} (t_Y^{v-1})^{-1}(w_i), & k_{i \mod |k|} = 0 \\ (t_Z^{v-1})^{-1}(w_i), & k_{i \mod |k|} = 1 \end{cases}, \tag{22}$$

$$d_i = D(v_{i-1}, v_i, r_{i \mod |r|}) = (t_Q^{v-1}(v_i) - r_{i \mod |r|}) \mod |\mathcal{A}|$$

for every $i \in \{0, \ldots, s\}$ (assuming again $v_{-1} = 0$). Analogously complexity of computing the value v_i is $\mathcal{O}(|\mathcal{A}|)$ and computing the value d_i is $\mathcal{O}(1)$. As previously each two consecutive runs of $\overrightarrow{\text{dec}_{k,r}}$ function are separated by computation of inv function, whose complexity is $\mathcal{O}(s)$. Summarising, the complexity of computation $\text{Dec}_n(w, k, r)$ is also $\mathcal{O}(|\mathcal{A}|sn)$.

It is worth to mentioning that this algorithm can be improved e. g. by recording information about the inverse functions $(t_Q^v)^{-1}, (t_Y^v)^{-1}, (t_Z^v)^{-1}$, thus changing for every $a \in \mathcal{A}$ complexity of computing $(t_Q^v)^{-1}(a), (t_Y^v)^{-1}(a), (t_Z^v)^{-1}(a)$ to $\mathcal{O}(1)$ (hence changing complexity of Enc_n and Dec_n operations to $\mathcal{O}(sn)$). But this operation will double the initial cost of memory needed to store the adjacency matrices. Also algorithm can be changed to work back and forth instead of applying function inv, but this will not change the estimated bit complexity of algorithms.

3   Cipher Tests

This part of the paper tests the strength of the encryption algorithm that is being presented. For this purpose encryption and decryption procedures have been developed in the *Java* programming language. To be able to easily configure all the cipher settings and to demonstrate how it works there has been created an applet which was deployed on the page written in the *HTML* language. The program has been embedded in this applet. In order to conduct tests there was created an additional package containing classes for generating a random system configuration and for testing. The HTML page with the embedded applet is available at url: http://jedu.cba.pl/pd/index.html.

To verify the strength of the encryption algorithm the tests collected and implemented in C programming language by the National Institute of Standards and Technology (NIST) were used.

One of the most basic and the most important assumptions concerning the cryptographic systems is that generated cryptotext should be indistinguishable from randomly-generated sequence, i. e. there is probability that in a particular position in the sequence a particular letter should be the same for all letters. In other words, the knowledge of a part of cryptotext should not provide information about the following part of cryptotext.

3.1   Asumptions

Tests were conducted in an analogous way to that in the in competition organized by NIST (*National Institute of Standards and Technology*) for the best cryptographic algorithm called AES (*Advanced Encryption Standard*). To verify that a given text can be considered as indistinguishable from randomly-generated one the set of statistical tests developed and implemented (in C language) by NIST was used. The tests set was prepared to evaluate randomness of binary sequences produced by the pseudo-random number generators. Each test investigates a given text with regard to a specific feature which should be posses by a truly random sequence. If the tested sample exposed deviations from the expected norm, it was considered as non-random by the test. Otherwise it was treated as a random one. Before using this set of tests, the cryptotext obtained by the encryption procedure had to be converted to a binary sequence. Moreover, parameters of cipher being examined had to be established. Thus, there was applied the following procedure:

- Input alphabet B consisted of 32 letters,
- Each letter was represented as 5-bit sequence,
- 100-run encryption and decryption operations were established, i. e. following four-tuple: $(B^*, \Sigma, Enc_{100}, Dec_{100})$ was used,
- Text was converted to a binary sequence by substituting letters with their binary representation.

The detailed description of each test in [9] contains recommendations about a minimal length of binary sequence being tested, which must be preserved in order to obtain meaningful results (brief description of each test can be found in [10,11]). To achieve sufficient length sets of binary sequences were joined into one sequence. To acquire accurate and reliable results, each test was preformed on many sequences. For every sequence being tested lt-graph was generated separately in a random way.

When examining strength of cryptographic algorithm not only the cryptotext obtained using the presented cipher was tested, but also dependence between the plaintext and the cryptotext derived from it or between two cryptotexts derived from very similar plaintexts. Thus test sets were divided into 9 groups, each group examining a different way of testing cryptographic algorithm strength. All groups are presented in Table 3. They were prepared in an analogous way to that in the NIST competition. The description of each group can be found in [11].

3.2   Preparation for Tests

As it was mentioned before, all analyzed sequences were split into 9 groups depending on the algorithm feature being tested. Table 3 presents the information about a length of each of 60 binary sequences in each group. 188 tests results were obtained from each binary sequence, unless the number of cycles in a sequence

Table 3. Test set groups and sequence lengths in each test group

Group No.	Feature being tested	Sequence length
1	Key avalanche	1146880
2	Plaintext avalanche	1146880
3	Plaintext-ciphertext correlation	1024000
4	Cipher Block Chaining mode	1024000
5	Electronic CodeBook mode	1024000
6	Low density plaintext	5284480
7	High density plaintext	5284480
8	Low density keys	10568960
9	High density keys	10568960

Table 4. NIST testing program along with parameter values

Test	parameter (designation)	value
Block Frequency Test	block length (M)	16384
Non-periodic Templates Test	block length (m)	9
Overlapping Template Test	block length (m)	9
Approximate Entropy Test	block length (m)	9
Serial test	block length (m)	14
Linear Complexity Test	block length (M)	1000

was too small to perform a random excursions test and a random excursions variant test (for details about these tests see [9]).

The testing program implemented by NIST had a few parameters, which were needed to be set before conducting tests. They are shown in Table 4 (explanation of parameters can be found in [9]).

Tests were conducted at a significance level of $\alpha = 0,05$. It means that the probability of commiting a type I error was equal to 5%, i. e. theoretically 1 out of 20 sequences considered as non-random was in fact random. But this is the idealized case, so the analysis there was established an approach using the so-called confidence interval which determines the ratio of binary sequences that should be indicated by test as random at the significance level of α. The largest number of sequences considered as non-random is given by the formula [11]:

$$n_s = s\left(\alpha + 3\sqrt{\frac{\alpha(1-\alpha)}{s}}\right), \tag{23}$$

where s is the number of binary sequences in each group (sample size).

For a group of 60 sequences this quantity is equal to $n_{60} \approx 8,1$. It means that if in the examined group the number of binary sequences indicated by tests as non-random was not greater than 9, then the group was considered to originate from generator producing random sequences (in program provided by NIST the number n_s was always rounded up).

3.3   Interpretation of the Results

Tests results conducted by the program provided by NIST were in convenient way summarized in the file named `finalAnalysisReport.txt`. For each test result there was a row consisting of i. a. a column containing the number of sequences from each group that were considered by the test as random (in relation to the size of the group) and a column indicating the p-value of χ^2 test, which was used to check whether the obtained results followed the uniform distribution (as it should be in the case of the group containing a sample from the generator producing random binary sequences). If the number of sequences indicated as non-random by the test exceeded the admissible quantity n_s or p-value of the χ^2 test for uniform distribution of results was too small, then in the appropriate column there was additionally present a star to emphasize that fact. If at least one of the columns had a star, it meant that the test indicated non-randomness of a group.

In order to get a statistically significant result of χ^2 test, there needed to be at least 55 p-values for each test result available. Unfortunately, due to the fact that performing the random excursions test and the random excursions variant test was dependent on a number of cycles in a given random walk represented by a binary sequence (see [9]), those tests were not executed for every binary sequence from the group, but only for those which met this requirement. Hence though each group consisted of 60 binary sequences, a minimal number of sequences to be able to interpret p-values obtained from those two tests was not reached. Thus those results should not be under analysis. For any other of 13 tests, since there were produced 60 p-values for each result, the outcome of χ^2 test is credible.

After the analysis of files `finalAnalysisReport.txt` obtained by testing each group there has been stated that on groups:

- 3, 4, 5, 8 and 9 — algorithm passed successfully all tests,
- 6 and 7 — the number of binary sequences indicated by result of one test was equal to $\lceil n_{60} \rceil + 1$ (for one out of 188 results in both groups), the other results did not show any reason to reject hypothesis about randomness of both groups,
- 1 — only the linear complexity test, random excursions test and random excursions variant test indicated that the group is random (in two last as it was pointed out before, due to too small number of sequences on which those tests could be performed, the p-value of test χ^2 was not taken into account), in the other cases, except non-overlapping template matching test for the template 101111000, all results indicated that obtained p-values follow the uniform distribution and about half of the results (including non-overlapping template matching test for the template 101111000) indicated too high ratio of sequences considered as non-random by each test,
- 2 — except linear complexity test all other tests (excluding random excursions test and random excursions variant test, which were performed only for 3 sequences, because for the other sequences the requirement about a number of cycles in the random walk represented by those binary sequences

Table 5. Tests results and corresponding numbers on charts

Test	Number(s)
Frequency Test	1
Frequency Test within a Block	2
Cumulative Sums Test	3, 4
Runs Test	5
Test for the Longest Run of Ones in a Block	6
Binary Matrix Rank Test	7
Discrete Fourier Transform Test	8
Non-overlapping Template Matching Test	9 – 156
Overlapping Template Matching Test	157
Maurer's 'Universal Statistical' Test	158
Approximate Entropy Test	159
Random Excursion Test	160 – 167
Random Excursion Variant Test	168 – 185
Serial test	186, 187
Linear Complexity Test	188

Table 6. Result numbers for group 1 and 2, in which test χ^2 rejected null hypothesis

Group No.	Result numbers
1	1 – 102, 104 – 160, 164, 167, 178, 186, 187
2	1 – 159, 186, 187

was not met) due to both ratio of the sequences indicated as non-random and the distribution of obtained p-values clearly indicated that the examined sequences were created by a random sequences generator.

The ratio of the number of sequences, for which the hypothesis about randomness was not rejected due to the groups size was presented as charts in picture 3.4. The horizontal line denotes the threshold 0.8333 (Indicating each of the 60 random sequences as non-random by test with significance level $\alpha = 0.05$ can be treated as a random variable following the binomial distribution with the probability of success equal to α. In such a model the probability of achieving not more than 83.33% of failures (i. e. correctly considering random sequence as random) is less than 0.001). Table 5 includes the assignment of test results to the numbers in the charts. The result numbers, for which randomness of sequences was rejected by χ^2 test are shown int Table 6. This test rejected randomness of sequences only in groups 1 and 2[1], so only these two groups are included in this table.

---

[1] χ^2 test in group 2 was not performed for random excursions test and random excursions variant test because there were obtained to few p-values (only 3 for every result) to verify their distribution. Thus in Table 6 results numbers 160 – 185 are not displayed.

3.4   Conclusions

The results of groups 3, 4, 5, 8 and 9 without doubts assert that they contain sequences indistinguishable from the random generated binary sequence. Only one result in each of groups 6 and 7 for non-overlapping template matching test (for templates 001010101 and 000011111 respectively) indicated non-randomness of a sample, but this indication was not clear since the test result is on the verge of rejecting the null hypothesis about randomness of a sample.

It means that the non-periodic bit sequence 001010101 (respectively 000011111) occurred too many times in the sequences from group 6 (respectively 7). It is very likely that this result is a statistical error. There is no reason for this algorithm to produce such sequences more likely than any other. To support this conclusion it would be worth performing an additional test with significantly increased sample size, to avoid the importance of the potential I type error connected with the established significance level $\alpha = 0,05$.

As far as the results in groups 6 and 7 could be treated as anomalies, so the results in groups 1 and 2 indicate that sequences in each group could not be treated as an output from a random binary sequences generator. Particularly almost all results (except the linear complexity test) in group 2 clearly rejected the hypothesis about randomness of sequences both by χ^2 test for p-values and by the ratio of the number of sequences considered as random to the group size. In the case of random excursions test and random excursions variant test, only 3 sequences from group 2 were examined by them. Although for each result the ratio of sequences considered as random (equal to $\frac{2}{3}$ or $\frac{3}{3}$) theoretically is high enough to consider the sample as random, the number of sequences which could not be examined by those tests suggests that the sample did not contain random binary sequences.

In group 1 approximately half of the results did not indicate the non-randomness of a sample through the ratio of the sequences considered as random to the group size, and those tests which indicated that the hypothesis did not do that clearly (in most cases the number of sequences indicated as non-random was around 12, so only 3 more than the threshold the $\lceil n_{60} \rceil = 9$). However, for almost all tests results (except 24) non-randomness of a sample was clearly indicated by χ^2 test. Only the results $161 - 163, 165, 166, 168 - 177, 179 - 185, 188$ considered the sample as random. Yet 165 tests rejected the hypothesis that the sequences from group 1 were indistinguishable from the random binary sequence (74 of them both by χ^2 test and ratio of the sequences considered as random to the sample size), which clearly stated that group 1 consisted of non-random sequences.

The tests detected an evident lack of randomness in groups 1 and 2. The presented algorithm satisfies neither the key nor the plaintext avalanche requirement. Correctness of this proposal seems to result from the fact that in groups 3 and 5 non-randomness was not indicated — it means that the binary representation of cryptotext (obtained from the random plaintext) itself is indistinguishable from the random bit sequence (which was examined in group 5), as well as the symmetric difference between bit representations of cryptotext and plaintext from which it was created also imitated the random sequence well

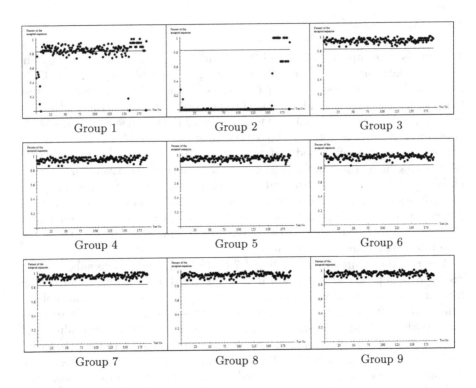

Fig. 2. Ratio of the sequences considered as random by each test to the group size

(what confirmed the examination of group 3). Thus non-randomness in groups 1 and 2 indeed result from the similarity of keys or plaintexts.

The encryption algorithm was resistant to the situations in which (as it was tested in groups 6, 7, 8 and 9) keys or plaintext contained a large number of one of the two bits — it behaved the same as in the case of encoding random plaintexts using random keys, i. e. in the bit representation of cryptotext there could not be found any traces of increased number of one of the bits — it contained a similar number of both bits. The cryptotext was indistinguishable from random bit sequences even when the encryption procedure was iterated i. e. it was working in the CBC mode (which was examined in group 4).

4   Remarks

The cipher presented in this work have many desired features, which should characterize such algorithms. The bit representations of cryptotexts generated by it are indistinguishable from the random bit sequences, whether it works in CBC or ECB mode. Its cryptographic strength does not shrink even when the plaintext bit representation consists mainly of zeroes (or ones). The cryptotext is in any manner similar to plaintext from which it was obtained.

Still, this cipher requires some refinement. There is need to invent some modification, which will cause that changing of one bit in plaintext or in one of the keys r or k will entail that two cryptotexts obtained in this way will not be similar to each other. Tests of this cipher were performed with fixed configuration described in subsection 3.1, i. a. there was established the 100-run encryption and decryption operations . Thus the first step to take seems to be to test how algorithm behaves when the number of iteration n is increased, which, in fact, is intended to blur the information about common letters of plaintexts being encrypted. In other words consideration of the cipher e. g. $(\mathcal{B}^*, \Sigma, Enc_{200}, Dec_{200})$ for alphabet $\mathcal{B}$ defined in subsection 3.1 seems to be justified. Another approach can be doubling the size of alphabet. Larger lt-graph implies increase of the number of paths in it, thus reducing the probability that two paths for similar plaintexts will be partially overlapped. To improve the results there can be also made some modifications in the algorithm itself, e. g. taking in the encryption process the position of letter being currently encrypted in the plaintext being processed.

References

1. Foryś, W., Oprocha, P.: Pseudo-random walks on graphs and cryptography. In: Proceedings of the 2009 International Conference on Foundations of Computer Science, FCS 2009, Las Vegas, Nevada, USA (2009)
2. Kapitaniak, T.: Controlling chaos. Theoretical and practical methods in non-linear dynamics. Academic Press, London (1996)
3. Kotulski, Z., Szczepański, J.: Discrete chaotic cryptography. Ann. Physics 6, 381–394 (1997)
4. Lind, D., Marcus, B.: Introduction to Symbolic Dynamics and Coding. Cambridge University Press (1995)
5. Maskanen, T.: On finite automaton public key cryptosystem. TUCS, Technical Raport, 408 (2001)
6. Masuda, N., Aihara, K.: Cryptosystems based on space-discretization of chaotic maps. IEEE Trans. Circuits Systems I Fund. Theory Appl. 49, 329–334 (1983)
7. Menezes, A., van Oorshot, P., Vanstone, S.: Handbook of applied cryptography. CRC Press Inc., Boca Raton (1997)
8. Quiquater, J.-J.: Cryptology and graph theory. UCL Crypto Group, EIDMA (2005)
9. Rukhin, A., Soto, J., Nechvatal, J., Smid, M., Barker, E., Leigh, S., et al.: A Statistical Test Suite for Random and Pseudorandom Number Generators for Cryptographic Applications. NIST Special Publication 800-22 Revision 1a, U.S. Department of Commerce, National Institute of Standards and Technology, Gaithersburg (2010)
10. Soto, J., Bassham, L.: Randomness Testing of the Advanced Encryption Standard Finalist Candidates. U.S. Department of Commerce, National Institute of Standards and Technology, Gaithersburg (2000)
11. Soto, J.: Randomness Testing of the Advanced Encryption Standard Candidate Algorithms. U.S. Department of Commerce, National Institute of Standards and Technology, Gaithersburg (1999)
12. Vithanage, A., Shimizu, T.: FIPS 140-2 (Change Notice 1), Random Number Tests. HM-RAE 103-0403, FDK Corporation (2003)
13. Zwierko, A.: Testowanie generatorów pseudolosowych — wybrane programowe pakiety testów statystycznych. In: Enigma 2003 — VII Krajowa Konferencja Zastosowań Kryptografii, Warszawa (2003)

On LDPC Codes Based on Families of Expanding Graphs of Increasing Girth without Edge-Transitive Automorphism Groups

Monika Polak and Vasyl Ustimenko

Institute of Mathematics, Maria Curie-Sklodowska University,
pl. M. Curie-Sklodowskiej 5, 20-031 Lublin, Poland
monika.katarzyna.polak@gmail.com, vasyl@hektor.umcs.lublin.pl

Abstract. We introduce new examples of Low Density Parity Check codes connected with the new families of regular graphs of bounded degree and increasing girth. Some new codes have an evident advantage in comparison with the $D(n, q)$ based codes [9]. The new graphs are not edge transitive. So, they are not isomorphic to the Cayley graphs or those from the $D(n, q)$ family, [14]. We use computer simulation to investigate spectral properties of graphs used for the construction of new codes. The experiment demonstrates existence of large spectral gaps in the case of each graph. We conjecture the existence of infinite families of Ramanujan graphs and expanders of bounded degree,existence of strongly Ramanujan graphs of unbounded degree. The lists of eigenvalues can be used for various practical applications of expanding graphs (Coding Theory, Networking, Image Processing). We show that new graphs can be used as a source of lists of cospectral pairs of graphs of bounded or unbounded degree.

Keywords: expanding graphs, Ramanujun graphs, LDPC codes, families of graphs of increasing girth, spectral gap, cospectral graphs.

We consider the results of computer simulations of graphs of increasing girth for the studies of the following problems:

i) construction of LDPC codes,
ii) expanding properties,
iii) search for families of cospectral graphs.

The specific feature of our research is the usage of graphs which are not edge transitive. Sec. 1 is a brief survey of the results on the edge transitive graphs of large girth and their applications for construction of LDPC codes. In Sec. 1.1 we observe the known results on the families of expanding graphs, Ramanujan graphs and their applications to the Coding Theory. Sec. 1.2 gives brief survey of construction of families of graphs of increasing girth and their applications. Sec. 2 contains the detailed description of the families which we are going to investigate. Sec. 3 is devoted to the properties of presented graphs and evaluation

Z. Kotulski et al. (Eds.): CSS 2014, CCIS 448, pp. 74–88, 2014.

of their second largest eigenvalues by computer simulations. Sec. 4 is devoted to error correcting codes. Constructions of new codes are described there and their general properties are given. Sec. 5 contains the results of BER simulations on the codes via computer simulations. In Sec. 6 we discuse the property of being strongly Ramanujan graphs and give a non trivial example of such graphs. In addition we present the results which show that new graphs are novel examples of families of cospectral graphs. In general a cospectral pair of graphs is easy to find but this is a hard problem to found a cospectral families of graphs. An example of such cospectral families of graphs can be find in [26]. Sec. 7 is a brief summation.

1   On the Edge Transitive Graphs of Large Girth and LDPC Codes

The theory of LDPC codes started with the Tanner's observation (the fact?) that the bipartite graphs without cycles C_4 and other short cycles can be successfully used for the construction of good Hamming codes, [29]. Recall that the error correcting code is $A \subset \mathbb{F}_{2^N}$, where $\mathbb{F}_2 = \{0, 1\}$ and codewords are in the classical Hamming metric: $d(\boldsymbol{x}, \boldsymbol{y}) = |\{i : x_i \neq y_i\}|$. Later on Gallager used this approach to define a class of codes currently known as Low Density Parity Check Codes (LDPC codes), [7]. For other important results see for example: [25], [18], [19], [17], [27].

The first codes obtained by Tanner were based on the generalized polygons i. e. the graphs of diameter m and girth $2m$ for a number m. Recall, that the *girth* is the length of the shortest cycle in a graph, [4].

Guinand and Lodge obtained good LDPC codes based on the members of the family of graphs of large girth, [9]. Recall, that the simple graphs G_i of degree k_i and order v_i with girth g_i form a *family of graphs of large girth* if $g_i \geq \gamma \log_{k_i} v_i$, where γ is the constant independent of i (see [2], [3]).

In 1959 Paul Erdős proved the existence of the family of graphs of large girth with the arbitrary large but bounded degree $k_i = k$ and $\gamma = 1/4$ by his famous probabilistic method, [6]. First explicit constructions of such the families of small (or bounded) order were given in [21], see also [36],[11], [3],[16], [5], [2]. A very special case is the studies of graphs of large girth and with arbitrary large degree (unbounded order). Basically, only two explicit constructions of the families of connected graphs of large girth and superlinear size (number of edges is a nonlinear function from the order) are known.

In 1988 G. A. Margulis showed the first explicit construction of such a family, denoted by $X(p, q)$, where p and q are primes, [20]. For every prime p, Margulis constructed an infinite sequence $\{X_i\}$ of finite undirected regular graphs of the degree $p + 1$ such that $g(X_i) \geq (\frac{4}{3} - o(1)) \log_p n(X_i)$, where $c(X_i)$ and $n(X_i)$ are respectively the girth and the order in the graph X_i. The family of *Cayley graphs* defined by G. Margulis was investigated further by several authors, [16], [11], [3], [22] and others. Notice, that M. Morgenstern [22] proposed an interesting generalisation of this family. M. Morgenstern ([22]) used prime powers instead of primes (Cayley graphs $SL_2(\mathbb{F}_{p^m})$, $m \geq 2$, p is a prime number, were considered instead of $SL_2(p)$).

The second explicit construction of the family of graphs of large girth and superlinear size are the algebraic graphs $CD(n, q)$ given by the nonlinear system of equations over the finite field $\mathbb{F}_q$, [13]. They are connected components of graphs $D(n, q)$, [14]. The polarity graphs of $CD(n, q)$ (see [15]) have an induced subgraph of the degree $q - 1$ which is a family of graphs of large girth with arbitrary large degree (it is shown in [31]). The above mentioned results form a list of major known examples till 2013.

Margulis and other authors investigated the error correcting LDPC codes based on the graphs from the family $X(p, q)$, but in 2003 D. MacKay together with M. Postol showed the weaknesses of this construction [19]. These codes include the codewords of small weight, thus they can not be used in practice. Guinand and Lodge in their work in 1997, [9], showed that the LDPC codes corresponding to graphs $CD(n, q)$ have very good properties. These codes were used in real satellite communications by NASA. Analysis of $CD(n, q)$ based LDPC codes did not bring results with indication of weak properties of such codes. So constructing new economic codes obtained from other families of graphs of increasing girth is hopeful.

1.1 Correlation with Expansion Properties

There is another important bridge between Graph Theory and Coding Theory. It is connected with the idea of expanding graphs used in Coding Theory (superconcentrators, magnifiers and etc, [10] and others).

We say that a family of regular graphs of the bounded degree q of the increasing order n *has an expansion constant c, $c > 0$* if for each subset A of the vertex set X, $|X| = n$ with $|A| \leq n/2$ the inequality $|\partial A| \geq c|A|$ holds. The expansion constant of the family of q-regular graphs can be estimated via the upper limit $q - \lambda_n$, $n \to \infty$, where λ_n is the second largest eigenvalue of family representative of the order n.

By the theorem of Alon and Boppana, large enough members of an infinite family of q-regular graphs with the constant degree q satisfy the inequality $\lambda \geq 2\sqrt{q-1} - o(1)$, where λ is the second largest eigenvalue in the absolute value. So, in the class of families of graphs of bounded degree, the largest possible spectral gap is $q - 2\sqrt{q-1}$. The Ramanujan graphs are q-regular graphs for which the inequality $\lambda \leq 2\sqrt{q-1}$ holds.

It is clear that for applications we need families of graphs with unbounded degree (social network "two persons know each other", the graph of relations of two persons who have e-mail exchange and etc). In fact known families of the Ramanujan graphs of the unbounded degree play an important role in the theory of finite geometries. The above mentioned known regular generalised m-gons of degree $q + 1 > 2$, where q is prime power, and affine generalised polygons of degree q are the examples of the infinite families of the Ramanujan graphs with the spectral gap strictly large with the difference of degree $k + 1$ and doubles square root of k. The other examples of "geometrical expanders" can be found in [1].

We will call further families of graphs G_i of the increasing degree k_i as strongly Ramanujan graphs if the upper limit α of $\lambda_i/2\sqrt{k_i - 1}$ is less than 1 (new definition). The natural examples of strongly Ramanujan graphs are projective regular generalised m-gons and their affine parts. For instance the finite projective plane $PG_2(q)$ (generalised 3-gon) has the degree $q + 1$ and the second largest eigenvalue $\sqrt{q}$. So we can take the infinite family of classical edge transitive graphs $PG_2(p^i)$, where p is the fixed prime and the integer i is unbounded, and form the family of strongly Ramanujan graphs with $\alpha = \frac{1}{2}$.

Conjecture 1. The minimal constant α for all the families of strongly Ramanujan graphs is $\alpha = \frac{1}{2}$.

It turns out that there is an interesting correlation between the high girth and the expanding properties of graphs. For example, both families $X(p,q)$ and $D(n,q)$ are expanding graphs. Lubotzky, Phillips and Sarnak [16] proved that the Cayley graphs $X(p,q)$, where p and q are the primes, introduced by G. Margulis [20] satisfy the Ramanujan graphs definition. For each member of the family $D(n,q)$ of the degree q the second largest eigenvalue λ_1 is bounded by $2\sqrt{q}$. We refer to such graphs as *almost Ramanujan graphs*.

1.2 Intransitive Graphs of Increasing Girth and Corresponding Codes

It is well known that random graphs are good expanders. A random graph is never vertex transitive. So, we hope that the idea to find families of graphs of large girth (or simply graphs with growing girth) and families of expanders among intransitive graphs can lead to good quality LDPC codes.

The first family of intransitive graphs $A(n,q)$ is connected with the following optimization problem. For each vertex w of a graph Γ we consider the minimal length $l(w)$ of cycle through w. We refer to the maximal value $l(w)$ among all vertices as *girth indicator* $\mathrm{gind}(\Gamma)$ of the graph. Obviously, inequality $\mathrm{gind}(\Gamma) \neq g(\Gamma)$ assure that graph is not transitive. Let $ex_{\mathrm{gind}}(v,n)$ be the maximal size (number of edges) for the graph of the order v and the gird indicator $> 2n$. In [33] it was proved that $ex_{\mathrm{gind}}(v,n) = Cv^{1+1/n}$, where C is independent of v. The sharpness of the bound is the corollary of the statement that girth indicator of $A(n,q)$ is $\geq 2n$. This graphs appears in [31] as the homomorphic images of $D(n,q)$ (or $CD(n,q)$) useful for the studies of dynamic systems corresponding to the families of large girth. Authors of [31] realised the self importance of graphs $A(n,q)$ and used their properties in cryptographic applications (see [34], [35]).

Notice that the result on the magnitude of $ex_{\mathrm{gind}}(v,n)$ has certain similarity with Even Circuit Theorem formulated by Paul Erdős (see [4]), which states that the maximal size $ex(v, C_{2n})$ of the graph of the order v is: $\leq cv^{1+1/n}$. Notice that the bound for $ex(v, C_{2n})$ is known to be sharp only for $n = 2, 3$ and 5. The well defined projective limit of graphs $A(n,q)$, $q \neq 2$, $n \to \infty$ is a q-regular tree. So these graphs form a family of connected graphs of the increasing girth in the case of fixed q, $q > 2$. It can be proved that such graphs form, in fact, a family of small world graphs.

The properties of LDPC codes related to the graphs $A(n, q)$ were investigated in [23]. Notice, that the question whether or not the graphs $A(n, q)$, $n = 2, 3, \ldots$ form a family of large girth is still open. The graphs $A(n, q)$ and $CD(n, q)$ are almost the Ramanujan ones.

For the graphs G belonging to the families $D(n, q), CD(n, q)$ and $A(n, q)$ in terms of related dynamic systems the "derivative operator" $G \to G'$ was introduced. In [32] the constructions of new graphs $A'(n, q)$, $A''(n, q)$, $D'(n, q)$ and $D''(n, q)$ associated with the previously known graphs $D(n, q)$ and $A(n, q)$ are given. We know that $D'(n, q)$, $D''(n, q)$ are the families of graphs of large girth (see [32]) and $A'(n, q)$ and $A''(n, q)$ are the families of graphs of the increasing girth but the question on their second eigenvalue was open. In this paper we present the results for the second largest eigenvalues λ_1 of this graphs obtained via computer calculations. The graphs $D'(n, q)$, $D''(n, q)$, $A'(n, q)$ and $A''(n, q)$ form families of graphs of the increasing girth. It can be proved that all these graphs are intransitive, the graphs $D'(q)$ and $D''(q)$ form families of graphs of large girth. The graphs $D'(n, q)$, $D''(n, q)$, $A'(n, q)$ and $A''(n, q)$ are applicable to Coding Theory.

The main goal of our paper is to show that new intransitive graphs $D'(n, q)$, $D''(n, q)$, $A'(n, q)$ and $A''(n, q)$ can be used in practice for the creation of good error correcting codes. We show that the LDPC codes compare well with the properties of codes related to $CD(n, q)$ and $A(n, q)$. We present the results for the second largest eigenvalues λ_1 of the graphs obtained via computer calculations. It turns out, that our graphs are very good expanders. In particular for the small parameters q and n experiments show that we have obtained the Ramanujan graphs. In means that these graphs can be effective for construction of superconcentrators and magnifiers. The spectrum of a graph is the multiset of eigenvalues of its adjacency matrix. Two graphs of different structures are called cospectral if they have the same spectrum. There are numerous constructions of cospectral pairs of graphs but there are only a few large families of cospectral graphs. In [32] it was shown that the families $D(n, q)$, $D'(n, q)$, $D''(n, q)$ and $A(n, q)$, $A'(n, q)$, $A''(n, q)$ have different structures. Computer simulations show that the presented families are large families of cospectral graphs.

2   Construction of Families for the Investigation

Let us recall some basic definitions of Graph Theory. The distance between the vertices w_1 and w_2 in the graph is the length of minimal path from w_1 to w_2. A graph is connected if for an arbitrary pair of vertices w_1, w_2, there is a path from w_1 to w_2. We refer to the bipartite graph $\Gamma(V_1 \cup V_2, E)$ as biregular one if the number of neighbours for the representatives of each partition set is the constants a and b (bidegrees). We call a graph regular in the case $a = b$. Let $\mathbb{F}_q$, where q is the prime power, be a finite field.

Traditionally in the graph theory one subset of vertices in the bipartite graphs is denoted by $V_1 = P$ and called a set of points and another one $V_2 = L$ is called a set of lines. Let P and L be two copies of Cartesian power $\mathbb{F}_q^n$, where $n \geq 2$ is an integer. Brackets and parenthesis will allow the reader to distinguish points and lines. In this paper we concentrate on the finite bipartite graphs on the vertex set $P \cup L$, where P and L are two copies of $\mathbb{F}_q^n$. If $z \in \mathbb{F}_q^n$, then $(z) \in P$ and $[z] \in L$. First, we introduce the bipartite graph $D(q)$, described in [14], with the following points and lines, which are infinite dimensional vectors over $\mathbb{F}_q$ written in the following way:

$$
\begin{aligned}
(p) &= (p_{1,0}, p_{1,1}, p_{1,2}, p_{2,1}, p_{2,2}, p'_{2,2}, p_{2,3}, ..., p_{i,i}, p'_{i,i}, p_{i,i+1}, p_{i+1,1}...), \\
[l] &= [l_{0,1}, l_{1,1}, l_{1,2}, l_{2,1}, l_{2,2}, l'_{2,2}, l_{2,3}, ..., l_{i,i}, l'_{i,i}, l_{i,i+1}, l_{i+1,1}...].
\end{aligned}
\tag{1}
$$

The point (p) is incident with the line $[l]$ (we denote it as $(p)I[l]$), if the following relations between their coordinates hold:

$$
\begin{cases}
l_{1,1} - p_{1,1} = l_{0,1}p_{1,0} \\
l_{1,2} - p_{1,2} = l_{1,1}p_{1,0} \\
l_{2,1} - p_{2,1} = l_{0,1}p_{1,1} \\
l_{i,i} - p_{i,i} = l_{0,1}p_{i-1,i} \\
l'_{i,i} - p'_{i,i} = l_{i,i-1}p_{1,0} \\
l_{i,i+1} - p_{i,i+1} = l_{i,i}p_{1,0} \\
l_{i+1,i} - p_{i+1,i} = l_{0,1}p'_{i,i}
\end{cases}
\tag{2}
$$

where $i \geq 2$. The set of vertices of the graph $D(q)$ of this infinite structure is $V = P \cup L$ and the set of edges consisting of all pairs $\{(p), [l]\}$ for which $(p)I[l]$.

For each positive integer $n > 2$ we obtain a finite incidence structure $(P_n, L_n, I_n)_D$ as follows. Firstly, P_n and L_n are obtained from P and L, respectively, by projecting each vector onto its n initial coordinates with respect to the natural order. The incidence I_n is then defined by imposing the first $n - 1$ incidence equations and ignoring all others. The graph corresponding to the finite incidence structure (P_n, L_n, I_n) is denoted by $D(n, q)$. $D(n, q)$ becomes disconnected for $n \geq 6$. The graphs $D(n, q)$ are edge transitive. It means that their connected components are isomorphic. The connected component of $D(n, q)$ is denoted by $CD(n, q)$. Notice that all connected components of the infinite graph $D(q)$ are q-regular trees.

Let us consider an alternative way of presentation of q-regular tree via equations over finite field $\mathbb{F}_q$. We consider an infinite graph $A(q)$ introduced in [35] with the points and lines:

$$
\begin{aligned}
(p) &= (p_{1,0}, p_{1,1}, p_{1,2}, p_{2,2}, p_{2,3}, ..., p_{i,i}, p_{i,i+1}, ...), \\
[l] &= [l_{0,1}, l_{1,1}, l_{1,2}, l_{2,2}, l_{2,3}, ..., l_{i,i}, l_{i,i+1}, ...].
\end{aligned}
\tag{3}
$$

$A(q)$ is a graph of infinite incidence structure $(P, L, I)_A$ such that point (p) is incident with the line $[l]$ $((p)I[l]$, if the following relations between their coordinates hold:

$$
\begin{cases}
l_{i,i} - p_{i,i} = l_{0,1}p_{i-1,i} \\
l_{i,i+1} - p_{i,i+1} = l_{i,i}p_{1,0}
\end{cases}
\tag{4}
$$

It turns out that $A(q)$ is connected in the case of odd q. It means that $A(q)$ is q regular tree.

Like in the case of $D(q)$ for each positive integer $n > 2$ we obtain an finite incidence structure $(P_n, L_n, I_n)_A$ where P_n and L_n are obtained from P and L, respectively, by projecting each vector onto its n initial coordinates with respect to the natural order. The incidence I_n is then defined by imposing the first $n-1$ incidence equations and ignoring all others. The graph corresponding to the finite incidence structure (P_n, L_n, I_n) is denoted by $A(n, q)$. A family $A(n, q)$ of increasing girth, superlinear size and degree q is given by the nonlinear system of equations. The graphs $A(n, q)$ are not edge transitive. They are connected if $q \geq 2$. In fact, $A(n, q)$ forms a family of small world graphs. There is a conjecture that $CD(n, q)$ is another family of small world graphs.

The described families of graphs can be used to obtain new families with different structures. It can be done by the use of simple cubical operator on the vertex set of the graph from one of the families, such operator allows us to define new relations. Let $(v) = (v_1, v_2, ...v_n)$ denote the point, $[v] = [v_1, v_2, ...v_n]$ denote line and $N_t(v)$ be the operator of taking neighbour of vertex v where the first coordinate is $v_1 + t$:

$$
\begin{aligned}
N_t(v_1, v_2, v_3, ...v_n) &\to [v_1 + t, *, *, ..., *], \\
N_t[v_1, v_2, v_3, ...v_n] &\to (v_1 + t, *, *, ..., *) .
\end{aligned}
\tag{5}
$$

The remaining coordinates can be determined uniquely using original relations defining the used graph. As it follows from the equations each vertex has exactly one neighbour of chosen color t. It is easy to see that N_t is an invertible operator on the set of vertices. To create a new family we can use the composition of two such operators $N_t \circ N_0$ on two copies of the same graph or $N_t \circ N_0 \circ N_0$ directly on the based graph (it is also possible to take other composition of such operators). For the arbitrary graph G described above let I' denote the incidence relation defined by using the composition $N_t \circ N_0$ and let I'' denote the incidence relation defined by using the composition $N_t \circ N_0 \circ N_0$. Take two copies of G and denote point in the first copy by (p) and in the second by $\langle z \rangle$. $(p)I' \langle z \rangle$ if for some $t \in \mathbb{F}_q$ relations $(p)I[l]I \langle z \rangle$ hold, where I is the incidence relation ((2) or (4)) in the based graph $A(n, q)$or $D(n, q)$ described above. Both families of graphs have natural coloring of vertices ρ. We simply assume that the color $t = \rho(v)$ of the vertex v (point (p) or line $[l]$) is its first coordinate $p_{1,0}$ or $l_{0,1}$. Let us define a new binary relation on two copies of graph $A(n, q)$: $(p)I' \langle z \rangle$ $\Leftrightarrow$ when there exists $t \in \mathbb{F}_q$ such that the following relations holds:

$$
\begin{cases}
p_{1,0} = z_{0,1} - t \\
p_{1,1} = z_{1,1} + tz_{1,0} \\
p_{1,2} = z_{1,2} + tp_{1,1} + tz_{0,1}p_{1,0} \\
p_{2,2} = z_{2,2} - tz_{0,1}p_{1,1} - tz_{0,1}^2 p_{1,0} \\
p_{i,i+1} = z_{i,i+1} + tp_{i,i} + tz_{0,1}p_{i-1,i} \\
p_{i+1,i+1} = z_{i+1,i+1} - tz_{0,1}p_{i,i} - tz_{0,1}^2 p_{i-2,i-1}
\end{cases}
\tag{6}
$$

for $i \geq 2$. Let us denote the graph described by this system of equations as $A'(n, q)$. Let us define a new binary relation on $A(n, q)$: $(p)I'' \langle l \rangle$ $\Leftrightarrow$ when if and only if there exists $t \in \mathbb{F}_q$ such that the following relations hold:

$$\begin{cases} p_{1,0} = l_{0,1} - t \\ p_{1,1} = l_{1,1} - p_{1,0}l_{0,1} \\ p_{1,2} = l_{1,2} - p_{1,0}p_{1,1} - p_{1,0}p_{1,0}l_{0,1} \\ p_{2,2} = l_{2,2} - l_{0,1}p_{1,2} \\ p_{i,i+1} = l_{i,i+1} - p_{1,0}p_{i,i} - p_{1,0}p_{i-1,i}l_{0,1} \\ p_{i+1,i+1} = l_{i+1,i+1} - l_{0,1}p_{i-1,i} \end{cases} \qquad (7)$$

for $i \geq 2$. Let us denote the graph described by this system of relations as $A''(n,q)$. The graph $D'(n,q)$ with the notation for point and line as for $D(n,q)$ is described by the following relations (for $t \in \mathbb{F}_q$):

$$\begin{cases} p_{1,0} = z_{1,0} - t \\ p_{1,1} = z_{1,1} + tz_{0,1} \\ p_{1,2} = z_{1,2} + tp_{1,1} + tz_{0,1}p_{1,0} \\ p_{2,1} = z_{2,1} - tz_{1,0}z_{1,0} \\ p_{i,i} = z_{i,i} - tz_{0,1}p_{i-1,i-1} - tp_{i-2,i-1}z_{0,1}^2 \\ p'_{i,i} = z'_{i,i} + tp_{i,i-1} + tz_{0,1}p'_{i-1,i-1} \\ p_{i,i+1} = z_{i,i+1} + tp_{i,i} + tz_{0,1}p_{i-1,i} \\ p_{i+1,i} = z_{i+1,i} - tz_{0,1}p_{i,i-1} - tz_{0,1}^2 p_{i-1,i-1} \end{cases} \qquad (8)$$

for $i \geq 2$ and $p'_{1,1} = p_{1,1}$. Let us define a new binary relation on $D(n,q)$: $(p)I''\langle l\rangle$ $\Leftrightarrow$ when if and only if there exists $t \in \mathbb{F}_q$ such that the following relations hold:

$$\begin{cases} p_{1,0} = l_{0,1} - t \\ p_{1,1} = l_{1,1} - p_{1,0}l_{0,1} \\ p_{1,2} = l_{1,2} - p_{1,0}p_{1,1} - p_{1,0}^2 l_{0,1} \\ p_{2,1} = l_{2,1} - l_{0,1}p_{1,1} \\ p_{i,i} = l_{i,i} - l_{0,1}p_{i-1,i} \\ p'_{i,i} = l'_{i,i} - p_{1,0}p_{i,i-1} - p_{1,0}p'_{i-1,i-1}l_{0,1} \\ p_{i,i+1} = l_{i,i+1} - p_{1,0}p_{i,i} - p_{1,0}p_{i-1,i}l_{0,1} \\ p_{i+1,i} = l_{i+1,i} - l_{0,1}p'_{i,i} \end{cases} \qquad (9)$$

for $i \geq 2$ and $p'_{1,1} = p_{1,1}$. Let us denote a graph described by this system of relations as $D''(n,q)$. The all above mentioned constructions form simple undirected families of graphs. The inverse functions of $N_t \circ N_0$ and $N_t \circ N_0 \circ N_0$ are of the form: $N_0 \circ N_{-t}$ and $N_0 \circ N_0 \circ N_{-t}$ accordingly. For each chosen vertex x from the graphs $A'(n,q)$ or $D'(n,q)$ we have $N_t(N_0(x)) = y$ and $N_0(N_{-t}(y)) = x$. For each chosen vertex x from the graphs $A''(n,q)$ or $D''(n,q)$ we have $N_t(N_0(N_0(x))) = y$ and $N_0(N_0(N_{-t}(y))) = x$.

3 On General Properties and Evaluation of Spectral Gap

The presented families are simple, undirected bipartite graphs. Each representative from the families $A'(n,q)$, $A''(n,q)$, $D'(n,q)$ and $D''(n,q)$ is a q-regular, bipartite graph with $|V| = 2q^n$ vertices and $|E| = q^{n+1}$ edges. the graphs belonging to the family of $A'(n,q)$ or $A''(n,q)$ are connected. For $n \geq 4$ the graphs from the family $D'(n,q)$ and $D''(n,q)$ can be disconnected. as $CD'(n,q)$ and $CD''(n,q)$ we denote the connected components of the graphs $D'(n,q)$ and $D''(n,q)$ accordingly. These families have representation as very sparse adjacency matrices. Because the graphs are bipartite the adjacency matrices are of the form:

$$A = \begin{pmatrix} 0 & M \\ M^T & 0 \end{pmatrix}. \tag{10}$$

The matrix M is the q-regular $q^n \times q^n$ matrix. The ratio of those to the total number of elements in the matrix M is $(q \cdot q^n)/(q^n \cdot q^n) = q^{1-n}$.

In [24] the reader can find the percentage of the number of ones in matrix M, which is a part of adjacency matrix, for some values of q and n.

The graph corresponding to the sparse adjacency matrix (with a small number of those) is sparse. The sparse graph has a small number of edges in comparison to the number of vertices. The simple relationship describing the density of the graph $\Gamma(V, E)$ is:

$$D = \frac{2|E|}{|V|(|V| - 1)}, \tag{11}$$

where $|E|$ is the number of edges of graph Γ and $|V|$ is the number of vertices. The maximal density is $D = 1$ when the graph is complete and the minimal density is 0 (Coleman & Moré 1983). For the presented families of graphs the density is: $D = (2q^{n+1})/(2q^n(2q^n - 1)) = q/(2q^n - 1)$.

Proposition 1. *The families $A'(n,q)$, $A''(n,q)$, $D'(n,q)$ and $D''(n,q)$ are q-regular sparse graphs and their density is according to (11) is $\dfrac{q}{2q^n - 1}$.*

The following theorems about the girth of the families of graphs presented here are from [32]. We remark that the lack of short cycles is a very important property for the derived LDPC codes.

Theorem 1 [32]. *The families $A'(n,q)$ and $A''(n,q)$, $D'(n,q)$ and $D''(n,q)$ are the families of graphs of the increasing girth (with growing n). For all $n \geq 2$ there are no cycles of length 4. $D'(n,q)$ and $D''(n,q)$ form families of a large girth.* □

Theorem 2 [32]. *There are no edge acting transitive groups on the graphs $A'(n,q)$, $A''(n,q)$, $D'(n,q)$ and $D''(n,q)$.* □

In this paper we present the results for the second largest eigenvalues λ_1 of these families of graphs. Via computer calculations in MATLAB (function eig) we obtained the results which allow us to formulate the following conjecture:

Conjecture 2. This families of the graphs: $A'(n,q)$, $A''(n,q)$, $D'(n,q)$ and $D''(n,q)$ are expander graphs with the second eigenvalues $\lambda_1 \leq 2\sqrt{q}$.

The details of our calculations are available in [24].

4   Corresponding LDPC Codes

In order to improve the transmission quality error correcting codes can be used. An error-correcting code (ECC) is a system of adding r extra bits-redundant data, to a k bits message. Moreover, checksums and correction codes are used in the information technology and telecommunications to protect the integrity of the data. As a result of this action we get the codewords $y \in C$ of the length N. Such a code has $r = N - k$ parity checks equations and is denoted by $[N; k]$. The ratio k/N is called code rate and is denoted by R_C. There are three ways to represent linear error correcting codes: generator matrix G, parity check matrix H or Tanner graph $\Gamma(V, E)$. There is a standard way to create error correcting codes from a bipartite, biregular Tanner graph. The parity check matrix H and the adjacency matrix A are closely related:

$$A = \begin{pmatrix} 0 & H \\ H^T & 0 \end{pmatrix}. \tag{12}$$

The matrix H uniquely determines the code.

LDPC code is one of the powerful classes of error correcting codes $C = \{y \in \mathbb{F}_2^N : Hy^T = 0\}$, which was discovered by Robert Gallanger in his work Low-Density Parity-Check Codes [7]. They were forgotten for twenty years to get back in the nineties, for example see [8,9,27]. The ability to use graphs in construction of LDPC was first discussed by Tanner [29]. Construction of efficient Tanner type codes based on the expander graphs was considered for example by Sipser and Spielman [27], Guinanad and Lodge [8,9].

The presented construction leads us to the families of graphs that can be successfully used in the coding theory to create a LDPC codes because they:

i)   are simple undirected graphs,
ii) do not have cycles of length less than 6 for arbitrary n,
iii) are families of graphs of the increasing girth,
iv) have structures that allow us to obtain the arbitrary code rate R_C,
v)   work with the existing decoding algorithm,
vi) have representation as very sparse matrices H.

To create the LDPC code with the codeword of length N we use $A'(n, q)$, $A''(n, q)$, $D'(n, q)$ or $D''(n, q)$, where $n^q > N$. Each of these graphs are already bipartite but q-regular instead of biregular, so parity check matrix is quadratic. To obtain biregularity and bigger code rate we can put restrictions on the $p_{i,j}$ or $l_{i,j}$ coordinates of lines or points for fixed i and j. We can make it by the method described for graphs $D(n, q)$ in [14]. To obtain the desired bidegree (e, f) we must put restriction on coordinates. Let $E \subset \mathbb{F}_q$ and $F \subset \mathbb{F}_q$ be an e-element and f-element subsets respectively ($e \neq f$) and let V_P and V_L be sets of points and lines in a new bipartite graph. They are the following sets:

$$V_P = \{(p) \in P | p_{i,j} \in E\}, \quad V_L = \{[l] \in L | l_{i,j} \in F\}.$$

The bigger set described above corresponds to the codeword bits and the smaller to the parity checks. By this method we can obtain a bipartite, biregular graph with the adjacency matrix: $\begin{pmatrix} 0 & H \\ H^T & 0 \end{pmatrix}$, which is a subgraph of graph corresponding to adjacency matrix $\begin{pmatrix} 0 & M \\ M^T & 0 \end{pmatrix}$. Bidegree reduction can only increase the girth so there are not short cycles. After bidegree reduction the graph can be disconnected and divided into several components. To create a parity checks matrix we use to only one component. We decide to put one or zero in a parity check matrix by checking if the relations (6),(7),(8) or (9) on the coordinates of individual points and lines are satisfied.

To obtain parity check matrix $H_{r \times N}$, where $r \leq \frac{N}{2}$ (code rate R_C more than $\frac{1}{2}$) we can reduce the bidegree of graph to (e, f) for $3 \leq e < \frac{f}{2} \leq \frac{q}{2}$ for $n \geq 3$ ($2 \leq e < \frac{f}{2} \leq \frac{q}{2}$ for $n = 2$; for bigger n value $e = 2$ can produce columns of weight 1 in parity check matrix H). Reducing the bidegrees to $e < f \leq q$ gives ensemble of regular $C^{e,f}(N, k)$ codes satisfying the following properties: each row has f ones, each column has e ones, the parity check matrix H is sparse, code rate is $1 - \frac{e}{f}$.

The matrix H, which is a part of adjacency matrix A after the bidegree reduction corresponding to (e, f)-regular graph is $eq^{n-1} \times fq^{n-1}$ matrix. The ratio of those to the total number of elements in the matrix H is $(e \cdot fq^{n-1})/(eq^{n-1} \cdot fq^{n-1}) = q^{1-n}$. We see that the density of the matrix H does not depend on the parameters e and f. The density for fixed n and q is the same as for the matrix M used to create code.

It has been proved in [32] that these new families of graphs have the increasing girth (with the increasing n) and are not edge transitive, so we can call them pseudorandom in some sense. This is the reason why the obtained codes have different properties for different chosen parameters (subsets A and B described below). In the case of the graphs $D(n, q)$ it does not matter which elements contain the subsets A and B, we are only interested in how many elements they contain. The graphs from these families do not have short cycles (length 4 or less) so this fact provides the convergence of decoding algorithm.

The *minimum distance* of an error correcting code is the smallest Hamming distance between two distinct codewords. This is one of the most important parameter of code design that determines the maximum number of errors that can be corrected under any decoding algorithm. The minimum distance analysis for the codes corresponding to the described graphs is following. the presented families of graphs have the increasing girth so we can construct the LDPC codes with arbitrary large girth. In [29] there was proved the following lower bound on d_{min} in terms of girth g and bit node degree e:

$$d_{min} \geq \frac{2[(e-1)^{g/4} - 1]}{e - 2} \text{ , where } g/2 \text{ is even,}$$

$$d_{min} \geq \frac{[e(e-1)^{\lfloor g/4 \rfloor} - 2]}{e - 2}, \text{ where } g/2 \text{ is odd .}$$

(13)

Combining Theorem 1 and the above mentioned inequalities, we can see that LDPC codes, corresponding to the presented families of graphs, can be designed to have the arbitrarily large minimum distance d_{min}.

5   Resulting Codes

The presented codes are Low-Density Parity-Check Codes (LDPC) because they have representation as the sparse parity check matrix H. In addition, families of graphs $A'(n, q)$ and $A''(n, q)$ are graphs of increasing girth while the families of graphs $D'(n, q)$ and $D''(n, q)$ are the graphs of large girth. Graphs $D(n, q)$ have been successfully applied to the construction of LDPC codes in the nineties by Guinand & Lodge. Due to the above the proposed families of graphs are good candidates for the construction of error correcting codes.

Our simulations were done using the BPSK modulation over the AWGN channel and simple belief-propagation (BP) decoder implementation with 10 iterations. The efficacy of the BP algorithm is only slightly worse than the optimum MAP decoding. Let y be the obtained codeword. MAP decoder works accordingly to the rule which returns an output value $\hat{x}$ of a code word x for which the *posteriori* probability $P = (x|y, H)$ is maximized. The BP algorithm consists in calculating the approximate values of the *a posteriori* probabilities $P = (x_i|y, H)$ for the different receiver bits of the codeword x until the hard decisions taken on the basis of these probabilities will indicate one of the possible code words or the maximum number of iterations will be reached. The use of iterative decoding is especially useful in the case of LDPC codes as the computational complexity of the decoding process for the sparse matrix depends linearly on the length of the codeword.

In accordance with Proposition 1 we can see that the presented codes have very sparse parity check matrices. The less short cycles in the used graph the approximate *a posteriori* probability values are more accurate. The presented families of graphs are sparse and have the increasing girth so it means that error correction capability of the code is very good and encoding, decoding are efficient.

In order to compare quality of codes which are obtained from the graphs from the family $D(n, q)$ and new families: $D'(n, q)$, $D''(n, q)$ $A'(n, q)$, $A''(n, q)$, with the same parameters accordingly, we made BER simulations. In [24] the reader can find properties of sample described codes and results of the corresponding BER simulations. the codes based on the families $A'(n, q)$ and $D'(n, q)$ have similar properties to those based on the families $A''(n, q)$ and $D''(n, q)$. In general, the codes based on the representatives of new described families, have better error correcting properties than those based on $D(n, q)$. This fact is supported by a dozen numbers of conducted simulations for the randomly selected subsets of E and F.

6   Strongly Ramanujan Graphs and Cospectral Graphs

Recall that the spectrum of a graph is the multiset of eigenvalues of its adjacency matrix. Suppose G_i and F_i are the families of simple graphs. We say that the families G_i and F_i are *families of cospectral graphs* if for each i graph G_i has the same spectrum as graph F_i. The interesting fact is that the family of graphs $CD(n, q)$ is edge transitive, however the graphs $CD''(n, q)$ are intransitive. In the case of the graphs $A(n, q)$ and $A'(n, q)$ these families are not cospectral because they have different second largest eigenvalue for the parameters $n = 3, 4$ and $q = 9$. The graphs $D(n, q)$ and $D'(n, q)$ have the same eigenvalues but their multiples are different. We made calculations by using MATLAB (function eig) to an accuracy of 10^{-15}. The details of our calculations are available in [24]. Based on the calculations we claim that the following properties for the arbitrary large parameters n and q are true:

Conjecture 3. For each chosen n and q pair $D(n, q)$ and $D''(n, q)$ is a pair of nonisomorphic graphs with the same spectrum.

Conjecture 4. For each chosen n and q pair $A(n, q)$ and $A''(n, q)$ is a pair of nonisomorphic graphs with the same spectrum.

The expanding properties of the graphs D' and D'' are better than for A' and A''. Based on the calculations we formulated the following conjectures. Recall that the families of graphs G_i of the increasing degree k_i are called strongly the Ramanujan graphs if the upper limit α of $\lambda_i/2\sqrt{k_i - 1}$ is less than 1.

Conjecture 5. Suppose $\mathbb{F}_q$ is a number field with characteristic $\neq 2$. The families $D'(4, q)$ and $D''(4, q)$ are q-regular Ramanujan graphs.

Conjecture 6. The graphs $D'(3, q) = A'(3, q)$ and $D''(3, q) = A''(3, q)$ are q-regular strongly Ramanujan graphs with the second eigenvalues $\lambda_1 = 2\sqrt{\frac{q}{2}} \leq 2\sqrt{q-1}$ and the constant $\alpha = \frac{\sqrt{2}}{2}$.

7 Conclusions

We use computer simulation to investigate the LDPC codes corresponding to intransitive graphs. These graphs form infinite families of graphs of the increasing girth. The computer experiments demonstrated existence of good LDPC codes with better parameters than in the previously studied codes based on the $D(n, q)$ graphs. We also use computer simulations to investigate extreme properties of our intransitive graphs. It allows us to formulate interesting conjectures on infinity families of expanders, Ramanujan graphs, strongly Ramanujan graphs, pairs of cospectral graphs of arbitrary degree.

This construction can be successfully used with other families of graph which can be described by a system of equations such as affine generalized polygons, [30]. Generalized m-gons are connected, biregular, bipartite graphs with the girth $2m$ and the diameter m. Traditionally, in the case of generalised m-gon $\Gamma(V_1 \cup V_2, E)$ one partition set $V_1 = P$ is called the set of points and the other $V_2 = L$ is called the set of lines. When two vertices point (p) and line $[l]$ are connected by the edge we call this incidence pair (p, l) a flag. We define the distance from flag (p, l) to the vertex $v \in V$ as the sum of distances from p

to v and l to v. Affine generalized m-gon can be obtained by choosing a flag (p, l) in the generalised m-gon and by removing all points and lines except those which are in the maximal distance from the flag. Instead of using composition of operators $N_t \circ N_0$ or $N_t \circ N_0 \circ N_0$ we can use $N_\alpha \circ N_\beta$, $N_\alpha \circ N_\beta \circ N_\gamma$ and their composition: $(N_\alpha \circ N_\beta)^k$, $(N_\alpha \circ N_\beta \circ N_\gamma)^k$, where α, β, γ are the elements from $\mathbb{F}_q$ and k is the positive integer.

We hope this will attract attention of mathematicians and our mathematical conjectures will be proved. Moreover, we hope our facts are interesting for specialists in Computer Science and cryptographers. One can use better computer or algorithm do find better codes or try to disprove our conjectures.

References

1. Alon, N.: Eigenvalues, geometric expanders, sorting in rounds and Ramsey theory. Combinatorica 6(3), 207–219 (1986)
2. Biggs, N.L.: Algebraic Graph Theory, 2nd edn. Cambridge University Press (1993)
3. Biggs, N.L.: Graphs with large girth. Ars Combin. In: Eleventh British Combinatorial Conference, London, vol. 25(C), pp. 73–80 (1988)
4. Bollobas, B.: Extremal Graph Theory. Academic Press, London (1978)
5. Chiu, P.: Cubic Ramanujan graphs. Combinatorica 12(3), 275–285 (1992)
6. Erdős, P.: Graph theory and probability. Canad. Math. Monthly 11, 34–38 (1959)
7. Gallager, R.G.: Low-Density Parity-Checks Codes. Monograph. M.I.T. Press (1963)
8. Guinand, P., Lodge, J.: Graph theoretic construction of generalized product codes. In: IEEE International Symposium on Information Theory, ISIT 1997, Ulm, Germany, June 29-July 4, p. 111 (1997)
9. Guinand, P., Lodge, J.: Tanner type codes arising from large girth graphs. In: Canadian Workshop on Information Theory CWIT 1997, Toronto, Ontario, Canada, pp. 5–7 (1997)
10. Hoory, S., Linial, N., Wigderson, A.: Expander graphs and their applications. Bull. Amer. Math. Soc. (N.S.) 43(4), 439–561 (2006)
11. Imrich, W.: Explicit construction of regular graphs without small cycles. Combinatorica 4(1), 53–59 (1984)
12. Lazebnik, F., Ustimenko, V., Woldar, A.J.: Polarities and 2k-cycle-free graphs. Discrete Mathematics 197-198, 503–513 (1999)
13. Lazebnik, F., Ustimenko, V., Woldar, A.J.: A characterization of the components of the graphs $D(k, q)$. Discrete Mathematics 157, 271–283 (1996)
14. Lazebnik, F., Ustimenko, V., Woldar, A.J.: A new series of dense graphs of high girth. Bulletin (New Series) of the AMS 32(1), 73–79 (1995)
15. Lazebnik, F., Ustimenko, V., Woldar, A.J.: Polarities and 2k-cycle-free graphs. Discrete Mathematics 197-198, 503–513 (1999)
16. Lubotsky, A., Philips, R., Sarnak, P.: Ramanujan graphs. Combinatorica 8(3), 261–277 (1988)
17. Luby, M.G., Mitzenmacher, M., Shokrollahi, M.A., Spielman, D.A.: Improved Low-Density Parity-Check Codes Using Irregular Graphs and Belief Propagation. In: ISIT 1998-IEEE International Symposium of Information Theory, Cambridge, USA, p. 171 (1998)

18. MacKay, D.J.C., Neal, R.M.: Good Codes Based on Very Sparse Matrices. In: Boyd, C. (ed.) Cryptography and Coding 1995. LNCS, vol. 1025, pp. 100–111. Springer, Heidelberg (1995)

19. MacKay, D., Postol, M.: Weakness of Margulis and Ramanujan Margulis Low Dencity Parity Check Codes. Electronic Notes in Theoretical Computer Science, vol. 74 (2003)

20. Margulis, G.A.: Explicit group-theoretic constructions of combinatorial schemes and their applications in the construction of expanders and concentrators. Problemy Peredachi Informatsii 24(1), 51–60 (1988)

21. Margulis, G.A.: Explicit construction of graphs without short cycles and low density codes. Combinatorica 2, 1–78 (1982)

22. Morgenstern, M.: Existence and explicit constructions of $q+1$-regular Ramanujan graphs for every prime power q. J. Combin. Theory Ser. B 62(1), 44–62 (1994)

23. Polak, M., Ustimenko, V.: On LDPC codes Corresponding to Infinite Family of Graphs $A(n, K)$. In: Proceedings of Federated Conference on Computer Science and Informations Systems, Wrocław, Poland, September 9-12, pp. 567–570 (2012)

24. Polak, M., Ustimenko, V.: Appendix for article On LDPC codes based on families of expanding graphs of increasing girth without edge-transitive automorphism groups. University of Maria Curie Skłodowska (2014),
http://umcs.pl/pl/zaklad-algebry-i-matematyki-dyskretnej,1336.htm

25. Richardson, T.J., Urbanke, R.L.: The Capacity of Low-Density Parity Check Codes Under Message-Passing Decoding. IEEE Transaction on Informarion Theory 47(2), 599–618 (2001)

26. Akos, S.: Large Families of Cospectral Graphs. Designs, Codes and Cryptography 21(1-3), 205–208 (2000)

27. Sipser, M., Spielman, D.A.: Expander codes. IEEE Trans. on Info. Theory 42(6), 1710 (1996)

28. Shannon, C.E., Warren, W.: The Mathematical Theory of Communication. University of Illinois Press (1963)

29. Tanner, R.M.: A recursive approach to low density codes. IEEE Transactions on Information Theory IT 27(5), 533–547 (1984)

30. Ustimenko, V., Woldar, A.: Extremal properties of regular and affine generalized polygons as tactical configurations. Eur. J. Combinator. 24, 99 (2003)

31. Ustimenko, V.: On linguistic dynamical systems, families of graphs of large girth, and cryptography. Zapiski Nauchnykh Seminarov POMI 326, 214–234 (2005)

32. Ustimenko, V.: On the K-theory of graph based dynamical systems and its applications. Dopovidi Natsional'noi Akademii nauk Ukrainy 8, 44–51 (2013)

33. Ustimenko, V.: On extremal graph theory and symbolic computations. Dopovidi Natsional'noi Akademii nauk Ukrainy 2, 42–49 (2013)

34. Romańczuk, U., Ustimenko, V.: On the key exchange protocol with new cubical maps based on graphs. Annales UMCS Informaticea XI, 11–29 (2011)

35. Ustimenko, V., Romańczuk, U.: On Extremal Graph Theory, Explicit algebraic constructions of extremal graphs and corresponding Turing encryption machines. In: Yang, X.-S. (ed.) Artificial Intelligence, Evolutionary Computing and Meta-heuristics. SCI, vol. 427, pp. 257–285. Springer, Heidelberg (2013)

36. Weiss, A.: Girths of bipartite sextet graphs. Combinatorica 4(2-3), 241–245 (1984)

Analysis of the Data Flow in the Newscast Protocol for Possible Vulnerabilities

Jakub Muszyński[1], Sébastien Varrette[1],
Juan Luis Jiménez Laredo[2], and Pascal Bouvry[1]

[1] Computer Science and Communication (CSC) Research Unit, Luxembourg
{jakub.muszynski,sebastien.varrette}@uni.lu
[2] Interdisciplinary Centre for Security Reliability and Trust (SnT),
University of Luxembourg, 6, rue Richard Coudenhove-Kalergi,
L-1359 Luxembourg, Luxembourg

Abstract. Newscast is a model for information dissemination and membership management in large-scale, agent-based distributed systems. It deploys a simple, peer-to-peer data exchange protocol. The Newscast protocol forms an overlay network and keeps it connected by means of an epidemic algorithm, thus featuring a complex, spatially structured, and dynamically changing environment. It has recently become very popular due to its inherent resilience to node volatility as it exhibits strong self-healing properties. In this paper, we analyze the robustness of the data flow within the Newscast model against a set of vulnerabilities that have not been taken into account in previous analysis. In particular, we perform an attack based on a cache content corruption which is able to defeat the protocol by breaking the network connectivity. Concrete experiments are performed using a framework that implements both the protocol and the corruption model considered in this work.

Keywords: newscast, fault tolerance, peer-to-peer.

1   Introduction

The popularity of P2P systems has increased since their advent in the 2000's. A key issue in these systems is that distribution of data and control across processes is symmetric: tasks or work loads are distributed between peers which are equally privileged, equipotent participants in the distributed application. Thus a well-designed P2P system can easily scale to millions of processes, each of which can join or leave whenever it pleases without seriously disrupting the system's overall quality of service. One of the main characteristics of classical P2P architecture remains its heterogeneity and, again, the extreme volatility of the resources as their owners may reclaim them without warning, leading therefore to what is commonly referred to as *crash faults*. Consequently, a large part of research on P2P systems focuses on routing protocols and self-managing systems to handle group membership and communications in an automated and distributed way. This is generally performed in two directions. On one side, an overlay network is

Z. Kotulski et al. (Eds.): CSS 2014, CCIS 448, pp. 89–99, 2014.

built in the application layer on top of an existing network such as the Internet. Each joining peer has an assigned identifier mapped over a structured topology (as in Chord [10] for instance) which is used to route messages. Another strategy consists in exploiting randomness to disseminate information across a large set of computing resources to maintain a high connectivity within this pool of nodes even in the event of major disasters. Such P2P algorithms fall in the category of epidemic (or gossiping) protocols that do not rely on a predefined structure, but on the emerging overlay network which is used to disseminate information virally. This comes with a bigger overhead in terms of routing performances, counter balanced by a high fault resilience and self-healing properties inherited from the epidemic nature of the protocol. A well-known example based on this paradigm is Newscast [6], a self-organized gossiping protocol for the maintenance of dynamic unstructured P2P overlay networks. Newscast displays a scalable and robust behavior which emerges from the interaction of a simple set of rules: nodes exchange pieces of routing information among randomly selected neighbors. Due to this simplicity, the protocol has been rapidly adopted in academic research: as a platform for distributed optimization [7], as a framework for peer-sampling services [4] or as a way for monitoring the status of large-scale decentralized systems [5]. While the robustness of the Newscast model against *crash faults* has been demonstrated successfully in many previous works [6,12], this paper investigates other attacks and possible vulnerabilities that have not yet been studied in a context of this protocol.

This paper is organized as follows: Section 2 details the background of this work and reviews related works. Possible vulnerabilities, experimental setup and the implementation details are provided in Section 3. Experimental results are discussed in Section 4 where we demonstrate that the Newscast protocol **is not resilient** against the considered attack. Finally, Section 5 concludes the paper with a summary of our results and provides future directions.

2   Context and Motivations

This section aims at providing general insights into the Newscast protocol and its inherent properties as defined in the seminal paper [6]. Then, some general concepts on fault-tolerance are introduced before reviewing the proposed approaches in the literature addressing this domain in the context of the Newscast model.

Overview of the Newscast Model. Newscast is a gossiping protocol for interconnecting large-scale distributed systems. Without any central services or servers, Newscast differs from other similar approaches [3,10,9] by its simplicity. The membership management follows an extremely simple protocol: in order to join the system, a node only needs to contact a connected node from which it gets a list of neighbors. Additionally, to leave the system, the node only requires to stop communicating for a predefined time. The dynamics of the system follow a probabilistic scheme able to keep a self-organized equilibrium. Such an equilibrium emerges from the loosely-coupled and decentralized run of the protocol within the different and independent nodes. The emerging graph behaves as a small-world topology [13] allowing a scalable information dissemination. This also contributes to make the system suitable for distributed computing. Despite the simplicity of the scheme, Newscast is particularly fault-tolerant against crash failures and exhibits a graceful degradation without requiring an extra mechanism other than its own emergent behavior [12].

Algorithm 1. Newscast protocol in $node_i$

1: Active Thread
2: **while** true **do**
3:    wait t_r
4:    $node_j \Leftarrow$ selected node from $Cache_i$ // *a cache is a vector of c node entries*
5:    send $Cache_i$ to $node_j$
6:    receive $Cache_j$ from $node_j$
7:    $Cache_i \Leftarrow$ Aggregate ($Cache_i,Cache_j$)
8: **end while**
9:
10: Passive Thread
11: **while** true **do**
12:    wait until $Cache_k$ is received from $node_k$
13:    send $Cache_i$ to $node_k$
14:    $Cache_i \Leftarrow$ Aggregate ($Cache_i,Cache_k$)
15: **end while**
16:
17: $Cache_{aggregated} \Leftarrow$ Aggregate($Cache_a,Cache_b$)
18: $Cache_{aggregated} \Leftarrow Cache_a \cup Cache_b$
19: Keep the c freshest items in $Cache_{aggregated}$ according with the time-stamp

---

Algorithm 1 shows the pseudo-code of the protocol. Each node keeps its own set of neighbors in a cache that contains $c \in \mathbb{N}$ entries, referring to c other nodes in the network without duplicates. Each entry provides a reference to the node in which it was created and a time-stamp of the entry creation (allowing the replacement of old items). There are two different tasks that the algorithm carries out within each node. The active thread which pro-actively initiates a cache exchange once every cycle (one cycle takes t_r time units) and the passive thread that waits for data-exchange requests. Every cycle, each $node_i$ initiates a cache exchange. It selects randomly a neighbor $node_j$ from its $Cache_i$ with uniform probability. Then $node_i$ and $node_j$ exchange their caches and merge them following an aggregation function, consisting of picking the freshest c items from $Cache_i \cup Cache_j$ and merging them into a single cache. Since this function applies in both nodes (the one initiating the request and the one serving the request), the result is that $node_i$ and $node_j$ will have in common the same entries in their respective caches.

Fault Tolerance and Robustness in Distributed Systems. Fault tolerance can be defined as an ability of a system to behave in a well-defined manner once a failure occurs. A failure is due to an error of the system which is a consequence of a fault. Different kinds of faults are usually distinguished in function of their origin and their temporal duration [1]. They could be intentional or not, software or hardware, *e.g.* modify the processing time of an operation, provide a wrong result or return no result at all.

When a given system is resilient to a given type of fault, one generally claims that this system is *robust*.

Fault-Tolerance of the Newscast Protocol. One of the important issues regarding P2P computing is the robustness of the underlying protocols, as they need to provide a coherent view of a large-scale — and potentially — unreliable distributed system. In that sense, the Newscast protocol establishes the dynamics of a changing communication graph which requires to persistently maintain a small-world connectivity. As a first assessment of its robustness, Jelasity and van Steen [6] showed that Newscast maintains such property regardless of the scale or the initial state of the system (*i.e.* the protocol is able to bootstrap from any graph structure and consistently converges to a small-world graph). Nevertheless, two additional issues still need to be considered for characterizing a protocol as robust. The first is related to the spontaneous partitioning of the communication graph, and the second to the resilience of the protocol to failures. The spontaneous partitioning of the communication graph refers to the probability of a subgraph to become disconnected from the system as a consequence of the protocol dynamics. In Newscast, the probability of a spontaneous partitioning is mainly influenced by the cache size c. Jelasity and van Steen [6] conclude that, while a partition in Newscast may happen if $c < 20$, the probability of spontaneous partitioning is almost negligible for $c \geq 20$ regardless of the size of the network. Previous results, however, do not take into account node failures, which is an inherent feature of large-scale distributed systems. In that sense, Spyros et al. [12] analyse the robustness of Newscast in a failure-prone scenario in which the nodes are removed until none is left. The study leads to the following conclusions: (1) despite failures, the Newscast graph remains connected until a large percentage of nodes are removed, *e.g.* for $c = 40$, almost 90% of the nodes have to be removed to split the graph; (2) when a partition finally takes place, most of the nodes still remain connected in a large cluster. From previous findings, Newscast can be said to be robust against crash-faults: the protocol consistently maintains the desired connectivity, even if considering a high percentage of nodes crashing. However, large-scale distributed systems are also subject to other potential sources of risks. Specifically, malicious users may pose a threat to the system, finding its vulnerabilities and exploiting them to disrupt the connectivity of the graph. This type of failures (*i.e. cheating faults*) also need to be considered for defining a protocol as fully robust. Assessing — and eventually enabling — security in Newscast is, therefore, a necessary step for promoting the uses of the protocol beyond the academic environment.

3   Toward Novel Vulnerabilities in Newscast

Newscast protocol was designed with emphasis on the ease of membership management as it was supposed to be used in a highly dynamic, decentralized P2P environment. Every client (node) can join and leave the network at any time without prior notification. The fact that the cache content received during the connection is by default assumed to be correct, leaves a space for abuse.

Cache merge operation and possible misuse. In previous works [8,11], the model of *cheating faults* has been introduced. It is a kind of byzantine fault, where the attacker falsifies the message of the protocol, if possible unnoticeably *i.e.* conform to the protocol. In the context of Newscast it could be caused by sending correctly constructed messages containing freshest possible entries, referring to random (and most likely) non-existing peers. In this paper we explain why such attack is possible by analyzing some of the Newscast features focused on the performed data-flow. We show that the build-in properties of the protocol allow to carry out such an attack successfully.

Experimental setup and implementation details. In order to better understand the data-flow during the protocol execution and to assess the impact of cheating faults on Newscast, we implemented the protocol, the cheating model and a set of monitoring sensors able to track the complete network state together with the data-flow characteristics. The resulting framework is based on the GRAPH-STREAM [2] (version 1.1.2) Java library for the modeling and analysis of dynamic graphs. This tool allows gathering network statistics (*e.g.* connectivity, biggest cluster size, etc.) and is able to graphically display the dynamics of the system.

The whole simulation is divided into steps (called *simulation* or *synchronization steps*). In each simulation step, every node is selected once — in random order — to initiate a cache-exchange according to the protocol's specification [6]. That includes every peer establishing an outgoing connection, sending its cache, receiving a cache from destination and performing the merge (see Section 2 for further details). At the onset of every experiment (step 0), the network is initialized as a bidirectional grid lattice. Then we let the protocol run during 50 steps for the network to bootstrap into a stable configuration. All measurements and external interactions (like cache alteration) are made after this initial period, *i.e.* starting at the 51st step.

4   Experimental Results

The experiments presented in this section are divided into two groups. Firstly, data-flow characteristics are measured in the original, unmodified network (Fig. 1–3). In the second group (Fig. 4 and 5), the impact of deliberately corrupted entries on connectivity and data-flow is measured. In all cases, it is worth to mention that the presented results were obtained by performing around four weeks of computations on the HPC platform of the UL for a total of 44594117 CPU-hours[1].

---

[1] This would have taken 1 year 151 days 3 hours 15 minutes 17 seconds on a single core machine.

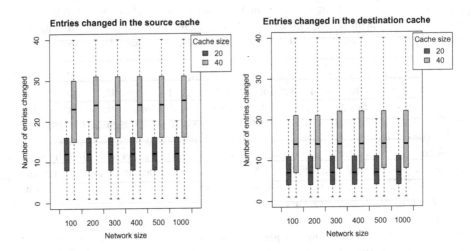

Fig. 1. Amount of entries changed during a single connection in the *source* and the *destination* caches. Values are measured over 100 executions (for the first 1000 merges) for all the parameter combinations to be considered statistically significant

Fig. 1 presents the amount of data actually exchanged between the nodes during a connection. This exchange is understood as the actual amount of entries changed in the cache of both parties not as the raw data transferred between the nodes. As visible, it is independent of the network size. What might be surprising, is the lack of the symmetry between the source and the destination. The average number of entries changed for cache size equal to 20 is around 12 (on the source cache) and 8 (on the destination cache) — respectively 23 and 14 for a cache size equal to 40. The results spread is maintained in both cases. The above mentioned differences indicate that, on average, the source of the connection has older entries in the cache than the destination.

Actually, this lack of symmetry is caused by the distribution of indegree in the connection graph — see example distribution on Fig. 2. Outdegree is omitted, as it is always equal to the cache size. High values of indegree are observed for more than half of the nodes, which makes them more probable to become a destination of some connection. Therefore causing more frequent cache merges and fresher content.

Fig. 3 presents different statistics for the cache entries: number of visited nodes, time spent in the network and number of usages to establish a connection. As visible, all measured values are on the average independent from the network size and depend only on the cache size. Whiskers on the figures mark extreme values. For small networks, some cache entries may spread to most of the nodes in the network (see the maximum value obtained for the network size equal to 200). However on average they reach 9 (resp. 19) nodes — for the cache size equal to 20 (resp. 40). Mean amount of synchronization steps required to completely remove the entry is equal to 3 for all the test cases, and in the worst case — 6.

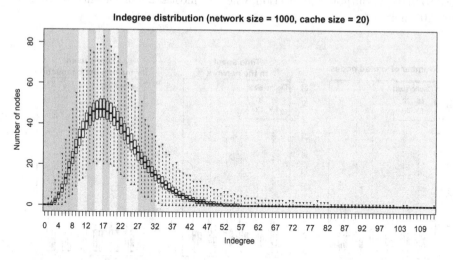

Fig. 2. Example of the indegree distribution for a network consisting of 1000 nodes with the cache size set to 20. The values are measured at the beginning of the simulation step for 1000 steps (after bootstrap) for 100 executions. Altered colors in the background correspond to the number of nodes equal to 10% of the original network

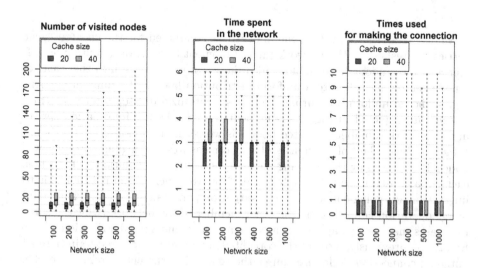

Fig. 3. Cache entries statistics measured for the first 10000 entries fully removed from the network for 100 executions for all the parameter combinations

Majority of the cache entries created during the protocol's execution are never used to make an outgoing connection, where at most some of the entries are used only 10 times.

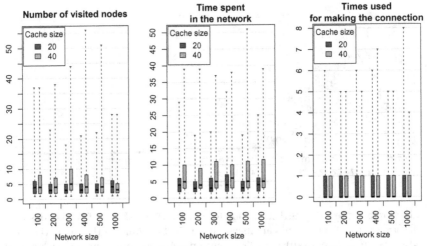

Fig. 4. Cache entries statistics similar to the ones presented in Fig. 3 measured for the cheated entries. Cache size of them are injected into the cache of a randomly chosen node at the random moment during the 51st synchronization step (*i.e.* after bootstrap). Only the fully removed entries are included in the figures. Simulation was executed 100 times for each combination of the parameters

Similar analysis (as to this one above) was conducted for the cheated cache entries — freshest in the network (at the moment of creation), containing references to a random set of nodes. Such data is injected once into the cache of a node chosen according to a uniform distribution law, at the random moment (again chosen uniformly), during the first synchronization step after bootstrap. Results are depicted in Fig. 4. As immediately visible, the information spread in the network (number of visited nodes) is worse than previously — maximum values are below half of previously obtained measures and averages are below 5 nodes. It is caused by the cheating model applied in the simulation — the whole cache of a chosen node is corrupted, therefore after such action it is not able to initiate any outgoing connection. This situation persists until the first successful merge operation is invoked by the other member of the network (which in some rare cases may never happen, as a consequence of indegree distribution — see Fig. 2). As previously, most of the corrupted entries are never used to initiate an outgoing connection — failure causes the removal of the entry from the cache. Therefore cheated data is present in the network until replacement with fresher information.

Fig. 5 presents results obtained when content of the cache of a randomly chosen node is flooded with cheated entries at every simulation step. The time

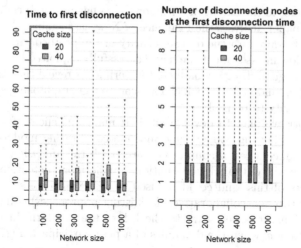

Fig. 5. Time to the first disconnection in the network and the number of disconnected nodes measured for all the combinations of simulation parameters over 100 executions. Randomly chosen node (fixed during the execution) is flooded with the cheated entries at every simulation step

required to disconnect any node is surprisingly short since it averages on 8 simulation steps for cache size equal to 20 (resp. 10 for the cache size equal to 40), for all the network sizes. In some extreme cases even 90 synchronization steps are needed (see result obtained for the network consisting of 400 nodes with cache size capacity set to 40). It is worth to notice that not always the flooded node is disconnected as the first and only one. Average number of nodes affected by the cheating during the experiments oscillates between one and two. The maximum value obtained — 9 — occurred for a network consisting of 1000 nodes with cache size set to 20. For every single execution, at least one node got disconnected.
In all cases, this demonstrates that the exhibited attack based on a cache corruption scheme is able to defeat the protocol by breaking the network connectivity in a very short period of time, even if the attack is performed by a single (malicious) node of the network.

5   Conclusion

Newscast is a P2P protocol designed to build up connectivity in distributed systems. To that end, nodes exchange routing information and establish an overlay network with the shape of a small-world graph. The emergent graph structure grants scalable access to information and makes the system suitable for distributed applications. In that context, the robustness of the protocol must secure the graph connectivity despite failures or attacks. While in some previous studies Newscast has proved to be resilient against crash faults (*i.e.* when nodes simply fail, stop working or disconnects), the possibility of the protocol being attacked by malicious users, to the extent of our knowledge, has not been considered yet. Therefore, this paper analyses the resilience of Newscast against cheating faults with a purpose to raise an issue on the security of the protocol. In this context, in order to provide an assessment, we have successfully exploited build-in vulnerabilities of the original design. Conducted experiments reveal that the protocol is sensitive to this kind of faults, which can lead to the graph being split *i.e.* the network connectivity to be broken.

In future work we plan to develop efficient malicious clients for the Newscast protocol — following cooperating and non-cooperating models. Secondly, we plan to introduce a set of countermeasures with the analysis of their influence on the properties of the original solution. Furthermore, detection techniques of malicious acts of this kind could be used to remove cheaters from the network, typically through collaborative blacklisting approaches). Finally, having the set of solutions, it is necessary to check how they perform in more realistic environments, *e.g.* when the dynamics of a peer participation (*e.g.* churn) is present.

Acknowledgments. The experiments presented in this paper were carried out using the HPC facility of the UL – `hpc.uni.lu`.

References

1. Avizienis, A., Laprie, J.C., Randell, B., Landwehr, C.E.: Basic Concepts and Taxonomy of Dependable and Secure Computing. IEEE Transactions on Dependable and Secure Computing 1, 11–33 (2004)
2. Dutot, A., Guinand, F., Olivier, D., Pigné, Y.: GraphStream: A Tool for bridging the gap between Complex Systems and Dynamic Graphs. In: Emergent Properties in Natural and Artificial Complex Systems. Satellite Conference within the 4th European Conference on Complex Systems (ECCS 2007), Dresden, Allemagne (2007-2010), `http://hal.archives-ouvertes.fr/hal-00264043`, ANR SARAH
3. GDF, The Gnutella Developer Forum: The annotated gnutella protocol specification v0.4 (2001),
   `http://rfc-gnutella.sourceforge.net/developer/stable/index.html`
4. Jelasity, M., Guerraoui, R., Kermarrec, A.-M., van Steen, M.: The peer sampling service: Experimental evaluation of unstructured gossip-based implementations. In: Jacobsen, H.-A. (ed.) Middleware 2004. LNCS, vol. 3231, pp. 79–98. Springer, Heidelberg (2004), `http://dl.acm.org/citation.cfm?id=1045658.1045666`
5. Jelasity, M., Montresor, A., Babaoglu, O.: Gossip-based aggregation in large dynamic networks. ACM Trans. Comput. Syst. 23(3), 219–252 (2005),
   `http://doi.acm.org/10.1145/1082469.1082470`
6. Jelasity, M., van Steen, M.: Large-scale newscast computing on the Internet. Tech. Rep. IR-503, Vrije Universiteit Amsterdam, Department of Computer Science, Amsterdam, The Netherlands (October 2002),
   `http://www.cs.vu.nl/pub/papers/globe/IR-503.02.pdf`
7. Laredo, J., Eiben, A., Steen, M., Merelo, J.: Evag: a scalable peer-to-peer evolutionary algorithm. Genetic Programming and Evolvable Machines 11(2), 227–246 (2010), `http://dx.doi.org/10.1007/s10710-009-9096-z`

8. Muszyński, J., Varrette, S., Bouvry, P., Seredyński, F., Khan, S.U.: Convergence Analysis of Evolutionary Algorithms in the Presence of Crash-Faults and Cheaters. Intl. Journal of Computers and Mathematics with Applications (CAMWA) 64(12), 3805–3819 (2012),
   http://www.sciencedirect.com/science/article/pii/S089812211200209X
9. Rowstron, A., Druschel, P.: Pastry: Scalable, decentralized object location, and routing for large-scale peer-to-peer systems. In: Guerraoui, R. (ed.) Middleware 2001. LNCS, vol. 2218, pp. 329–350. Springer, Heidelberg (2001)
10. Stoica, I., Morris, R., Karger, D., Kaashoek, F., Balakrishnan, H.: Chord: A scalable Peer-To-Peer lookup service for internet applications. In: Proceedings of the 2001 ACM SIGCOMM Conference, pp. 149–160 (2001),
   citeseer.ist.psu.edu/stoica01chord.html
11. Varrette, S., Tantar, E., Bouvry, P.: On the Resilience of [distributed] Evolutionary Algorithms against Cheaters in Global Computing Platforms. In: Proc. of the 14th Intl. Workshop on Nature Inspired Distributed Computing (NIDISC 2011), Part of the 25th IEEE/ACM Intl. Parallel and Distributed Processing Symposium (IPDPS 2011), May 16-20, IEEE Computer Society, Anchorage (2011),
   http://www.ipdps.org/
12. Voulgaris, S., Jelasity, M., van Steen, M.: A Robust and Scalable Peer-to-Peer Gossiping Protocol. In: Moro, G., Sartori, C., Singh, M.P. (eds.) AP2PC 2003. LNCS (LNAI), vol. 2872, pp. 47–58. Springer, Heidelberg (2004)
13. Watts, D., Strogatz, S.: Collective dynamics of "small-world" networks. Nature 393, 440–442 (1998)

Efficient Verifiable Multi-Secret Sharing Based on Y.C.H Scheme

Appala Naidu Tentu and Allam Appa Rao

CR Rao Advanced Institute of Mathematics, Statistics, and Computer Science,
University of Hyderabad Campus,
Hyderabad-500046, India
{naidunit,apparaoallam}@gmail.com

Abstract. In this paper, we propose an efficient verifiable multi-secret sharing protocol based on an identity based signature scheme, that uses identities for its participants. The scheme makes use of advantages of identity based signature scheme and hash function for the verifiability which does not require much computation. It checks either dealer or participant(s) honesty, that means a corrupted dealer may provide a fake secret or a participant may provide a fake share to the other participants in the reconstruction phase. In the previous proposed schemes, dealer [15] (or) participants [12,16] could communicate with each other securely before the secret distribution phase for sending secret shadows and they used exponential functions for verification. In our scheme, we do not require pre-secure communication between a dealer and participants, although we use a two-variable way for the distribution purpose but we do not prevent from any exponential functions for the verification phase. Our scheme resist a dealer/participant(s) cheating behaviour efficiently.

Keywords: threshold, secret sharing, multi-secret sharing, verifiable, identity based signature, hash function.

1 Introduction

Secret sharing is normally used when there is either a lack of trust in a single person or the responsibility of a single person has to be delegated to a group during the absence of the person. This can be obtrained by taking a secret key and sharing it among a number of participants. Secret sharing can be also seen as a collective ownership of the secret by participants who hold shares of it. Secret sharing was first proposed by Shamir [14] and Blakley [1]. The scheme by Shamir [14] consists in the standard Lagrange polynomial interpolation, whereas the scheme by Blakley [1] is based on the geometric idea that uses the concept of intersecting hyper planes.

The family of authorized subsets is known as the access structure. An access structure is said to be monotone if a set is qualified then its superset must also be qualified. Several access structures are proposed in the literature. They include the (t, n)-threshold access structure, the Generalized access structure and the

Z. Kotulski et al. (Eds.): CSS 2014, CCIS 448, pp. 100–109, 2014.

Multipartite access structure. In the (t, n)-threshold access structure there are n shareholders, an authorized group consists of any t or more participants and any group of at most $t - 1$ participants is an unauthorized group. A (t, n) threshold scheme is a method whereby n pieces of information of the secret key K, called shares are distributed to n participants so that:

- The secret can be reconstructed from the knowledge of any t or more shares.
- The secret cannot be reconstructed from the knowledge of fewer than t shares.

Detection of cheaters: The verifiable secret-sharing scheme [11] is to provide the shareholder with the abilities to verify that (a) the secret shadows obtained from the dealer are derived consistently from the same secret: and (b) the secret shadows obtained from the other shareholder in the secret reconstruction process are genuine ones. These abilities are very important. For example, a dishonest dealer can cheat some shareholders by giving them fake shadows. Communication errors (i.e., noise) can also result in fake shadows. A shareholder may also cheat the others in the secret reconstruction process by presenting a fake shadow to prevent others from obtaining the real secret.

1.1   Related Work

In every secret sharing process only one secret can be shared. This secret sharing is the one-time-use scheme, in other words once the secret has been reconstructed, a dealer must redistribute a fresh shadow over a secure channel to every participant. In both of them it is supposed that the dealer and participants are honest but in fact, it is impossible in the real word and a dishonest dealer [11] may distribute a fake shadow to a certain participant or a malicious participant may provide a fake share to other participants.

A multi-secret sharing scheme is an extension of a Shamir's [14] secret sharing. In these [14,1] schemes several problems occure like, in every secret sharing process only one secret can be shared and this algorithm is the one-time use scheme. To overcome the above problems He and Dawson[7,8] proposed a MSS to share multiple secrets based on one-way function. In 2004, Yang et.al (Y.C.H) [15] proposed an efficient MSS, which is based on the two variable one-way function [7]. Chien et.al [4] presented a practical multi-secret sharing based on the block codes and matrices. In [12], Shao and Cao proposed a new efficient VMSS based on Y.C.H and the intractability of the discrete logarithm. In 2007, Zhao et al. [16] and M.H. Dehkordi et al. [2] proposed a practical verifiable multi-secret sharing based on the Y.C.H and Hwang-Chang (HC) [9] schemes. The verification phase of Zhao's scheme is the same as that of HC scheme.

1.2   Our Contribution

In this paper, we propose a verifiable multi-secret sharing protocol based on an identity based signature scheme, that uses the identities of the participants. In a practical scenario, we cannot believe the honesty of others. That means, a dealer may cheat in secret distribution (or) corrupted participants may provide a fake share to other participants in the reconstruction phase.

In the previous proposed schemes [12,16] a dealer (or) participants could communicate with each other securely before the secret distribution phase for sending secret shadows. Also they used the exponential funtions for the purpose of the verification. In our scheme we use a multi-secret sharing scheme proposed by Y.C.H [15]. In this scheme, we do not require pre-secure communication between dealer and participants. Also, we do not use any exponential calculation functions like one-way functions, two variable one-way functions, RSA and discrete logarithmic functions in the verification phase. We use a hash function and an identity based signature scheme to generate a signature which allows a dealer and participants to share verification.

1.3   Organization of the Paper

The rest of the paper is organized as follows: Section 2 presents some of the preliminaries used in the construction. Section 3 explains the overview of the multi-secret sharing scheme proposed by [15]. Our proposed verifiable multi-secret sharing scheme was discribed in section 4. Conclusions are in section 5.

2   Preliminaries

2.1   One-Way Functions

One-way functions, namely functions that are *easy* to compute and *hard* to invert, are an extremely important cryptographic primitive. Namely, any probabilistic polynomial time (PPT) algorithm attempt to invert the one-way function into an element in its range, will succeed with no more than *negligible* probability, where the probability refers to the elements in the domain of the function and the coin tosses of the PPT attempting the inversion. Formally, a function $f : \{0,1\}^* \rightarrow \{0,1\}^*$ is one-way if f can be computed by a polynomial time algorithm, but for every randomized algorithm $\mathcal{A}$ which runs in the polynomial time in $n = |x|$, every polynomial $p(n)$, and all sufficiently large n

$$\Pr[f(\mathcal{A}(f(x))) = f(x)] < \frac{1}{p(n)}, \tag{1}$$

where the probability is over the choice of x from the uniform distribution on $\{0,1\}^n$, and the randomness of $\mathcal{A}$.

2.2   Hash Function

A cryptographic hash function [10] is a function that takes an arbitrary block of data and returns a fixed-size bit string, the cryptographic hash value, such that any (accidental or intentional) change to the data will (with very high probability) change the hash value. The data to be encoded are often called the *message*, and the hash value is sometimes called the *message digest* or simply *digest*. The cryptographic hash function $H : \{0,1\}^* \leftarrow \{0,1\}^n$, where $n > 0$ has four main properties:

1. Computability - It is easy to compute the hash value for any given message,
2. Pre-image resistance - It is infeasible to generate a message that has a given hash,
3. Second pre-image resistance - It is infeasible to modify a message without changing the hash,
4. Collision-resistance - It is infeasible to find two different messages with the same hash.

2.3 Identity Based Signature Scheme

An Identity Based Signature (IBS) scheme consists of four algorithms:

- **Setup(1^λ)** : A probabilistic polynomial time algorithm run by a private key generator (PKG) that takes a security parameter 1^λ as input and outputs a master secret key MSK and public parameters $Params$,
- **KeyGen($ID, MSK, Params$)** : A probabilistic polynomial time algorithm run by PKG which takes identity ID, master secret key MSK and public parameters $Params$ as input and outputs a secret key SK_{ID} associated to the identity ID,
- **Sign($m, SK_{ID_{Sen}}, ID_{Sen}, Params$)** : A probabilistic polynomial time algorithm that takes a message m, the sender's secret key $SK_{ID_{sen}}$, the sender's identity ID_{Sen} and public parameters $Params$ as input and outputs a signature σ,
- **Verify($m, \sigma, ID_{Sen}, Params$)** : A deterministic polynomial time algorithm that takes a message m, a signature σ, sender's identity ID_{Sen} and public parameters $Params$ as input and outputs true if σ is a valid signature of the message m, else outputs $\perp$ (false).

2.4 Shamir's (t, n) Threshold Secret Sharing Scheme [6]

In Shamir [14] (t, n) threshold scheme uses polynomial interpolation. Let secrets be taken from the set $S \in GF_q$ where GF_q is a finite Galois field with q elements. Shamir scheme uses two algorithms: the dealer and the combiner. The dealer sets up the scheme and distributes shares to all participants $P = \{P_1, P_2, \cdots, P_n\}$ via secure channels. The combiner collects shares from collaborating participants and computes the secret only if the set of cooperating participants is of size t or larger. To set up a (t, n) threshold scheme the dealer chooses n distinct nonzero elements $x_1, x_2, \cdots, x_n \in GF_q$ and publishes them. Next for a secret S, the dealer randomly chooses $t - 1$ elements $a_1, a_2, \cdots, a_{t-1}$ from GF_q and forms the following polynomial $f(x) = S + \sum_{i=1}^{t-1} a_i x^i$.

The share of the participant P_i is $S_i = f(x_i)$. The secret $S = f(0)$. Note that a_i are randomly chosen from all elements of GF_q, so in general, $f(x)$ is of degree at most $t - 1$. During the reconstruction phase, the combiner takes shares of at least t participants $s_{i_1}, s_{i_2}, \cdots, s_{i_t}$, use the Lagrange interpolation formula which gives the expression for the secret S. It is known that the Shamir scheme is perfect. That is, if a group of fewer than t participants collaborate, their original uncertainty about S remains unchanged.

3   Multi-secret Sharing Scheme (Y.C.H)

In this section, we briefly explain the multi-secret sharing scheme proposed by Yang et.al [15]. Here, the function $f(r, s)$ denotes any two variable one-way function that maps a secret shadow s and a value r onto a bit string $f(r, s)$ of a fixed length. The scheme is a (t, n) threshold scheme, $p_1, p_2, \cdots, p_k$ denote k secrets to be shared. Function $f(r, s)$ denotes any two-variable one-way function. In this phase, the dealer D randomly chooses n secret shadows $s_1, s_2, \cdots, s_n$ and distributes them to every participant M_i by a security channel. Then D randomly chooses a value r and computes $f(r, s_i)$ for $i = 1, 2, \cdots, n$.

3.1   If $k \leq t$

Distribution Phase

- Choose a prime q and construct $(t - 1)^{th}$ degree polynomial $h(x) mod q$:

$$h(x) = p_1 + p_2 x + \cdots + p_k x^{k-1} + a_1 x^k + \cdots + a_{t-k} x^{t-1} mod q , \quad (2)$$

  where $0 < N, p_1, p_2, \cdots, p_k, a_1, a_2, \cdots, a_{t-k} < q$,
- Compute $y_i = h(f(r, s_i)) mod q$ for $i = 1, 2, \cdots, n$,
- Publish $(r, y_1, y_2, \cdots, y_n)$.

Reconstruction Phase

- If $M = \{M_1, M_2, \cdots, M_t\}$ members of M will recover the secrets $p_1, p_2, \cdots, p_k$, they pool their shares $f(r, s_i)$ for $i = 1, 2, \cdots, t$, then the polynomial $h(x) mod q$ can be uniquely determined as follows:

$$h(x) = \sum_{i=1}^{t} y_i \prod_{j=1, j \neq i}^{t} \frac{x - f(r, s_j)}{f(r, s_i) - f(r, s_j)} mod q, \quad (3)$$

$$h(x) = p_1 + p_2 x + \cdots + p_k x^{k-1} + a_1 x^k + \cdots + a_{t-k} x^{t-1} mod q .$$

3.2 If $k > t$

Distribution Phase

- Choose a prime q and construct $(k-1)^{th}$ degree polynomial $h(x) mod q$:

$$h(x) = p_1 + p_2 x + \cdots + p_k x^{k-1} mod q, \tag{4}$$

where $0 < p_1, p_2, \cdots, p_k < q$,
- Compute $y_i = h(f(r, s_i)) mod q$ for $i = 1, 2, \cdots, n$,
- Compute $h(i) mod q$ for $i = 0, 1, 2, \cdots, (k-t)$,
- Publish $(r, y_1, y_2, \cdots, y_n, h(1), h(2), \cdots, h(k-t))$.

Reconstruction Phase

$$h(x) = \sum_{i=1}^{t} y_i \prod_{j=1, j \neq i}^{t} \frac{x - f(r, s_j)}{f(r, s_i) - f(r, s_j)} + \sum_{i=1}^{k-t} h(i) \prod_{j=1, j \neq i}^{k-t} \frac{x - j}{i - j} mod q, \tag{5}$$

$$h(x) = p_1 + p_2 x + \cdots + p_k x^{k-1} mod q .$$

4 Proposed Scheme

Let a group of n participants participates in the secret sharing scheme. In this mutli-secret sharing scheme, the dealer having a couple of secrets which he would like to share with a group of n participants. The dealer fixes a prime $q > n$, and n participants denoted as $p_1, p_2, \cdots, p_n$ and let t be a positive integer such that $1 \leq t \leq n$. We choose $t - k$ distinct points $a_1, a_2, \cdots, a_{t-k} \in \mathbb{F}_q$. Let $(s_1, s_2, \cdots, s_k) \in \mathbb{F}_q$ be the K secrets to be shared to the n participants.

4.1 Initialization Phase

Each participant is assigned with a unique identity $ID_i, i = 1, 2, \cdots, n$. In this, Dealer D runs the *Setup* polynomial time algorithm that takes a secure parameter 1^λ as an input and outputs a master secret key MSK and public parameters *params* is as follows:

$$Setup(1^\lambda) \to (MSK, params) . \tag{6}$$

Now a dealer executes the polynomial time algorithm which takes identity ID_i, master the secret key MSK and public parameters *params* as input and outputs a secret key SK_{ID_i} associated with the identity ID_i is as follows:

$$KeyGen(ID_i, MSK, params) \to (SK_{ID_i}, params) . \tag{7}$$

Then a dealer chooses an integer r and computes $f_i = f(r, SK_{ID_i})$ for $i = 1, 2, \cdots, n$ and he publishes r publicly. Since the secret key SK_{ID_i} is the distance for every participant, $f_i \neq f_j, i \neq j$.

Compute $Sign$ probabilistic polynomial time algorithm that takes a secret share f_i, the sender's secret key SK_{ID_i}, the sender's identity ID_i and public parameters $params$ as input and outputs of the signature σ_i for each participant is as follows:

$$Sign(f_i, SK_{ID_i}, ID_i, params) \to (\sigma_i, params) . \tag{8}$$

The $Verify$ algorithm is availble to all participants publicly. The dealer show how to the execute secret sharing algorithm in two separate cases:

4.2   If $k \le t$

Distribution Phase

- Choose a prime q, distinct $ID_i \in \mathbb{F}_q$ of the participants and construct $(t-1)^{th}$ degree polynomial $h(x) mod q$:

$$h(x) = s_1 + s_2 x + \cdots + s_k x^{k-1} + a_1 x^k + \cdots + a_{t-k} x^{t-1} mod q, \tag{9}$$

  where $0 < s_1, s_2, \cdots, s_k, a_1, a_2, \cdots, a_{t-k} < q$,
- Compute $y_i = h(f_i) mod q$ for $i = 1, 2, \cdots, n$,
- Dealer sends SK_{ID_i} as share to the participant p_i secretly,
- Also, he computes $h_{1i} = H(ID_i \| SK_{ID_i})$, here $H(.)$ denotes the hash function,
- Publish $(y_i, \sigma_i, h_{1i}, ID_i, params)$ for every participant p_i.

Verification Phase

- Participants can then verify consistency of the shares provided by the dealer using the following $Verify$ algorithm as follows:

$$h_{1i} = H(ID_i \| SK_{ID_i}), 1 \le i \le n, \tag{10}$$

- Received secret shares SK_{ID_i} from the participant i, the reconstructor can calculate $f_i = f(r, SK_{ID_i})$, then he verifies whether other participants provide correct share or not (Here $Verify$ algorithm is available publicly),

$$Verify(f_i, \sigma_i, ID_i, params), \tag{11}$$

If the output is true, return f_i , else outputs $\perp$ (null).

Reconstruction Phase

- At least t participants pool their secret shares SK_{ID_i} then the reconstructor can calculate $f_i = f(r, SK_{ID_i})$. By using the Lagrange interpolation polynomial, with the knowledge of t pairs the $(t-1)^{th}$ degree polynomial $f(x) mod q$ can be uniquely determined as follows:

$$h(x) = \sum_{i=1}^{t} y_i \prod_{j=1, j\neq i}^{t} \frac{x - f_i}{f_i - f_j} modq,$$

(12)

$$h(x) = s_1 + s_2 x + \cdots + s_k x^{k-1} + a_1 x^k + \cdots + a_{t-k} x^{t-1} modq .$$

4.3 If $k > t$

Distribution Phase

- Choose a prime q and construct $(k-1)$th degree polynomial $h(x) modq$:

$$h(x) = s_1 + s_2 x + \cdots + s_k x^{k-1} modq,$$

(13)

where $0 < s_1, s_2, \cdots, s_k < q$,
- Compute $y_i = h(f_i) modq$ for $i = 1, 2, \cdots, n$,
- Dealer sends SK_{ID_i} as secret shares to a participant p_i secretly.
- Compute $h(i) modq$ for $i = 1, 2, \cdots, (k-t)$,
- Also, he computes $h_{1i} = H(ID_i || SK_{ID_i})$, here $H(.)$ denotes the hash function,
- Publish $y_i, \sigma_i, h_{1i}, ID_i)$ for every participant p_i and additionally parameters $h(1), h(2), \cdots, h(k-t)$ and $params$.

Verification Phase

- Participants can then verify consistency of the shares provided by the dealer using the $Hash$ algorithm as follows:

$$h_{1i} = H(ID_i || SK_{ID_i}), 1 \leq i \leq n,$$

(14)

- Received secret shares f_i from the participant i, the reconstructor can calculate $f_i = f(r, SK_{ID_i})$, then he verifies whether other participants provide correct share or not (Here $Verify$ algorithm is available publicly):

$$Verify(f_i, \sigma_i, ID_i, params) .$$

(15)

If the output is true, return f_i , else outputs $\perp$ (null).

Reconstruction Phase

- Threshold number (t) of participants provides their secret shares SK_{ID_i} then a reconstructor can calculate $f_i = f(r, SK_{ID_i})$. Then they will be able recover multiple secrets using the following equation:

$$h(x) = \sum_{i=1}^{t} y_i \prod_{j=1, j\neq i}^{t} \frac{x - f_i}{f_i - f_j} + \sum_{i=1}^{k-t} h(i) \prod_{j=1, j\neq i}^{k-t} \frac{x - j}{i - j} modq,$$

(16)

$$h(x) = s_1 + s_2 x + \cdots + s_k x^{k-1} modq .$$

4.4   Privacy and Performance Analysis

Secret sharing schemes must provide the privacy in a secure way, thwarting the activities of corrupted participants. Moreover, the solution must prevent the disclosure of the secrets to unauthorized parties.

Privacy: The following theorem shows, that $t - 1$ or less, then participants collaborating learn absolutely nothing about secrets, where as t or more participants are able to reconstruct the secrets efficiently.

Theorem 1. *The secrets can be recovered by the recovery phase described above in polynomial time if the set of participants recovering the secrets is an authorized set.*   □

Proof. It is obvious that the proposed scheme can be projected into the threshold secret sharing scheme the same as Shamir's secret sharing. In the Shamir's threshold secret sharing scheme, a secret can be stored at the constant position of the selected $(t - 1)^{th}$ degree polynomial. Our proposed scheme is also the threshold scheme, but the multiple secrets can be stored as selected polynomial coefficients. If the required threshold number of nodes provides their secret shares then by using the Lagrange's interpolation, we are able to find the secret polynomial where the secrets are stored (same as Y.C.H scheme). As the set of actual unknowns was chosen independently with uniform distribution, hence for every secrets $s_i \in \mathbb{F}_q$, the selecting probability is $1/q$. If fewer than threshold t number of nodes provides their secret shares probability of guessing other secret share is $1/q$ same as exhaustive search. That means we are not able to find a unique polynomial where the secrets are stored. So, that $t - 1$ or fewer nodes collaborating learns nothing about secrets that belong to an unauthorized set.   □

Performance Analysis. In our Verifiable multi-secret sharing scheme a dealer cannot be a cheater and participant p_i can check whether others' secret shares are valid or not. In the previous proposed schemes they requires at most $t - 1$ exponentiations. So our verification phase is faster than that of Shao and Cao [12] verification phase. Summarizing, our VMSS scheme has the advantages of Shao and Cao scheme [12] such as: The secrets are reconstructed only by using Lagrange interpolation polynomial equation. Furthermore our scheme has the following advantages:

1. In our scheme, either a dealer or participants do not require any pre-communication (i.e., sending secret shadow's either side).
2. Every participant can verify their validity of shares provided by the dealer and the participant can check honesty of other participants in the secret reconstruction.
3. Our scheme also prevents the participants from cheating behavior efficiently. There is no need for the use of any exponentiations. Fast computation is also an advantage.

5 Conclusions

This paper presents verifiable multi-secret sharing based on the Y.C.H, intractability of an identity based signature scheme and hash function. In our proposed scheme, we do not require pre-secure communication between a dealer and participants. Our scheme is based on the Y.C.H scheme. We do not use exponentiate calculation functions in the reconstruction phase. Our share verification algorithm runs in the deterministic polynomial time algorithm which tests honesty of the participants. So our verification phase is faster than that of Shao and Cao [12] verification phase. To extend our work future, we are searching reduction of public information used in this secret sharing scheme to avoid storage problem.

References

1. Blakley, G.R.: Safeguarding cryptographic keys. In: AFIPS Conference Proceedings, vol. 48, pp. 313–317 (1979)
2. Dehkordi, M.H., Mashhadi, S.: An efficient threshold verifiable multi-secret sharing. Computer Standards and Interfaces 30, 187–190 (2008)
3. Chan, C.W., Chang, C.C.: A Scheme for Threshold Multi secret Sharing. Applied Mathematics and Computation 166(1), 1–14 (2005)
4. Chien, H.Y., Jan, J.K., Tseng, Y.M.: A practical (t,n) multi-secret sharing scheme. IEICE Trans. Fundamentals E83-A 12, 2762–2765 (2000)
5. Goldwasser, S., Bellare, M.: http://cseweb.ucsd.edu/~mihir/papers/gb.pdf
6. Ghodosi, H., Pieprzyk, J., Safavi-Naini, R.: Secret Sharing in Multilevel and Compartmented Groups. In: Boyd, C., Dawson, E. (eds.) ACISP 1998. LNCS, vol. 1438, pp. 367–378. Springer, Heidelberg (1998)
7. He, J., Dawson, E.: Multistage secret sharing based on one-way function. Electronics Letters 30(19), 1591–1592 (1994)
8. He, J., Dawson, E.: Multi secret-sharing scheme based on one-way function. Electronics Letters 31(2), 93–95 (1995)
9. Hwang, R.-J., Chang, C.-C.: An on-line secret sharing scheme for multi-secrets. Computer Communications 21(13), 1170–1176 (1998)
10. Menezes, A., Oorschot, P., Vanstone, S.: Handbook of applied cryptography. CRC Press (1996)
11. Stadler, M.: Publicly verifiable secret sharing. In: Maurer, U.M. (ed.) EUROCRYPT 1996. LNCS, vol. 1070, pp. 190–199. Springer, Heidelberg (1996)
12. Shao, J., Cao, Z.-F.: A new efficient (t,n) verifiable multi-secret sharing (VMSS) based on Y.C.H scheme. Applied Mathematics and Computation 168, 135–140 (2005)
13. Shamir, A.: Identity-Based Cryptosystems and Signature Schemes. In: Blakely, G.R., Chaum, D. (eds.) CRYPTO 1984. LNCS, vol. 196, pp. 47–53. Springer, Heidelberg (1985)
14. Shamir, A.: How to share a secret. Comm. ACM 22, 612–613 (1979)
15. Yang, C.-C., Chang, T.-Y., Hwang, M.-S.: A (t,n) multi-secret sharing scheme. Applied Mathematics and Computation 151, 483–490 (2004)
16. Zhao, J., Zhang, J., Zhao, R.: A practical verifiable multi-secret sharing scheme. Computer Standards and Interfaces 29(1), 138–141 (2007)
17. Chien, J.H.-Y., Tseng, J.-K., et al.: A practical (t,n) multi-secret sharing. IEICE Transactions on Fundamentals of Electronics. Communications and Computer Sciences E83-A (12), 2762–2765 (2000)

A Lightweight Authentication Protocol for RFID

Ferucio Laurenţiu Ţiplea*

Department of Computer Science,
Al.I.Cuza University of Iaşi,
Iaşi 700506, Romania
fltiplea@info.uaic.ro

Abstract. In this paper, a novel lightweight authentication protocol for RFID systems is proposed. The protocol is based on a non-linear feedback shift register sequences generated by the position digit algebra function, which has a large average period lengths. This function uses only the radix r additions (for some $r \geq 2$), which makes it very efficient from a computational point of view, and suitable enough to be implemented in the RFID tags' logic. The protocol appears to have good privacy and security properties.

1 Introduction

Radio-frequency identification (RFID) is a wireless non-contact technology that uses radio-frequency electromagnetic fields to perform identification of physical objects. This technology has been around since the late 1960s and is largely used in commerce (payment by mobile phones, asset management, inventory systems, product tracking, access control), transportation and logistics, infrastructure management and protection, passports, animal and human identification, hospitals and healthcare, libraries, museums, schools and universities, sports, telemetry and so forth.

The RFID system consists of three main components: the RFID tag (also called transponder), the RFID reader (also called transceiver), and the back-end server. The RFID tag is a small identification device, located on the object to be identified. It contains a microchip and an antenna coil that is used to receive power from a reader and to send back information. The RFID reader is a device that can provide a number of functions to the RFID tags, such as an interrogation, powering, identification, reading, and writing. The RFID readers can have ample storage and communication and processing capabilities. The RFID readers query tags by broadcasting a radio-frequency signal, read their responses and transmit them to the back-end server for further processing. The server maintains a data base which contains data for each tag it manages. Tag data can be retrieved only when the tag is identified.

* Work supported by the *"Executive Unit for Financing Education, Higher Research, Development, and Innovation"* of Romania, under the grant 704/2013-2014 of bilateral cooperation between Romania and France.

Z. Kotulski et al. (Eds.): CSS 2014, CCIS 448, pp. 110–121, 2014.
© Springer-Verlag Berlin Heidelberg 2014

The RFID tags can be passive, semi-passive, or active. An active tag has an on-board battery and can initiate its own communication. Semi-passive tags have small batteries on board and are activated when in the presence of an RFID reader. Passive tags do not have their own power supply; they use the radio energy transmitted by the reader as an energy source. Passive tags are of more interest to retailers for various reasons such as: they exhibit indefinite operational lifetime, require no battery, and can be made small enough to fit almost everywhere.

The communication between tags and readers is the subject to eavesdropping. As a conclusion, any identification or authentication protocol for RFID systems should focus on securing this part of the communication. One may also take into account the fact that the low-cost tags cannot implement yet strong cryptographic protocols. Although the communication between readers and servers can be assumed to be secure because both readers and servers are more powerful devices and can support protocols based on strong cryptographic primitives, an issue of efficiency should be addressed here. Namely, the server should be able to efficiently disambiguate the tag among many concurrent encrypted tag responses. Two general security goals that should be true for any RFID identification or authentication protocol are privacy and tracking [9,13,21,7,18]: privacy means that no secret information should leak from the tag that can help in identifying tag contents or the bearer of the tag, while tracking (also called the location privacy), refers to the fact that the movement of the tag can or cannot be monitored.

Many identification and authentication protocols for RFID systems have been proposed. The distinction between them is usually made by the computational power of the tag. Tags with good computational capabilities can implement protocols based on the strong cryptographic primitives [8,2,3,15,18] but they can be too costly to be adopted in most retailer operations which are envisioned as major applications of the RFID technology. A large amount of research has been dedicated to the design of the RFID authentication protocols based on hash functions, hash function chains, pseudo-random functions, and random number generators [33,10,17,1,16,28,18]. Lightweight and ultra-lightweight authentication protocols for RFID systems only require to perform primitive operations such as random number generation, arithmetic bit-wise operations, cyclic redundancy code checksum, or even light hash or pseudo-random functions [31,12,14,20,19,5,24,4,22,18,23,6]. There is an widespread view that the lightweight and ultra-lightweight authentication protocols will be the best candidate technology for securing the future low-cost RFID systems.

1.1 Contribution and Related Work

In this paper we propose a lightweight RFID authentication protocol based on some special non-linear feedback shift register sequences. The starting point is a novel operation on bit sequences called the position digit algebra function (PDAF) which is already used as a low-level cryptographic function underlying on the Real Privacy Management (RPM) technology [25]. Given the radix $r \geq 2$, this function generates r-ary digit numbers by using two r-ary digit numbers, one of them being thought as a sequence of pointers into the other one. Therefore, starting with two r-ary digit numbers, the position digit algebra function generates a sequence of r-ary digit numbers whose average period length may be considerable large [30].

In our protocol, the position digit algebra function is used to generate three sequences of numbers. Two of them are used to randomize the tags' answers to avoid location traceability and reply attacks. The third sequence is used to synchronize the tag answer with the tag record maintained by server in its data base.

The idea of randomizing the tag answer is not new but most research papers implement it by hash functions and random numbers generated by the reader and the tag (see, for instance, [16,28]). Our protocol uses position digit algebra functions as pseudo-random number generators, which are based only on radix r additions. Moreover, two different seeds are used to generate two pseudo-random sequences, which are used with equal probabilities in the tag's answer.

Solutions to the synchronization between the tag and the server were proposed by many authors by giving the server the capability to maintain information about old transactions (see, for instance [16,28]). In our protocol, a third pseudo-random sequence is used just to inform the server about the number of tag queries from the last transaction with the server. In this way, the server is capable of updating the tag record in its data base. The server recovers the tag record from its data base by searching the data base record by record, as it is the case of most approaches proposed so far (see, for instance [33,16,28]).

Our protocol is very efficient from a computational point of view, due to the operations it is based on (radix r additions and no hash functions, no random number generators, no pseudo-random functions). At the same time, the protocol achieves good privacy and security properties, such as tag information and location privacy, resistance to reply attacks, resistance to denial of service attacks, as well as backward traceability and server impersonation.

1.2 Paper Organization

The paper is organized as follows. The first one is an introduction to the theory of RFID systems. Section 2 recalls basic concepts and results on the position digit algebra function, while the next one describes our protocol, and performs a security analysis. Conclusions are summarized in the fourth section.

2 The Position Digit Algebra Function

The protocol we are going to propose, is based on a low-level cryptographic function underlying the Real Privacy Management (RPM) technology [25], which we recall below. Our exposition follows [27,29,30,25,26].

The set of integers is denoted by $\mathbb{Z}$; given a positive integer r, $\mathbb{Z}_r$ stands for the ring of integers modulo r. The addition modulo r, also called r-XOR, is denoted by $\oplus_r$. When $r = 2$, the notation $\oplus_r$ is simplified to $\oplus$, which is the standard XOR.

Given $x \in \mathbb{Z}_r^n$, the ith r-ary digit of x will be denoted by x_i, for all $0 \leq i < n$.

The *position digit algebra function* (PDAF) [29,30,25,26], also called *the combining function* [27,25,26], is the function:

$$PDAF : \bigcup_{r \geq 2, n \geq 1} (\mathbb{Z}_r^n \times \mathbb{Z}_r^n) \rightarrow \bigcup_{r \geq 2, n \geq 1} \mathbb{Z}_r^n , \tag{1}$$

given by

$$PDAF(x, y)_i = x_i \oplus_r x_{i \oplus_n y_i} , \tag{2}$$

for all $r \geq 2$, $n \geq 1$, $x, y \in \mathbb{Z}_r^n$, and $0 \leq i < n$. Usually, r stands for the *radix* or *base* of the number system and n stands for the number of r-ary digits. Therefore, x and y are regarded as two r-ary n-digit numbers. x is called a *value key* and y an *offset key*. We will often simply write $x[y]$ instead of $PDAF(x, y)$.

This function has interesting properties [30]. Below recall the properties to be used in this paper. First, the following concepts from [30] are needed. Two r-ary n-digit numbers $x, x' \in \mathbb{Z}_r^n$ are called *value key equivalent*, abbreviated *VK-equivalent*, if $x[y] = x'[y]$, for some $y \in \mathbb{Z}_r^n$. Two r-ary n-digit numbers $y, y' \in \mathbb{Z}_r^n$ are called *offset key equivalent*, abbreviated *OK-equivalent*, if $x[y] = x[y']$, for some $x \in \mathbb{Z}_r^n$.

Proposition 1 ([30]). *Let x, x', y, y' be four r-ary n-digit numbers.*

1. *If r is even and $x'_i = x_i + r/2 \bmod r$, for all $0 \leq i < n$, then x and x' are VK-equivalent,*
2. *The probability of generating at random two VK-equivalent r-ary n-digit numbers is:*

$$\frac{1}{(r-1)^n} + \epsilon \tag{3}$$

for some negligible small number ϵ.
3. *y and y' are OK-equivalent if and only if, for all $0 \leq i < n$, one of the following holds:*

$$y'_i = y_i + jn, \text{ for some } 1 \leq j \leq \alpha_i, \text{where } \alpha_i = \left\lfloor \frac{r-1-y_i}{n} \right\rfloor \geq 1; \tag{4}$$

$$y'_i = y_i - jn, \text{ for some } 1 \leq j \leq \beta_i, \text{ where } \beta_i = \left\lfloor \frac{y_i}{n} \right\rfloor \geq 1. \tag{5}$$

4. *The probability of generating at random two OK-equivalent r-ary n-digit numbers is:*

$$\frac{\prod_{i=0}^{n-1}(\alpha_i + \beta_i + 1) - 1}{r^n} , \tag{6}$$

if $n < r$, and 0, otherwise.

The position digit algebra function can be naturally used to define *non-linear feedback shift-register* (NLFSR) *sequences* [30], as follows:

- choose initially at random two r-ary n-digit numbers x_0 and x_1,
- define $x_{i+2} = x_i[x_{i+1}]$, for all $i \geq 0$.

The period of this sequence depends on x_0 and x_1.

Proposition 2 ([30]). *The average period length of the NLFSR sequence of r-ary n-digit numbers is $(r-1)^n$.*

According to the Proposition 2, if one takes $r = 16$ and $n = 32$, the average period length will be 4.31×10^{37}, which is large enough for cryptographic purposes (and especially for RFID authentication).

3   The Protocol

Any RFID system must implement an identification or a unilateral authentication or a mutual authentication protocol. An identification protocol allows the RFID reader to obtain the identity of a tag without proving it. A unilateral authentication protocol allows the reader to obtain the identity of a tag together with a proof of the identity, and a mutual authentication protocol allows the reader to obtain the identity of the tag while both the reader and the tag authenticate each other. In this section we propose a mutual authentication protocol for RFID systems.

3.1   Protocol Description

Our protocol is based on NLFSR sequences generated by the position digit algebra function defined in the previous section, as a way to randomize the tags' answers and to synchronize with the server. The only operations performed by tags are PDAF computations, that is, base r additions for some radix r. From this point of view, the protocol can be regarded as a lightweight or even a ultra-lightweight protocol.

The initialization phase described below, sets the basic elements needed for the protocol to be run.

Initialization The following steps must be performed by a trusted party prior to using the protocol:

1. two integers $r \geq 2$ and $n \geq r$ and a hash function h are chosen. All these elements are public,
2. a private key K_R of some symmetric cryptosystem (such as AES) is chosen uniformly at random and securely distributed to the reader R,
3. for each tag T, the following steps are performed:
   (a) five values $K_{ST}, c_0, c_1, c_2, LT \in \mathbb{Z}_r^n$ are chosen independent and uniformly at random,

(b) the value $P(T) = h(\{ID(T)\}_{K_R} \| K_{ST})$ is computed, where $ID(T)$ is the tag T identity, $\{\cdot\}_{K_R}$ stands for encryption by K_R, and $\|$ stands for concatenation,

(c) $P(T), K_{ST}, c_0, c_1, c_2, LT$ are stored in the tag T,

(d) $P(T), \{ID(T)\}_{K_R}, K_{ST}, c_0, c_1, LT$ are stored in the server's data base.

Figure 1 pictorially represents how these parameters are distributed to the three participants of the protocol: tag, reader, and server (with its data base).

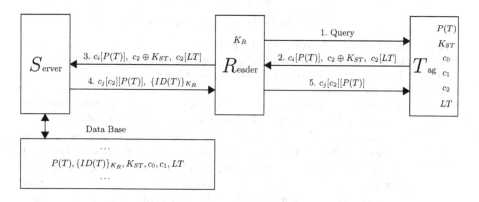

Fig. 1. The protocol

More explanations of them are in order. As one can see, the key K_R is used to encrypt the identity of all tags the server manages. Therefore, the server does not have access to the tags' identities. The random numbers c_0, c_1, and c_2 act as seeds for three NLFSR sequences:

- two NLFSR sequences derived from c_0 and c_1, used to randomize tags' answers;
- one NLFSR sequence derived from c_2 and used to randomize LT.

The parameter LT (last transaction) counts the queries performed by the readers to the tag. This parameter needs to be sent to the server for synchronization purposes.

Protocol description

1. $R \longrightarrow T$:   The reader R queries the tag T;
2. $T \longrightarrow R$:   The tag T chooses uniformly at random a bit $i \in \{0,1\}$ and computes $c_i[P(T)]$, $c_2[LT]$, and $c_2 \oplus K_{ST}$. Then, it sends

$$c_i[P(T)], \ c_2 \oplus K_{ST}, \ c_2[LT]$$

to the reader R. Finally, the tag increments LT by 1 and updates c_0, c_1, and c_2 as follows:

- $c_{k,aux} := c_k$, for all $0 \le k \le 2$;

- $c_0 := c_{1,aux}[c_{0,aux}]$;
- $c_1 := c_{0,aux}[c_{1,aux}]$;
- $c_2 := c_{j,aux}[c_{2,aux}]$,

  where j is the binary complement of i;

3. $R \longrightarrow S$:   When the reader receives the tag's message, it simply forward it to the server;

4. $S \longrightarrow R$:   On receipt of the reader message which is of the form "α, β, γ", the server searches the data base to find the record row associated to the tag. For each record row

$$P(T'), \{ID(T')\}_{K_R}, K_{ST'}, c_0', c_1', LT'$$

of the data base, the server does the following:

(a) extracts c_2 from β (by using $K_{ST'}$) and then obtains LT from γ;

(b) if $LT < LT'$ then it goes to the next record row;

(c) if $LT \geq LT'$ then

    i. temporarily updates $(LT - LT')$ times c_0' and c_1' (in the same way as the tag did). Let c_0'' and c_1'' be the results, respectively;

    ii. computes $c_0''[P(T')]$ and $c_1''[P(T')]$, and checks whether one of them coincides with α. If this is not the case, then it goes to the next record row; otherwise, the server concludes that the current record row corresponds to the tag which sent the message via the reader (that is, using our notation, $T' = T$); it also obtains the bit i. Then, it replaces LT' by LT, c_0' by c_0'', c_1' by c_1'', computes $c_j'[c_2][P(T')]$ and sends it, along with $\{ID(T')\}_{K_R}$, to the reader (j is the binary complement of i). Finally, it updates one more time c_0' and c_1' and increments LT' by one;

(d) if all record rows were searched and the property from the item above failed for all of them, then the server signals an error message to the reader;

5. $R \longrightarrow T$:   When the reader receives $c_j[c_2][P(T')]$ and $\{ID(T')\}_{K_R}$, it extracts the identity of the tag and forwards $c_j[c_2][P(T')]$ to the tag to perform authentication;

6. On receipt of $c_j[c_2][P(T')]$, the tag computes $c_2[P(T)]$ by using c_2 and $P(T)$ stored on its memory and compares it agains the message received from the reader (remark that $c_j[c_2]$ computed by the server should equal the current c_2 in the tag because the tag updated c_2 after performing the sending operation in step 2). If the test succeeds, then the authentication process passes. Otherwise, an error message is signaled.

The first five steps of the protocol described above are pictorially represented in Figure 1.

Remark 1. A few remarks about the protocol correctness and efficiency are in order.

1. The extraction of a unique LT from $c_2[LT]$ when c_2 is known (step (4) in the protocol description) is based on Proposition 1(4). Remark that, according to this Proposition, the inequality $n \geq r$ guarantees the uniqueness of LT).

2. The term $c_2 \oplus K_{ST}$ in steps (2) and (3) hides c_2 which is needed to compute $c_2[LT]$ at the server side. If c_2 is random, then $c_2 \oplus K_{ST}$ is random too (although K_{ST} is fixed for the tag).

3. If one bit of $c_2 \oplus K_{ST}$ is changed by an attacker, then c_2 cannot correctly be recovered at the server side. This leads to the fact that LT will be wrongly recovered from $c_2[LT]$ and, therefore, the step (4) in the protocol description will fail with high probability for all record rows. A similar conclusion can be drawn if at least one bit in $c_2[LT]$ or $c_i[P(T)]$ is changed. Changing bits in all sequences $c_i[P(T)]$, $c_2 \oplus K_{ST}$, and $c_2[LT]$ so that the search process in step (4) ends successfully, seems to be infeasible.

4. The only operations performed by the tag are base r additions and comparisons, which can efficiently be implemented in the tag's logic.

3.2 Protocol Analysis

The protocol can be efficiently implemented by the tag because only six r-ary n-digit numbers are needed to be stored in the tag memory and the operations are only radix r additions. For instance, if $r = 16$ and $n = 24$, then the tag needs to store six 96-bit numbers. Only three of these six numbers are rewritable; the other three store static data. In each transaction, the tag exchanges four numbers (it sends three and receives one). The server's data base stores six r-ary n-digit numbers for each tag.

We will informally argue below, that the protocol we have proposed has good privacy and security properties. The properties taken into consideration are: tag information privacy, tag location privacy, tag impersonation, reply attacks, denial of service, backward and forward traceability, and server impersonation.

Tag Information Privacy refers to the fact that no information should leak from the tag that can help in identifying tag contents or the bearer of the tag. In our protocol, tag's ID is only stored on the data base in an encrypted way so that the only entity which is able to recover the tag's ID is the reader. Assuming that the server is trusted and the reader authenticates itself to the server, we can say that the tag's ID is read only by the authorized entity. The $P(T)$ information stored in the tag T does not help at all at finding $ID(T)$ without accessing the server's data base and without knowing the key K_R.

Although $P(T)$ does not reveal tag's ID, one can also remark that even $P(T)$ is hard to obtain from tag's answer, because all the components of the answer are randomized (for each query).

Tag location privacy is an important privacy property whose role is to prevent tracking people by the tags they carry. Usually, this property is achieved by randomizing the tag's answer to the reader's query. This is the case of our protocol too. Each response of the tag to the reader's query is randomized by means of the NLFSR sequences computed by the tag. For instance, if:

$$c_i^1[P(T)], \ c_2^1 \oplus K_{ST}, \ c_2^1[LT^1] \tag{7}$$

is the tag T answer at the transaction t_1 and

$$c_j^2[P(T)], \quad c_2^2 \oplus K_{ST}, \quad c_2^2[LT^2] \tag{8}$$

is the tag T answer at the transaction t_2, where $t_2 > t_1$, then there is no way to see that $c_i^1[P(T)]$ and $c_i^2[P(T)]$, or $c_2^1 \oplus K_{ST}$ and $c_2^2 \oplus K_{ST}$, are built by using the common identifying element $P(T)$ or K_{ST}, respectively. Also remark that the equality $c_i^1[P(T)] = c_i^2[P(T)]$ may hold with a very small probability (Proposition 1(2)).

Therefore, no response of the tag can be linked by an attacker to previous responses of the tag (or any other particular tag). As a conclusion, it does not appear feasible to track the tag's location.

Tag Impersonation To impersonate a tag T in our protocol, an attacker needs the knowledge of the current c_0, c_1, and c_2. These numbers are initially chosen on a random basis and they are updated after each query and so, it seems hard to compute valid triples (c_0, c_1, c_2).

Replay Attacks An attacker who obtains the tag answer to some query cannot use this answer into another session with the reader because c_0, c_1, and LT are updated after each query both by the tag and the server. One can also note, that the attacker can not use the reader's answer $c_j[c_2][P(T)]$ in a new session with the reader.

Denial of Service in this scenario we aim to permanently desynchronize the server and the tag, by changing the internal state of the tag to be unrecognizable by the server. An attacker can try to desynchronize the tag and the server by querying the tag several times without sending the tag's answer to the reader. However, this does not affect the protocol because LT is increased with each query and it is sent in a safe way with a random c_2 which is also protected by K_{ST}. The server resynchronizes with the tag using LT.

Backward and Forward Traceability A clear distinction between backward and forward traceability was made in [16]. Backward traceability refers to the possibility of tracking the tag owner's past behavior by having knowledge of the tag's current internal state. In our protocol, the success of backward traceability depends on the computing c_0 and c_1 from $c_1[c_0]$ and $c_0[c_1]$. However, this seems quite hard.

Forward traceability refers to the impossibility of predicting future answers of the tag to the reader's queries by having knowledge of the tag's current internal state. Forward traceability is important in case of tag ownership transfer, without resetting the tag. Unfortunately, this property is not satisfied by our protocol because c_0, c_1, and c_2 can be easily updated by anyone who knows the internal state of the tag.

Server Impersonation If it is possible to impersonate a server to a tag, then the server and the tag can be desynchronized and, therefore, they can be incapable of further communication. In our protocol, to impersonate the server, an attacker needs knowledge of the legitimate server data base in order to compute the answer. Namely, the attacker needs c_j, c_2, $P(T)$, and $\{ID(T)\}_{K_R}$ because its answer $c_j[c_2][P(T)]$ is to be authenticated by the tag. Computing these elements without having access to the server's data base seems infeasible.

4 Conclusions

There is an increasing interest in lightweight and ultra-lightweight authentication protocols for RFID systems, because these kinds of protocols are envisioned as the best candidate technology for securing the future low-cost RFID systems. On the other side, the design of lightweight authentication protocols open a number of challenges due to the extremely limited storage and computational capabilities of low-cots RFID tags.

In this paper, a novel lightweight (or even ultra-lightweight) authentication protocol for RFID systems was proposed. The protocol is based on non-linear feedback shift register sequences generated by the position digit algebra function, which have a large average period lengths. The position digit algebra function uses only radix r additions (for some $r \geq 2$), which makes it very efficient from a computational point of view and suitable enough to be implemented in the RFID tags' logic.

The research carried out in this paper can be improved as follows:

1. extend the protocol to be resistant to forward traceability;
2. add formal privacy and security proofs based on privacy models such as those proposed in [32,11].

One may also try to generalize our protocol by replacing the NLFSR sequences based on the position digit algebra function by more general NLFSR sequences.

References

1. Avoine, G., Oechslin, P.: A scalable and provably secure hash-based RFID protocol. In: Third IEEE International Conference on Pervasive Computing and Communications Workshops, pp. 110–114 (March 2005)
2. Batina, L., Guajardo, J., Kerins, T., Mentens, N., Tuyls, P., Verbauwhede, I.: An elliptic curve processor suitable for RFID-tags (2006)
3. Batina, L., Guajardo, J., Kerins, T., Mentens, N., Tuyls, P., Verbauwhede, I.: Public-key cryptography for RFID-tags. In: Proceedings of the Fifth IEEE International Conference on Pervasive Computing and Communications Workshops, pp. 217–222. IEEE Computer Society, Washington, DC (2007)
4. Burmester, M., de Medeiros, B.: The security of EPC gen2 compliant RFID protocols. In: Bellovin, S.M., Gennaro, R., Keromytis, A.D., Yung, M. (eds.) ACNS 2008. LNCS, vol. 5037, pp. 490–506. Springer, Heidelberg (2008)

5. Chien, H.Y., Huang, C.W.: Security of ultra-lightweight RFID authentication protocols and its improvements. SIGOPS Oper. Syst. Rev. 41(4), 83–86 (2007)
6. Chien, H.Y., Huang, C.W.: A lightweight authentication protocol for low-cost RFID. J. Signal Process. Syst. 59(1), 95–102 (2010)
7. Dimitriou, T.: RFID security and privacy. In: Kitsos, P., Zhang, Y. (eds.) RFID Security: Techniques, Protocols and System-On-Chip Design, 1st edn. Springer Publishing Company, Incorporated (2008)
8. Feldhofer, M., Dominikus, S., Wolkerstorfer, J.: Strong authentication for RFID systems using the AES algorithm. In: Joye, M., Quisquater, J.-J. (eds.) CHES 2004. LNCS, vol. 3156, pp. 357–370. Springer, Heidelberg (2004)
9. Garfinkel, S., Juels, A., Pappu, R.: RFID privacy: an overview of problems and proposed solutions. IEEE Security Privacy 3(3), 34–43 (2005)
10. Henrici, D., Muller, P.: Hash-based enhancement of location privacy for radio-frequency identification devices using varying identifiers. In: Proceedings of the Second IEEE Annual Conference on Pervasive Computing and Communications Workshops, pp. 149–153 (March 2004)
11. Hermans, J., Pashalidis, A., Vercauteren, F., Preneel, B.: A new RFID privacy model. In: Atluri, V., Diaz, C. (eds.) ESORICS 2011. LNCS, vol. 6879, pp. 568–587. Springer, Heidelberg (2011)
12. Juels, A.: Minimalist cryptography for low-cost RFID tags (Extended abstract). In: Blundo, C., Cimato, S. (eds.) SCN 2004. LNCS, vol. 3352, pp. 149–164. Springer, Heidelberg (2005)
13. Juels, A.: RFID security and privacy: a research survey. IEEE Journal on Selected Areas in Communications 24(2), 381–394 (2006)
14. Juels, A., Weis, S.A.: Authenticating pervasive devices with human protocols. In: Shoup, V. (ed.) CRYPTO 2005. LNCS, vol. 3621, pp. 293–308. Springer, Heidelberg (2005)
15. Lee, Y.K., Sakiyama, K., Batina, L., Verbauwhede, I.: Elliptic-curve-based security processor for rfid. IEEE Transactions on Computers 57(11), 1514–1527 (2008)
16. Lim, C.H., Kwon, T.: Strong and robust RFID authentication enabling perfect ownership transfer. In: Ning, P., Qing, S., Li, N. (eds.) ICICS 2006. LNCS, vol. 4307, pp. 1–20. Springer, Heidelberg (2006)
17. Ohkubo, M., Suzuki, K., Kinoshita, S.: Cryptographic approach to "privacy-friendly" tags. In: RFID Privacy Workshop (2003)
18. Pantelić, G., Bojanić, S., Tomašević, V.: Authentication protocols in RFID systems. In: Zhang, Y., Kitsos, P. (eds.) Security in RFID and Sensor Networks, pp. 99–120. Auerbach Publications (April 2009)
19. Peris-Lopez, P., Hernandez-Castro, J.C., Estevez-Tapiador, J.M., Ribagorda, A.: EMAP: An efficient mutual-authentication protocol for low-cost RFID tags. In: Meersman, R., Tari, Z., Herrero, P. (eds.) OTM 2006 Workshops. LNCS, vol. 4277, pp. 352–361. Springer, Heidelberg (2006)
20. Peris-Lopez, P., Hernandez-Castro, J.C., Estevez-Tapiador, J.M., Ribagorda, A.: M^2AP: A minimalist mutual-authentication protocol for low-cost RFID tags. In: Ma, J., Jin, H., Yang, L.T., Tsai, J.J.-P. (eds.) UIC 2006. LNCS, vol. 4159, pp. 912–923. Springer, Heidelberg (2006)
21. Peris-Lopez, P., Hernandez-Castro, J.C., Estevez-Tapiador, J.M., Ribagorda, A.: RFID systems: A survey on security threats and proposed solutions. In: Cuenca, P., Orozco-Barbosa, L. (eds.) PWC 2006. LNCS, vol. 4217, pp. 159–170. Springer, Heidelberg (2006)

22. Peris-Lopez, P., Hernandez-Castro, J.C., Tapiador, J.M.E., Ribagorda, A.: Advances in ultralightweight cryptography for low-cost RFID tags: Gossamer protocol. In: Chung, K.-I., Sohn, K., Yung, M. (eds.) WISA 2008. LNCS, vol. 5379, pp. 56–68. Springer, Heidelberg (2009)

23. Peris-Lopez, P., Hernandez-Castro, J.C., Estevez-Tapiador, J.M., Ribagorda, A.: Lightweight cryptography for low-cost RFID tags. In: Zhang, Y., Kitsos, P. (eds.) Security in RFID and Sensor Networks, pp. 121–150. Auerbach Publications (April 2009)

24. Piramuthu, S.: Protocols for RFID tag/reader authentication. Decision Support Systems 43(3), 897–914 (2007)

25. The RPM Lab: Real Privacy Management (RPM). Reference Guide (2009), http://www.therpmlab.com/papers.htm

26. The RPM Lab: Real Privacy Management (RPM). Cryptographic Description (2010), http://www.therpmlab.com/papers.htm

27. Sherman, A.: An initial assessment of the 2factor authentication and key-management system (May 2005)

28. Song, B., Mitchell, C.J.: RFID authentication protocol for low-cost tags. In: Proceedings of the First ACM Conference on Wireless Network Security, pp. 140–147. ACM, New York (2008)

29. Tanaka, H.: Security-function integrated simple cipher communication system. In: Proceedings of the 2006 Symposium on Cryptography and Information Security (2006)

30. Tanaka, H.: Generation of cryptographic random sequences and its applications to secure enchipering. In: Proceedings of the 2007 Symposium on Cryptography and Information Security (2007)

31. Vajda, I., Buttyán, L.: Lightweight authentication protocols for low-cost RFID tags. In: Second Workshop on Security in Ubiquitous Computing – Ubicomp 2003 (2003)

32. Vaudenay, S.: On privacy models for RFID. In: Kurosawa, K. (ed.) ASIACRYPT 2007. LNCS, vol. 4833, pp. 68–87. Springer, Heidelberg (2007)

33. Weis, S.A., Sarma, S.E., Rivest, R.L., Engels, D.W.: Security and privacy aspects of low-cost radio frequency identification systems. In: Hutter, D., Müller, G., Stephan, W., Ullmann, M. (eds.) Security in Pervasive Computing. LNCS, vol. 2802, pp. 201–212. Springer, Heidelberg (2004)

Long-Term Secure Two-Round Group Key Establishment from Pairings

Kashi Neupane

Division of Science, Math, and Health Professions,
Atlanta Metropolitan State College,
1630 Metropolitan Parkway, Atlanta, GA 30310, USA
kneupane@atlm.edu

Abstract. In 2007, Bohli et al. introduced the concept of long-term security as resistance against attacks even if later, after completion of the protocol some security assumptions become invalid, and proposed a three-round long-term secure two-party key establishment protocol. Building on a two-party solution of Bohli et al., we present an authenticated two-round group key establishment protocol which remains secure if either a Computational Bilinear Diffie Hellman problem is hard or a server, who shares a symmetric key with each user, is uncorrupted.

Keywords: group key establishment, pairing, long-term security.

1   Introduction

The task of key establishment is one of the most important and also most difficult parts of a security system. It is a common practice to construct key establishment protocols based on either symmetric cryptosystems or public key cryptosystems. The usual requirement for the security of symmetric cipher is that the cost of breaking the scheme is close to exponential in the key length because its security is based on an assumption that no better attack than bruit force search is known. However, the prediction of the cost of breaking the scheme is far more challenging for public-key cryptography, which is usually much more structured as compared to symmetric ciphers because of algorithmic advances in solving the underlying problem. The major disadvantage of protocols based on the former one is that a trusted server who is not a group member knows the secret key, whereas the major drawback of protocols based on the latter one is that it will be no more secure in future when the underlying hardness assumption breaks. Bohli et. al [1] formally introduced a new concept, long-term security of key establishment protocols in cryptography. This new concept not only facilitates the option of combining the advantages of both types of cryptosystems mentioned above but also ensures the secrecy of data over long periods of time. More precisely, long-term secure protocols are based on two hardness assumptions, and the security of a protocol depends on both hardness assumptions independently. A combination of two different hardness assumptions allows the protocol to remain secure, even

Z. Kotulski et al. (Eds.): CSS 2014, CCIS 448, pp. 122–130, 2014.

if one of the hardness assumptions becomes invalid after the completion of the protocol.

Bohli et. al [1] proposed a long-term secure three-round two-party key establishment protocol based on DDH assumption and an assumption which is close to real-or-random indistinguishability of a symmetric encryption scheme. Müller-Quade and Unruh [2] extended the notion of long-term security in Universally Composable framework. Moreover, Unruh [3] defined a variant of the Universal Composability framework, everlasting quantum-UC, and showed that secure communication and general multi-party computation, using signature cards as trusted setup, can be implemented. Neupane and Steinwandt [4] proposed a long-term secure three-party key establishment protocol based on Bilinear Decisional Diffie-Hellman (BDDH) assumption, and also [5] extended Joux's three-party one-round protocol to an actively secure two-round group key establishment protocol. As a contribution to compiler construction, Neupane et. al [6] presented a compiler which allows to add perfect forward secrecy to any secure authenticated group key establishment which has at least one round at the cost of one more additional round. In this paper, we propose an authenticated long-term secure group key establishment protocol with two rounds. We use Bilinear Computational Diffie-Hellman (BCDH) assumption as an underlying hardness assumption for public key cryptosystem, whereas the notion of real-or -random indistinguishability has been used for the security of the underlying symmetric cipher.

2 Preliminaries

On the mathematical side, the main technical tool is a bilinear pairing. Following the formalization of Boneh and Franklin [7], in this section we quickly review the relevant terminology—for more details we refer to [7]. We also review the standard definitions of signature scheme, symmetric encryption, and then the main idea of real-or-random indistinguishability as discussed by Bellare et al. [8].

2.1 Bilinear Maps and the Bilinear Diffie Hellman Assumption

Let $(G_1, +)$, $(G_2, \cdot)$ be two groups of prime order q, such that $q > 2^k$ with the security parameter being k. We denote by $\hat{e} : G_1 \longrightarrow G_2$ an *admissible bilinear map*, i.e., $\hat{e}$ has all of the following properties:

Bilinear: For all $P, Q \in G_1$ and all $a, b \in \mathbb{Z}$ we have $\hat{e}(aP, bQ) = \hat{e}(P, Q)^{ab}$.

Non-degenerate: For P is a generator of G_1, we have $\hat{e}(P, P)$ is a generator of G_2, i.e., $\hat{e}(P, P) \neq 1$.

Efficiently computable: There is a polynomial time algorithm which for all $Q, R \in G_1$ computes $\hat{e}(Q, R)$.

To specify the Bilinear Computational Diffie-Hellman (BCDH) problem, we use a probabilistic polynomial time (ppt) algorithm $\mathcal{G}$: on input the security parameter 1^k, this *BCDH parameter generator* $\mathcal{G}$ outputs q and a description of G_1, G_2, and $\hat{e}$ as above; in slight abuse of notation we write $\langle q, G_1, G_2, \hat{e} \rangle \leftarrow \mathcal{G}(1^k)$. Descriptions output by $\mathcal{G}$ are assumed to specify polynomial time algorithms for efficiently computing in G_1, G_2 and for evaluating the bilinear map $\hat{e}$.

Next, for a ppt algorithm $\mathcal{A}$ we consider the following experiment:

1. The BCDH parameter generator is run, yielding BCDH parameters

$$\langle q, G_1, G_2, \hat{e} \rangle.$$

2. Values $a, b, c \leftarrow \{0, \ldots, q-1\}$ are chosen uniformly at random, and $\mathcal{A}$ obtains the output of $\mathcal{G}$ along with aP, bP and cP as input.
3. Now $\mathcal{A}$ outputs a value $g \in G_2$, and is successful whenever $g = \hat{e}(P, P)^{abc}$.

To measure the *advantage of $\mathcal{A}$ in solving the BCDH problem* we use the function $\mathrm{Adv}_{\mathcal{A}}^{\mathrm{bcdh}} = \mathrm{Adv}_{\mathcal{G}, \mathcal{A}}^{\mathrm{bcdh}}(k) :=$

$$\Pr \left[\mathcal{A}(q, G_1, G_2, \hat{e}, P, aP, bP, cP) = \hat{e}(P, P)^{abc} \left| \begin{array}{l} \langle q, G_1, G_2, \hat{e} \rangle \leftarrow \mathcal{G}(1^k), \\ P \leftarrow G_1 \\ a, b, c \leftarrow \{0, \ldots, q-1\} \end{array} \right. \right]. \quad (1)$$

Definition 1 (BCDH Assumption). *A BCDH instance generator $\mathcal{G}$ satisfies the BCDH assumption if for all ppt algorithms $\mathcal{A}$, the advantage $\mathrm{Adv}_{\mathcal{A}}^{\mathrm{bcdh}}$ is negligible (in k). In this case, we say that BCDH is hard in groups generated by $\mathcal{G}$.*

2.2   Digital Signature Scheme

A digital signature is a method to sign a message electronically by a user which can be verified by anybody later. A digital signature protects data from being altered, respectively enables the detection of modification. Because of page limits, we do not review the definition of a signature scheme—for more details we refer to [9].

2.3   Real-or-Random Indistinguishability

Our presentation of real-or-random indistinguishability follows the one of Bellare et al. in [8], and we refer to the latter paper for a more detailed discussion. We review the definition of symmetric encryption scheme before giving the definition of real-or random indistinguishability.

Definition 2 (Symmetric Key Encryption Scheme). *A symmetric key encryption scheme $\mathcal{SE} = (\mathsf{Gen}, \mathsf{Enc}, \mathsf{Dec})$ is a triple of polynomial-time algorithms:*

- *A randomized key generation algorithm Gen which takes the security parameter 1^k as its input, and returns a secret key $K \in \{0, 1\}^*$;*
- *A randomized encryption algorithm Enc which takes a secret key K and a message $M \in \{0, 1\}^*$ as its inputs, and returns a ciphertext $C \in \{0, 1\}^*$;*

- *A deterministic decryption algorithm* Dec *which takes the key* K *and a cipher-text* C *as its inputs, and returns either a message* M *or an error symbol* $\perp$.

The scheme is said to provide *correct decryption* if for any secret key K and any message M such that ciphertext $C \leftarrow \text{Enc}_K(M)$, it is the case $\text{Dec}_K(C) = M$. To formalize the security notion needed later, we use a *real-or-random oracle* $\mathcal{E}_K(\mathcal{RR}(\cdot, b))$ with the following properties: on input $b \in \{0, 1\}$ and a plaintext $M \in \{0, 1\}^*$,

- returns an encryption $C \leftarrow \text{Enc}_K(M)$ of M, if $b = 1$
- returns an encryption $C \leftarrow \text{Enc}_K(r)$ of a uniformly at random chosen bit-string $r \leftarrow \{0, 1\}^{|M|}$, if $b = 0$.

For a ppt algorithm $\mathcal{A}$ now consider the following experiment where $b \in \{0, 1\}$ is fixed and unknown to $\mathcal{A}$: a secret key $K \leftarrow \text{Gen}(1^k)$ is created, and $\mathcal{A}$ has unrestricted access to $\mathcal{E}_K(\mathcal{RR}(\cdot, b))$. Further, $\mathcal{A}$ has access to a decryption oracle $\mathcal{D}_K(\cdot)$ which executes $\text{Dec}_K(\cdot)$, subject to the restriction that no messages must be queried to $\mathcal{D}_K(\cdot)$ that have been output by the real-or-random oracle. We measure $\mathcal{A}$'s advantage as the difference $\text{Adv}_{\mathcal{A}}^{\text{ror}-\text{cca}} =$

$$\text{Adv}_{\mathcal{A}}^{\text{ror}-\text{cca}}(k) := \Pr\left[1 \leftarrow \mathcal{A}^{\mathcal{E}_K(\mathcal{RR}(\cdot,1)),\mathcal{D}_K(\cdot)}(1^k) \,\Big|\, K \leftarrow \text{Gen}(1^k)\right] - \\ \Pr\left[1 \leftarrow \mathcal{A}^{\mathcal{E}_K(\mathcal{RR}(\cdot,0)),\mathcal{D}_K(\cdot)}(1^k) \,\Big|\, K \leftarrow \text{Gen}(1^k)\right] . \quad (2)$$

Definition 3 (Real-or-random Indistinguishability). *A symmetric encryption scheme* $\mathcal{SE}$ *is secure in the sense of real-or-random indistinguishability* (ROR-CCA), *if for all ppt algorithms* $\mathcal{A}$, *the advantage* $\text{Adv}_{\mathcal{A}}^{\text{ror}-\text{cca}}$ *is negligible* (*in* k).

3 Security Model

Our security model is based on the one used by Bohli et al. [10] and [6], which in turn builds on work by Katz and Yung [11] and Bresson et al. [12,13].

Protocol Participants. We denote by S a trusted *server* and by $\mathcal{U} = \{U_0, \ldots, U_n\}$ a polynomial size set of *users*. Both server and users are modeled as ppt algorithms, and each $U \in \mathcal{U} \cup \{S\}$ can execute a polynomial number of protocol instances Π_U^s concurrently ($s \in \mathbb{N}$). User identities are assumed to be bitstrings of identical length k and to keep notation simple, throughout we will not distinguish between the bitstring identifying a user U and the algorithm U itself. To a protocol instance Π_U^s, the variables acc_U^s, pid_U^s, sk_U^s, sid_U^s, state_U^s, term_U^s, and used_U^s are associated.

Initialization. Before actual protocol executions take place, a trusted initialization phase *without adversarial interference* is allowed. In this phase, for each $U \in \mathcal{U}$ a (verification key, signing key)-pair $(pk_U, sk_U^{\text{sig}})$ for an existentially unforgeable (EUF-CMA secure) signature scheme is generated, sk_U^{sig} is given to U

only, and pk_U is handed to all users in $\mathcal{U}$ and to the adversary. In addition, for each user $U \in \mathcal{U}$, a secret key $K_U \leftarrow \mathsf{Gen}(1^k)$ for the underlying symmetric encryption scheme, $(\mathsf{Gen}, \mathsf{Enc}, \mathsf{Dec})$ is generated, where k is the security parameter for the symmetric encryption scheme. This generated key is given to U and the server S. Thus, after this initialization phase, the server shares a symmetric key K_U with each user $U \in \mathcal{U}$.

Adversarial Capabilities and Communication Network. The network is non-private, fully asynchronous and allows arbitrary point-to-point connections among users, and between users and the server. The adversary $\mathcal{A}$ is modeled as ppt algorithm with full control over the communication network. More specifically, $\mathcal{A}$'s capabilities are captured by the $\mathsf{Send}(U, s, M)$, $\mathsf{Reveal}(U, s)$, and $\mathsf{Corrupt}(U)$ *oracles*.

In addition to the mentioned oracles, $\mathcal{A}$ has access to a Test oracle, which can be queried only once: the query $\mathsf{Test}(U, s)$ can be made with an instance Π_U^s that has accepted a session key. Then a bit $b \leftarrow \{0, 1\}$ is chosen uniformly at random; for $b = 0$, the session key stored in sk_U^s is returned, and for $b = 1$ a uniformly at random chosen element from the space of session keys is returned.

Definition 4 (Partnering). *Two instances* $\prod_{U_i}^{s_i}$ *and* $\prod_{U_j}^{s_j}$ *are partnered if* $\mathsf{sid}_{U_i}^{s_i} = \mathsf{sid}_{U_j}^{s_j}$, $\mathsf{pid}_{U_i}^{s_i} = \mathsf{pid}_{U_j}^{s_j}$ *and* $\mathsf{acc}_{U_i}^{s_i} = \mathsf{acc}_{U_j}^{s_j} = \mathrm{TRUE}$.

Based on this notion of partnering, we can specify what we mean by a *fresh* instance, i.e., an instance where the adversary should not know the session key:

Definition 5 (Freshness). *An instance* $\prod_{U_i}^{s_i}$ *is said to be* fresh *if the adversary queried neither* $\mathsf{Corrupt}(U_j)$ *for some* $U_j \in \mathsf{pid}_{U_i}^{s_i}$ *before a query of the form* $\mathsf{Send}(U_k, s_k, *)$ *with* $U_k \in \mathsf{pid}_{U_i}^{s_i}$ *has taken place, nor* $\mathsf{Reveal}(U_j, s_j)$ *for an instance* $\prod_{U_j}^{s_j}$ *that is partnered with* $\prod_{U_i}^{s_i}$.

It is worth noting that the above definition allows an adversary $\mathcal{A}$ to reveal *all* secret signing keys without violating freshness, provided $\mathcal{A}$ does not send any messages after having received the signing keys. As a consequence security in the sense of Definition 6 below implies forward secrecy: We write $\mathsf{Succ}_{\mathcal{A}}$ for the event $\mathcal{A}$ queries Test with a fresh instance and outputs a correct guess for the Test oracle's bit b. By:

$$\mathrm{Adv}_{\mathcal{A}}^{\mathsf{ke}} = \mathrm{Adv}_{\mathcal{A}}^{\mathsf{ke}}(k) := \left| \Pr[\mathsf{Succ}] - \frac{1}{2} \right| \tag{3}$$

we denote the *advantage* of $\mathcal{A}$.

Definition 6 (Semantic Security). *A key establishment protocol is said to be* (semantically) secure, *if* $\mathrm{Adv}_{\mathcal{A}}^{\mathsf{ke}} = \mathrm{Adv}_{\mathcal{A}}^{\mathsf{ke}}(k)$ *is negligible for all ppt algorithms* $\mathcal{A}$.

In addition to the above standard security goal, we are also interested in *integrity* (which may be interpreted a form of "worst case correctness") and *strong entity authentication*:

Definition 7 (Integrity). *A key establishment protocol fulfills integrity if with overwhelming probability for all instances $\prod_{U_i}^{s_i}$, $\prod_{U_j}^{s_j}$ of uncorrupted users the following holds: if* $\mathsf{acc}_{U_i}^{s_i} = \mathsf{acc}_{U_j}^{s_j} = \text{TRUE}$ *and* $\mathsf{sid}_{U_i}^{s_i} = \mathsf{sid}_{U_j}^{s_j}$, *then* $\mathsf{sk}_{U_i}^{s_i} = \mathsf{sk}_{U_j}^{s_j}$ *and* $\mathsf{pid}_{U_i}^{s_i} = \mathsf{pid}_{U_j}^{s_j}$.

Definition 8 (Strong Entity Authentication). *We say that* strong entity authentication *for an instance $\prod_{U_i}^{s_i}$ is provided if* $\mathsf{acc}_{U_i}^{s_i} = \text{TRUE}$ *implies that for all uncorrupted $U_j \in \mathsf{pid}_{U_i}^{s_i}$ there exists with overwhelming probability an instance $\prod_{U_j}^{s_j}$ with $\mathsf{sid}_{U_j}^{s_j} = \mathsf{sid}_{U_i}^{s_i}$ and $U_i \in \mathsf{pid}_{U_j}^{s_j}$.*

4   The Proposed Group Key Establishment Protocol

The proposed protocol has two rounds with the help of a trusted server S, and makes use of a random oracle $H : \{0,1\}^* \to \{0,1\}^k$. To describe the protocol we use the notation from Section 2.1 with P being a generator of the additive group G_1 of prime order q, as used in the BCDH assumption. By Enc we denote the encryption algorithm of a symmetric encryption scheme that is secure in the sense of ROR-CCA, and by σ we denote an existentially unforgeable signature scheme. We write $U_0, \ldots, U_{n-1}$ for the protocol participants who want to establish a common session key. We assume the number n of these participants to be greater than three and even—if $2 \nmid n$, then U_{n-1} can simulate an additional (virtual) user U_n.

4.1   Description of the Protocol

We arrange the participants $U_0, \ldots, U_{n-1}$ in a circle such that $U_{(i-j) \bmod n}$ respectively $U_{(i+j) \bmod n}$ is the participant j positions away from U_i in counter-clockwise (left) respectively clockwise (right) direction. The proposed protocol for establishing a common group session key among users $U_0, \ldots, U_n$, invoking a server S, is described in Figure 1 (for ease of notation, we omit indices referring to a particular user instance and write only sid_U instead of sid_U^s etc.), to simplify notation, we do not explicitly refer to protocol instances $\prod_i^{s_i}$. The protocol has two rounds and makes use of random oracle $H : \{0,1\}^* \to \{0,1\}^k$ and a trusted server. In the first round, each user broadcasts one message for Joux's three-party key agreement protocol, and receives one messages from the server. In the second round, each user broadcasts either a signed messages with the signature or a signature on a string, which is known to each user. Finally, each user computes a common master key, and then computes a session key and a session id using the same master key.

4.2   Security Analysis

The security of the protocol in Figure 1 can be ensured "long-term" provided that the underlying signature scheme is existentially unforgeable and the invoked symmetric encryption scheme is secure in the sense of ROR-CCA. More specifically, we have the following.

Round 1:

　Computation Each U_i chooses $u_i \in \{0, \ldots, q-1\}$ uniformly at random and computes $u_i P$. The server S selects $k^{\mathsf{srv}} \leftarrow \{0,1\}^k$ uniformly at random and for $i = 1, \ldots, n$ computes $c_i := \mathsf{Enc}_{k_{U_i}}(\mathsf{pid}, k^{\mathsf{srv}})$.

　Broadcast Each U_i broadcasts $u_i P$ and the server broadcasts $(\mathsf{pid}, c_1, \ldots, c_n)$.

Round 2:

　Computation Each U_i computes

$$\begin{cases} t_i^L := H(e(P,P)^{u_{(i-2) \bmod n} u_{(i-1) \bmod n} u_i}) \text{ and} \\ t_i^R := H(e(P,P)^{u_i u_{(i+1) \bmod n} u_{(i+2) \bmod n}}) & , \text{if } i \text{ is odd} \\ t_i^M := H(e(P,P)^{u_{(i-1) \bmod n} u_i u_{(i+1) \bmod n}}) & , \text{if } i \text{ is even} \end{cases}$$

In addition, each U_i recovers k^{srv} from the message received in Round 1, computes $\mathsf{conf}_i := (k^{\mathsf{srv}} \| \mathsf{pid}_i \| u_0 P \| u_1 P \| \ldots \| u_{n-1} P)$ and

$$\begin{cases} \text{a signature } \sigma_i \text{ on } \mathsf{conf}_i \| T_i \text{ where } T_i := t_i^L \oplus t_i^R, \text{ if } i \text{ is odd} \\ \text{a signature } \sigma_i \text{ on } \mathsf{conf}_i & , \text{if } i \text{ is even} \end{cases}$$

　Broadcast Each U_i broadcasts (σ_i, T_i) (if $2 \nmid i$) respectively σ_i (if $2 \mid i$).

　Check Each U_i verifies $\sigma_0, \ldots, \sigma_{n-1}$ (using the $u_j P$ received in Round 1 and pid_i for the partner identifier) and checks if $T_1 \oplus T_3 \oplus T_5 \oplus \cdots \oplus T_{n-1} = 0$ holds. If any of these checks fails, U_i aborts.

　Key derivation: Each U_i recovers the values t_j^R for $j = 1, 3, \ldots, n-1$ as follows:

　– U_i with $2 \nmid i$ finds $t_j^R = t_i^L \oplus \bigoplus_{\substack{s=2 \\ 2 \mid s}}^{(i-j-2) \bmod n} T_{(j+s) \bmod n}$

　– U_i with $2 \mid i$ finds $t_j^R = t_i^M \oplus \bigoplus_{\substack{s=2 \\ 2 \mid s}}^{(i-j-1) \bmod n} T_{(j+s) \bmod n}$

Finally, each U_i computes the master key $K := (k^{\mathsf{srv}}, t_1^R, t_3^R, \ldots, t_{n-1}^R, \mathsf{pid}_i)$, sets $\mathsf{sk}_{U_i} := H(K\|0)$ and $\mathsf{sid}_{U_i} := H(K\|1)$.

Fig. 1. Long-term secure group key establishment

Proposition 1. *Suppose the signature scheme used in the protocol in Figure 1 is secure in the sense of* UF-CMA *and the symmetric encryption scheme is secure in the sense of* ROR-CCA. *Then the protocol in Figure 1 is semantically secure, fulfills integrity, and strong entity authentication holds to all involved instances provided that at least one of the following conditions holds:*

　– *The server S is uncorrupted.*
　– *The BCDH assumption for the underlying BCDH instance generator holds.*

The proposition is proved in two steps. First, we prove it where the BCDH assumption holds and therafter we show the case where the server is uncorrupted. We prove the security of the protocol in both cases by using a short sequence of games. Beause of the page limit we do not include a proof here.

　The protocol we have proposed is similar to the one suggested by Neupane et. al [6] in the sense of cyclic structure and security model, but the basic requirements and the goals are quite different, and it is worth highlighting some differences. Our protocol is a long-term secure protocol based on two security assumptions, while [6] allows to add perfect forward secrecy to a secure authenticated group key establishment protocol. We use Bilinear Computational Diffie-Hellman(BCDH) assumption as an underlying hardness assumption for public key cryptosystem, whereas the notion of real-or -random indistinguishability has been used for the security of the underlying symmetric cipher, but the security of the [6] is based on the security assumptions which have been used for the original protocol. We have constructed an authenticated two-round group key establishment protocol with Joux's three party key establishment protocol as the main building block and a use of a trusted server, while [6] is a compiler which is constructed from two existing protocols, a secure unauthenticated one-round two-party key establishment protocol and a secure authenticated group key establishment protocol which has at least one round.

5 Conclusion

The 2-round secure group key establishment we presented can be seen as expensive in the sense that shared keys with a server, signature scheme, and two hardness assumptions are involved. Nonetheless, the *long-term security* guarantee established is rather strong. The protocol uses Joux's protocol as fundamental building block—instead of a 2-party Diffie-Hellman key establishment. The protocol has attractive features that each user has to sign just a single message in comparison to other authenticated group key establishment protocols, and the hardness assumptions used in the protocols are quite acceptable compared to Bohli et al. three-round two-party solution.

References

1. Bohli, J.-M., Müller-Quade, J., Röhrich, S.: Long-Term and Dynamical Aspects of Information Security: Emerging Trends in Information and Communication Security. Long-term Secure Key Establishment, pp. 87–95. Nova Science Publishers (2007)
2. Müller-Quade, J., Unruh, D.: Long-Term Security and Universal Composability. In: Vadhan, S.P. (ed.) TCC 2007. LNCS, vol. 4392, pp. 41–60. Springer, Heidelberg (2007)
3. Unruh, D.: Everlasting multi-party computation. In: Canetti, R., Garay, J.A. (eds.) CRYPTO 2013, Part II. LNCS, vol. 8043, pp. 380–397. Springer, Heidelberg (2013)
4. Neupane, K., Steinwandt, R.: Server-assisted Long-term Secure 3-party Key Establishment. In: SECRYPT 2010 - Proceedings of the International Conference on Security and Cryptography, pp. 372–378. SciTePress (2010)
5. Neupane, K., Steinwandt, R.: Communication-Efficient 2-Round Group Key Establishment from Pairings. In: Kiayias, A. (ed.) CT-RSA 2011. LNCS, vol. 6558, pp. 65–76. Springer, Heidelberg (2011)
6. Neupane, K., Steinwandt, R., Corona, A.S.: Group Key Establishment: Adding Perfect Forward Secrecy at the Cost of One Round. In: Pieprzyk, J., Sadeghi, A.-R., Manulis, M. (eds.) CANS 2012. LNCS, vol. 7712, pp. 158–168. Springer, Heidelberg (2012)

7. Boneh, D., Franklin, M.: Identity-Based Encryption from the Weil Pairing. SIAM Journal of Computing 32, 586–615 (2003)
8. Bellare, M., Desai, A., Jokipii, E., Rogaway, P.: A Concrete Security Treatment of Symmetric Encryption, http://cseweb.ucsd.edu/~mihir/papers/sym-enc.html
9. Menezes, A., Van Oorschot, P., Vanstone, S.: Handbook of Applied Cryptography. CRC Press, Boca Raton (1996)
10. Bohli, J.-M., González Vasco, M.I., Steinwandt, R.: Secure group key establishment revisited. International Journal of Information Security 6, 243–254 (2007)
11. Katz, J., Yung, M.: Scalable Protocols for Authenticated Group Key Exchange. In: Boneh, D. (ed.) CRYPTO 2003. LNCS, vol. 2729, pp. 110–125. Springer, Heidelberg (2003)
12. Bresson, E., Chevassut, O., Pointcheval, D.: Provably Authenticated Group Diffie-Hellman Key Exchange - The Dynamic Case. In: Boyd, C. (ed.) ASIACRYPT 2001. LNCS, vol. 2248, pp. 290–309. Springer, Heidelberg (2001)
13. Bresson, E., Chevassut, O., Pointcheval, D., Quisquater, J.-J.: Provably Authenticated Group Diffie-Hellman Key Exchange. In: Proceedings of the 8th ACM Conference on Computer and Communications Security, CCS 2001, pp. 255–264. ACM (2001)

Optimizing SHA256 in Bitcoin Mining

Nicolas T. Courtois[1], Marek Grajek[2], and Rahul Naik[1,3]

[1] University College London, UK
n.courtois@cs.ucl.ac.uk
[2] Independent researcher and writer, Poland
[3] Royal Bank of Scotland, UK

Abstract. Bitcoin is a "crypto currency", a decentralized electronic payment scheme based on cryptography. It implements a particular type of peer-to-peer payment system. Bitcoin depends on well-known cryptographic standards such as SHA-256. In this paper we revisit the cryptographic process which allows one to make money by producing new bitcoins. We reformulate this problem as a specific sort of Constrained Input Small Output (CISO) hashing problem and reduce the problem to a pure block cipher problem, cf. Fig. 1. We estimate the speed of this process and we show that the amortized cost of this process is less than it seems and it depends on a certain cryptographic constant which is estimated to be at most 1.89. These optimizations enable bitcoin miners to save countless millions of dollars per year in electricity bills.

Keywords: electronic payment, crypto currencies, bitcoin, hash functions, SHA-256, bitcoin mining, CICO problem (Constrained Input Constrained Output), cryptanalysis of block ciphers.

1 What Are Bitcoins and Bitcoin Mining

Bitcoin is a collaborative virtual currency and a decentralized peer-to-peer payment system without trusted central authorities. It has been invented in 2008 [27] and launched in 2009. Ever since Bitcoin was launched in 2009, it has been presented by its technical architects as an experimental rather than mature electronic currency ecosystem. Initially bitcoin was a sort of social experiment, however bitcoins have been traded for real money for several years now. One year ago, in April 2013 the leading newspaper The Economist explains that bitcoin is here to stay, that it is a future of payments and calls it *digital gold* [14]. This has coincided with the total value of bitcoins in circulation exceeding 1 billion dollars. Bitcoin became a mainstream financial instrument.

In this paper we study bitcoin with particular attention paid to the process of bitcoin mining, which is the specialist term given to the process by which new bitcoins are created. Then later in Section 3 we are going to study in a lot of detail one particular technical question in symmetric cryptography to see if there exists an improved method which allows one to mine bitcoins faster.

Bitcoins are a type of digital currency which can be stored on a computer. Bitcoins use the concept of so called "Proofs of Work" which are solutions to

Z. Kotulski et al. (Eds.): CSS 2014, CCIS 448, pp. 131–144, 2014.

certain very hard cryptographic puzzles based on hash functions. However these solutions are NOT bitcoins. The puzzles are rather part of the bitcoin trust infrastructure. In fact the puzzles are connected together to form a chain and as the length of this chain grows, so does the security level. Bitcoins are simply awarded to people who produce these "Proofs of Work". Ownership of bitcoins is achieved through digital signatures: the owner of a certain private key is the owner of a certain quantity of bitcoins. This private key is the unique way to transfer the bitcoin to another computer or person.

The operation of so called *bitcoin mining* or creating bitcoins out of the thin air is not only possible. It is essential, it is encouraged, and it is a crucial and necessary part of the Bitcoin ecosystem.

Cryptographic computations executed in a peer-to-peer network with tens of thousands of independent hashing nodes are the heart of the security assurance provided by this virtual currency system. It would be very difficult and extremely costly for one entity to corrupt all these independent miners. The sum of all this collective computational work provides some sort of solid cryptographic proof and prevents attacks on this system. This is also how the network polices itself: miners are expected to approve only correctly formed transactions. Bitcoin implements a specific sort of distributed and decentralized electronic notary system without a central authority. Well almost. Certain decisions about how the system works, what exactly the bitcoin software does and how [3], are still pretty centralized. In particular mining activity concentrates in extremely few very large mining pools one of which controls more than 40 % of hash power, see Table 2 in [9].

In a nutshell, bitcoin miners make money when they find a 32-bit value which, when hashed together with the data from other transactions with a standard hash function gives a hash with a certain number of 64 or more leading zeros. This is an extremely rare event. It is in general believed that there is no way to produce these data otherwise than by very long and costly computations. This question of how to improve this process is the central question in this paper.

2 Detailed Study of Mining Internals

The goal of the miner is to solve a certain cryptographic puzzle which we will later call **a CISO Hash Problem**. The solution will be called **a CISO block**. Great majority of miners ignore what exactly they are doing, either running open source software, or having purchased specialized hardware to do mining very efficiently. However miners must know that the operation is very timely and that they need to be permanently connected to the network. The solutions to these puzzles are linked to each other and form a **unique** chain of blocks. This is usually called *the block chain*. The whole block chain is public and the whole of it can for example be consulted at `http://blockexplorer.com/`. All new blocks which are found need to be broadcast to all network participants as soon as possible. The miners need to be very reactive and they do it because it is in their interest. They need to listen to broadcasts in order to receive the data about recent transactions which they are expected to approve. Then they need to broadcast any solution (CISO block) which they have found as soon as they found it, because their solution is likely to be part of the *"main chain of blocks"* only if it is widely known. Once the solution is known it "discourages" other miners from searching for the same block. Instead they can concentrate on searching for the next block which will confirm the present block and will make the miner be able to claim his a reward for producing this CISO block.

Our goal is to clarify how this system works. In this paper we mostly consider this to be a static problem which needs to be solved. We refer to [8] for a discussion on how the difficulty of this problem changes with time.

The problem of bitcoin mining is very closely related to well known problems in cryptography. One crucial question is as follows: how does the bitcoin mining differ from traditional questions in cryptanalysis of block ciphers and hash functions and is there a more efficient way to mine bitcoins.

First we are going to briefly describe the problem as a static computation problem about a certain block cipher. Then we are going to look at how the problem evolves in time and how solutions to the CISO problem are converted to shares in the bitcoin currency. Finally we are going to study what the possible solutions and optimizations are.

2.1   Constrained Input Small Output (CISO) Hashing Problem

New bitcoins can be created when the miner hashes some data from the bitcoin network together with a 32-bit random nonce, and obtains a number on 256 bits which starts with a certain number of zeros. We call this problem CISO: Constrained Input Small Output.

This can be seen as a special case of a problem which is sometimes called CICO which translates into Constrained Inputs Constrained Outputs problem. This terminology has been introduced in the study of the most recently standardized U.S. government standard hash function SHA-3 a.k.a. Keccak. SHA-3 is the latest hash function in the SHA family and a successor to SHA-256 used in bitcoin [1]. It is possible to claim that this means that SHA-256 of Bitcoin is considered by the United States NIST and a broader cryptographic engineering community as NOT sufficiently secure for long term security. This sort of CISO/CICO problems are not new, they are very frequently studied in cryptanalysis of hash functions since ever, and endless variants of these problems exist for specific hash functions, some examples can be found in [1,11,26].

The exact details of the specific Constrained Input Small Output (CISO) problem which we have in bitcoin are described below. It can be obtained by the inspection of the bitcoin source code, see [3].

2.2   (CISO) Hashing Problem Internals

On Fig. 1 we show the cryptographic computation which is executed many many times by bitcoin miners. This picture emphasizes the internal structure inside SHA-256 hash function.

SHA-256 is a hash function built from a block cipher following the so called Davies-Meyer construction. The principle of the Davies-Meyer construction is that the input value is at the end added to the output and that it transforms an encryption algorithm into a "hashing" algorithm, a building piece of a standard hash function. The underlying block cipher has 64 rounds and thus a 2048-bit expanded internal key (64x32 bits). This key is obtained from the message block to be compressed, which has 512 bits at the input and is expanded four times to form this 2048-bit internal key for our block cipher. In one sense on Fig. 1 we convert the problem of bitcoin mining or of solving CISO hash puzzles, to a specific problem with three distinct applications of the block cipher which underlies SHA-256 connected together to form certain circuit.

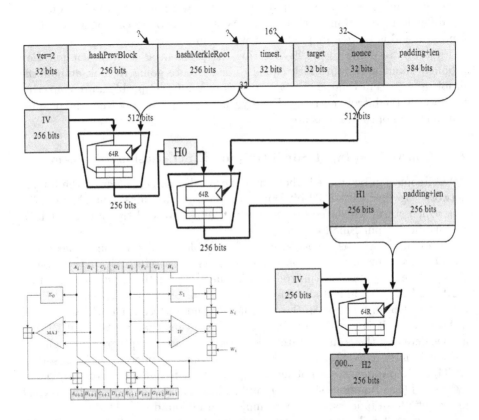

Fig. 1. The Block Hashing Algorithm of bitcoin revisited and seen as a Constrained Input Small Output (CISO) problem. We see two applications of SHA-256 together with internal details of the Davies-Meyer construction. We can view it as a triple application of a specific block cipher. An interesting question is whether there is a more efficient cryptographic shortcut or inversion attack or some non-trivial optimizations which allow to save a constant factor. Such optimizations, if they exist, could be worth some serious money as they would allow to produce bitcoins cheaper

2.3   The Main Objective of CISO Hashing

The goal of CISO hashing is to produce solutions which are correctly formed in the sense that they satisfy all the required conditions and constraints, which we are going to explain in details in Section 2.4. The miner is trying to find a solution to the CISO problem such that:

$$H2 < \texttt{target} . \tag{1}$$

Here `target` is a large integer which is a global variable for the whole bitcoin system worldwide, and on which all the participants worldwide are expected to agree. The value of `target` is adjusted approximately every 2 weeks, see [8] for more details. The job of bitcoin miners is to find these solutions and publish them. They are rewarded with some bitcoins for their work. In 2014 the reward is 25 BTC (25 bitcoins) per valid solution. The reward also changes very slowly with time, see [8].

It is generally believed that there is no other method to achieve success than trial and error; hashing at random as depicted on Fig. 1 until a result with a sufficient number of leading zeros is found. However this is unlikely to be true, there is always a better way, at least slightly, see Section 4.

2.4   The Inputs and Input Constraints In CISO Hashing

A number of data fields are present as inputs to the CISO problem, cf. Fig. 1. Some fields are fixed or change very slowly and these are indicated in green on Fig. 1. Other data need to be adjusted by the miner in order to obtain a solution however they still change very slowly. Such data are indicated in yellow on the main picture. Data which change the most frequently are indicated in red: these are "hot" data which need to be re-computed each time the nonce changes.

Bitcoin is a live distributed system and the exact conditions required for the data to be consider valid are essentially fixed and known, however they are likely to evolve with time in subtle ways. Rules have already been and are likely to be altered during the operation of the system. They depend on the consensus of participants in the system. We have:

1. **Version number on 32 bits.** Has been equal to 1 then it became 2.
2. **The previous block on 256 bits.** Or more precisely a hash on 256 bits of all the data of the last CISO block which was broadcast in the peer-to-peer network: the miner works to extend the chain of hashes by one more block. The process of generating new blocks is a sort of lottery and sometimes there will be ambiguity on which block to use (less than 1 % of the time cf. [9]). Miners in principle follow the longest chain or choose at random. However miners could also disagree for profit or in order to attack the network and there are endless subversive scenarios, see [8,9].
3. **The Merkle root on 256 bits**. This is a sort of an aggregated hash of many recent events in the bitcoin network which certifies that the system recognizes all of them simultaneously as being valid. It also contains the public key of

the future owner of this freshly created portion of bitcoin currency which this block is intended to embody. The current CISO block which the miner is trying to create by solving the current CISO problem and all subsequent CISO blocks will provide an accumulation of evidence about all these events. This security guarantee increases with time. In principle miners can decide which transactions are going to be recognized by the system. However the transaction fees which will be obtained by the miners for the transactions included in this block are an incentive to include every single transaction.

4. **Timestamp on 32 bits**. This is the current time in seconds.
5. **Target on 32 bits**. More precisely the global variable `target` is on 256 bits and what is stored here is a compressed version of `target` which is frequently called `difficulty`. We have `difficulty` = $6,119,726,089 \approx 2^{32.5}$ as of 14 April 2014. We have `difficulty` $\cdot 2^{32} = 1/\texttt{probability} = 2^{256}/\texttt{target}$.
6. **Nonce on 32 bits**. This nonce is freely chosen by the miner. Interestingly the nonce has only 32 bits while the current value of `target` makes that the probability of obtaining a suitable $H2$ by accident is as low as $2^{-64.5}$.
   This means that the miner needs to be able to generate different versions of the puzzle with a different Merkle root (or with other differences)
7. **Padding+ Len has 384 bits for H1 and 256 bits for H2**. Two constants due to the specification of SHA-256 hash function which is used here twice with data of different sizes: the input hashed has 640 and 256 bits respectively in each application of SHA-256. These two values never change.

With respect to the input data requirements and constraints above and the output constraint $H2 < \texttt{target}$ we have:

Definition 1 (CISO Problem). *We call the CISO Problem the problem of finding a valid Merkle root, 32-bit nonce and other data as illustrated on Fig. 1 which is correctly formed and such that $H2 < \texttt{target}$.*

3 How to Speed Up the Bitcoin Mining Process

In this part we look at a pure specialist question which pertains to symmetric cryptography, of whether there is a cryptographic "shortcut" attack: simply a method of mining bitcoins faster than brute force, or faster than the trivial method in which the SHA-256 hash function is a black box. The question is what is the fastest possible method for bitcoin mining, given the specific structure of Fig. 1. We were the first to develop such techniques openly and publish them.

Related Search: One could also try to solve this problem by formal coding and "a software algebraic attack", see [10,23,28].

Our analysis follows the NIST specification of SHA-256 [15] and the inspection of the Bitcoin source code [3]. SHA-256 is a hash function built from a block cipher following the well-known Davies-Meyer construction in which the input is at the end added to the output. This construction is one of the known methods to transform a block cipher into a compression function. A compression function is a building block of a hash function with a fixed input size. It is typically equal

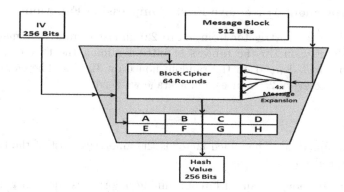

Fig. 2. One compression function in SHA-256. It comprises a 256-bit block cipher with 64 rounds, a key expansion mechanism from 512 to 2048 bits, and a final set of eight 32-bit additions

to twice the output size. In our case we have a compression function from 512 to 256 bits, cf. Fig. 2.

The block size in this block cipher is 256 bits, the key size is 512 bits which is expanded to 64 subkeys on 32 bits each for each of 64 rounds of the cipher. The first 16 subkeys for the first 16 rounds are identical to the message and are copied in the same order cf. [15] and later (Algorithm [1])

In addition in order to hash a full message, SHA-256 applies a Merkle-Damgard padding and length extension which makes it a secure hash function for messages of variable length. In the pre-processing stage, we must append one binary 1 and many zeros to the message in such a way that the resulting length is equal to 448 modulo 512, cf. [15]. Then we append the length of the message in bits as a 64-bit big-endian integer. Full SHA-256 is applied twice. In the first application of SHA-256 in bitcoin mining the message has a fixed length of 640 bits which requires two applications of the compression function. In the second application SHA-256 is applied to 256 bits.

It may therefore seem that a bitcoin miner needs to compute the compression function 3.0 times for each nonce and for each Merkle hash. In the following sections we are going to work on reducing this figure down to about 1.89.

We recall from Section 2.1 that new bitcoins can be created when the miner succeeds to hash some data from the bitcoin network together with a 32-bit random nonce and is able to obtain a number on 256 bits which starts with a certain number of 64 or more zeros. We called it **C**onstrained **I**nput **S**mall **O**utput problem or shortly the CISO problem, cf. Fig. 1. The process needs to be iterated with different values of MerkleRoot and different 32-bit nonces until a suitable "CISO configuration" is found in which the output satisfies $H2 <$ `target` as explained in Section 2.3.

3.1   Improvement 1: Remove First Compression Function

We can reduce the cost factor from 3.0 to 2.0 almost instantly by making the following observation. In the process of bitcoin mining the first compression function does **not** depend on the random nonce on 32 bits. Therefore we can compute it once every 2^{32} nonces. On average we need:

$$2.0 + \frac{1}{2^{32}} \tag{2}$$

compression functions. The added factor is the amortized cost of the first hash and can be neglected.

Discussion. In more advanced bitcoin mining algorithms the miner does **not** have to compute the output for every nonce. He can do it only for some well chosen nonces. They may be chosen in such a way as in order to obtain specific values which make the computation easier. Moreover, some well chosen nonces could be generated in some specific order in order to enable incremental computations. In an incremental computation some computations could made easier by reusing all the (known) internal values in one or several previous computations. There is a lot of highly non-trivial optimizations which can be developed. One simple example of incremental computation will be given in Section 3.4, another in Section 3.9.

3.2   Improvement 2: Save 3 Rounds at the End

We look at the computation of H2 on Fig. 1. The second computation of the hash function and the third compression function. A close examination reveals that in the last rounds of the underlying block cipher the two words on 32 bits in which we want to have at least 64 zeros, after addition of a suitable constant, are created at rounds 60 and 61 if we number from 0. We basically want to force values created at rounds $t = 60$ and 61 to two fixed constants which come from the SHA-256 IV constants, and which would produce zeros at the output. For this most of the time we just need to compute the first 61 rounds out of 64 and we can early reject most cases. Only in $1/2^{32}$ of cases we need to compute 62 rounds in the third compression function. Then only in some $1/2^{64}$ of cases where we have actually obtained at least 64 zeros, we would need compute the full 64 rounds. Thus overall one only needs to compute the whole compression function an equivalent of very roughly $1 + 61/64 \approx 1.95$ times on average. Most of the time one only needs to compute H1 and 61 rounds of H2 to early reject the 32-bit value obtained which must be equal to the IV constant.

3.3   Improvement 3: Gain Three Rounds at the Beginning

Now we look at the second computation of the hash function in the second compression function, the computation of H1 on Fig. 1. Here we use the observation that in SHA-256 the key for the first 16 rounds are exactly the 16 message blocks in the same order, cf. [15] and Algorithm [1]. It is possible that in the second compression function on Fig. 1 the nonce enters at round 3 (numbered from 0) and therefore in most cases we just need to compute the last 61 out of 64 rounds of the block cipher. The first three rounds are the same for every nonce and their (amortized) cost is nearly zero.

3.4   Improvement 4: Incremental Calculations in Round 3

This improvement requires us to delve more deeply into the structure of the block cipher inside SHA-256. We recall that the state of the cipher after round 2 is constant and does not yet depend on the value of the nonce. The 32-bit nonce will be precisely copied to become the session key for the round 3 of encryption. In the lower-left corner of Fig. 1 we show the circuit for one round of encryption where at round 3 the nonce enters as $W_3 = $ nonce as shown on later in Table 1. Here $\boxplus$ denotes one addition on 32 bits.

W_t is the key derived from the message and K_t is a certain constant [15]. For $t = 3$ we have $W_3 = $ nonce. Now it is obvious that the whole round 3 can be computed essentially for free in the incremental way. We just need two 32-bit increments instead of one whole round which is about 7 additions and 4 other 32-bit operations. Each time we increment the nonce we simply need to increment two values Thus we have saved one more round in each of our computations.

3.5   Improvement 5: Exploiting Zeros and Constants in the Key

The next improvement comes from the fact that the key in the first 16 rounds of the block cipher is an exact copy of the message. Many parts of this key are constants. Many are actually always equal to zero. This allows one to save a lot of additions in the computation of SHA-256.

3.6   Improvement 6: Saving Two More Additions with Hard Coding

It is easy to see that 2 more additions can be saved. Looking at Table 1 we should not count the three first constants on the left in yellow which are identical for all the 2^{32} different nonces. This is because this saving was already done in Section 3.3. However we have two additional constants in the last line in green. Then in these two last rounds, one in each computation, and because the K_t are constants and do not depend on the message being hashed, we can pre-compute the constants $KW_t = K_t \boxplus W_t$ on 32 bits which saves us 2 additions.

Remark 1. In Section 3.5 above and here in Section 3.6 we saved 18+2 additions. However these savings are illusory, because we can **save many more additions** by another method. On Fig. 3 we show that one only needs essentially 2 additions in order to implement the whole round function of SHA256, this instead of 6+1 full adders in each compression function cf. Fig. 1.

We are going to use Carry Save Adders (CSA) in order to delay the propagation of carries and save a lot of circuit area. The main idea which is attributed to

Table 1. Key in the first 16 rounds out of 64 in each computation and their provenance

Computation of $H1$			Computation of $H2$		
Round t	32 bit W_t	Description	Round t	32 bit W_t	Description
0	XXXXXXXX	last 32 bits of hash Markle Root	0	XXXXXXXX	$H1_0$
1	XXXXXXXX	timestamp	1	XXXXXXXX	$H1_1$
2	XXXXXXXX	target	2	XXXXXXXX	$H1_2$
		nonce (00000000	3	XXXXXXXX	$H1_3$
3	XXXXXXXX	to FFFFFFFF)	4	XXXXXXXX	$H1_4$
4	0x80000000	Padding starts	5	XXXXXXXX	$H1_5$
5	0x00000000		6	XXXXXXXX	$H1_6$
6	0x00000000		7	XXXXXXXX	$H1_7$
7	0x00000000				Padding
8	0x00000000		8	0x80000000	starts
9	0x00000000		9	0x00000000	
10	0x00000000		10	0x00000000	
11	0x00000000		11	0x00000000	
12	0x00000000		12	0x00000000	
13	0x00000000	Padding ends			Padding ends
14	0x00000000	length H	13	0x00000000	length H
15	0x00000280	length L	14	0x00000000	
			15	0x00000100	length L

John von Neumann, is to propagate the carries only locally delaying a complete propagation to the very end. This allows a dramatic reduction in the cost of implementing multiple additions: three or more additions do NOT cost much more than one single addition.

More precisely Carry Save Adders (CSA) allow to add n numbers for any $n \geq 3$ and to form two numbers which need to be added to obtain the final result. This is obtained by a successive transformation of 3 numbers into 2 numbers with a Carry Save Adder (CSA) which has a very low cost and a final addition of 2 numbers. A Carry Save Adder takes 3 integers a, b, c on k bits written in binary and outputs two numbers ps (partial sum) and sc (shift-carry) as follows:

$$
\begin{aligned}
ps_i &= a_i \oplus b_i \oplus c_i , \\
sc_{i+1} &= a_i b_i \vee a_i c_i \vee b_i c_i .
\end{aligned}
\tag{3}
$$

In the case of addition modulo 2^k there is a slight simplification as the most significant digits can be discarded but the result remains essentially the same.

Overall the application of Carry Save Adders (CSA) allows us to implement each round of SHA256 with only two full additions cf. Fig. 3.

Now we are also going to look beyond the 64 rounds of SHA256 seen as a block cipher. What remains is the key expansion which expands the message to be hashed into the 64x32 bit keys W_t.

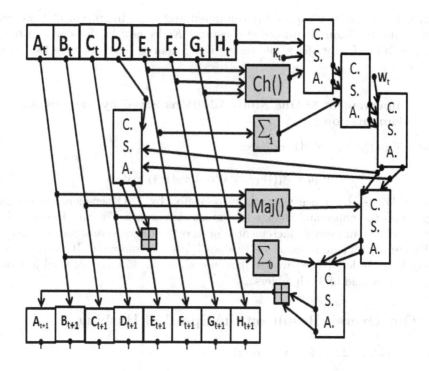

Fig. 3. How to compute one round of SHA-256 with just two full adders

3.7   Short Description of Message Expansion in SHA-256

Before we can propose additional optimizations, we need to explain how the
message expansion works in the NIST specification of SHA-256 [15]. We refer to
[15] for definitions of σ_0 and σ_1.

Algorithm 1. The message scheduler expanding a 512 message block into a
2048-bit key for the SHA-256 block cipher.

---

for $0 \leq t \leq 15$ **do**
   $W_t = M_t$
end for
for $16 \leq t \leq 63$ **do**
   $W_t = \sigma_1(W_{t-2}) \boxplus W_{t-7} \boxplus \sigma_0(W_{t-15}) \boxplus W_{t-16}$
end for

3.8   Improvement 7: Saving Two More Additions

We consider the computation of H1. It is possible to see that the first two non-
trivial keys W_{16} and W_{17} are also constants and do not yet depend on the

nonce. Therefore they can be pre-computed and as in Improvement 6 we can replace the traditional hard-coded constants K_t by new hard-coded constants $KW_t = W_t \boxplus K_t$ for the whole range of 2^{32} nonces. Thus we save two more additions.

3.9 Improvement 8: One More Additions Saved by Incremental Computation

Now still in the case of H1 we have:

$$W_{19} = \sigma_1(W_{17}) \boxplus W_{11} \boxplus \sigma_0(W_4) \boxplus W_3 . \tag{4}$$

Here W_3 is the nonce which is incremented by 1. Other elements do not depend on the nonce and change at a much slower rate. We can thus save one more addition and simply increment W_{19} directly for each consecutive nonce.

Summary: There remains 48-3 values W_t to be computed. If we use again Carry Save Adders (CSA) we see that in each of the 45 cases we need just one full adder instead of 3 full adders.

4   Our Overall Result on the Speed of Hashing

We have obtained the following result:

Theorem 1. *[Hash Speed] The amortized average cost of trying one output H2 to see if it has 64 or more leading zeros is at most about 1.89 computations of the compression function of SHA-256 instead of 3.0, which represents an improvement by 37%.*   □

Justification: We have saved about 7 rounds and many additions. However known ASIC implementations also save many additions and actually the designs which achieve the lowest possible area are not necessarily the fastest. Therefore we are just going to estimate the RELATIVE savings w.r.t. best standard ASIC implementations of full SHA256 such as in [5,12,13,16,17,18,19,20,21,25,29,30]. Thus overall cost minus savings are equivalent to a total of

$$\frac{64 + 64}{64} - \frac{7}{64} = 2 - \frac{7}{64} \approx 1.89 \tag{5}$$

compression functions.

This 1.89 compression functions is equivalent to saving of 37% compared to the initial cost of 3.0 compression functions as per Fig. 1. It also shows how much can be gained in bitcoin mining compared to using an optimized SHA256 ASIC implementation three times.

Remark 2. Our problem is essentially the same as a brute force attack on a block cipher. The same computation is done a very large number of times, yet cheaper, maybe just a small factor cheaper. It is not correct to believe that block ciphers are well understood in cryptography. On the contrary, it appears that for more or less any block cipher there may exist an attack which will be just slightly faster than brute force, see [24]. An efficient low-data software algebraic attack could also be a solution to this problem, cf. [10,23,28].

5 Conclusion

In this paper we explain how bitcoin electronic currency works and show that the profitability of bitcoin mining depends on a certain cryptographic constant which we showed to be at most 1.89. Normally very few people care about this sort of fine cryptographic engineering details. However here it is different. This observation allows bitcoin miners to save many millions of dollars each year.

References

1. Aumasson, J.-P., Khovratovich, D.: First Analysis of Keccak (2009), http://131002.net/data/papers/AK09.pdf
2. Barber, S., Boyen, X., Shi, E., Uzun, E.: Bitter to Better — How to Make Bitcoin a Better Currency. In: Keromytis, A.D. (ed.) FC 2012. LNCS, vol. 7397, pp. 399–414. Springer, Heidelberg (2012)
3. Nakamoto, S., et al.: Bitcoin QT: http://bitcoin.org/en/download
4. Boyar, J., Matthews, P., Peralta, R.: Logic Minimization Techniques with Applications to Cryptology. Journal of Cryptology 26, 280–312 (2013)
5. Chaves, R., Kuzmanov, G., Sousa, L., Vassiliadis, S.: Improving SHA-2 hardware implementations. In: Goubin, L., Matsui, M. (eds.) CHES 2006. LNCS, vol. 4249, pp. 298–310. Springer, Heidelberg (2006)
6. Courtois, N.T., Hulme, D., Mourouzis, T.: Solving Circuit Optimisation Problems in Cryptography and Cryptanalysis. In: Proceedings of SHARCS 2012 Workshop, UK, pp. 179–191 (2011)
7. Courtois, N.T., Hulme, D., Mourouzis, T.: Multiplicative Complexity and Solving Generalized Brent Equations With SAT Solvers. In: COMPUTATION TOOLS 2012, The Third International Conference on Computational Logics, Algebras, Programming, Tools, and Benchmarking. ARIA, Nice (2012)
8. Courtois, N.T., Grajek, M., Naik, R.: The Unreasonable Fundamental Incertitudes Behind Bitcoin Mining (2013), http://arxiv.org/abs/1310.7935
9. Courtois, N.T., Bahack, L.: On Subversive Miner Strategies and Block Withholding Attack in Bitcoin Digital Currency (2014), http://arxiv.org/abs/1402.1718
10. Courtois, N.T., Bard, G.V.: Algebraic Cryptanalysis of the Data Encryption Standard. In: Galbraith, S.D. (ed.) Cryptography and Coding 2007. LNCS, vol. 4887, pp. 152–169. Springer, Heidelberg (2007)
11. Courtois, N.T., Mourouzis, T.: Black-Box Collision Attacks on the Compression Function of the GOST Hash Function. In: Proceedings of 6th International Conference on Security and Cryptography SECRYPT, Spain (2011)
12. Dadda, L., Macchetti, M., Jeff Owen, J.: An ASIC design for a high speed implementation of the hash function SHA-256 384, 512. In: ACM Great Lakes Symposium on VLSI, pp. 421–425. ACM (2004)
13. Dadda, L., Macchetti, M., Owen, J.: The Design of a High Speed ASIC Unit for the Hash Function SHA-256 (384, 512). In: DATE 2004, pp. 70–75. IEEE (2004)

14. Virtual currencies: Mining digital gold, From the print edition: Finance and economics, The Economist (2013)
15. National Institute of Standards and Technology (NIST). FIPS PUB 180-2, SHA256 Standard (2002),
    http://csrc.nist.gov/publications/fips/
    fips180-2/fips180-2withchangenotice.pdf
16. Feldhofer, M., Rechberger, C.: A Case Against Currently Used Hash Functions in RFID Protocols. In: Meersman, R., Tari, Z., Herrero, P. (eds.) OTM 2006 Workshops. LNCS, vol. 4277, pp. 372–381. Springer, Heidelberg (2006)
17. Knezevic, M.: Efficient Hardware Implementations of Cryptographic Primitives. PhD thesis, Katholieke Universiteit Leuven (2011)
18. Lee, Y.K., Chan, H., Verbauwhede, I.: Iteration bound analysis and throughput optimum architecture of SHA-256 (384,512) for hardware implementations. In: Kim, S., Yung, M., Lee, H.-W. (eds.) WISA 2007. LNCS, vol. 4867, pp. 102–114. Springer, Heidelberg (2008)
19. Macchetti, M., Dadda, L.: Quasi-Pipelined Hash Circuits. In: IEEE Symposium on Computer Arithmetic, pp. 222–229 (2005)
20. Michail, H.E., Athanasiou, G., Kritikakou, A., Goutis, C.E., Gregoriades, A., Papadopoulou, V.G.: Ultra High Speed SHA-256 Hashing Cryptographic Module for IPSec Hardware/Software Codesign. In: SECRYPT, pp. 309–313 (2010)
21. Michail, H.E., Athanasiou, G., Gregoriades, A., Panagiotou, C.L., Goutis, C.E.: High Throughput Hardware/Software Co-design Approach SHA-256 Hashing Cryptographic Module. Global Journal of Computer Science and Technology 10, 15 (2010)
22. Guo, J., Matusiewicz, K.: Preimages for Step-Reduced SHA-2 (2008),
    http://eprint.iacr.org/2009/477.pdf
23. Heusser, J.: SAT solving - An alternative to brute force bitcoin mining (2013),
    http://jheusser.github.io/2013/02/03/satcoin.html
24. Huang, J., Lai, X.: What is the Effective Key Length for a Block Cipher: an Attack on Every Block Cipher (2012), http://eprint.iacr.org/2012/677
25. Kim, M., Ryou, J., Jun, S.: Efficient Hardware Architecture of SHA-256 Algorithm for Trusted Mobile Computing. In: Yung, M., Liu, P., Lin, D. (eds.) Inscrypt 2008. LNCS, vol. 5487, pp. 240–252. Springer, Heidelberg (2009)
26. Matusiewicz, K., Pieprzyk, J., Pramstaller, N.: Rechberger, Ch., Rijmen, V.: Analysis of simplified variants of SHA-256:
    http://www2.mat.dtu.dk/people/K.Matusiewicz/papers/SimplifiedSHA256.pdf
27. Nakamoto, S.: Bitcoin: A Peer-to-Peer Electronic Cash System:
    http://bitcoin.org/bitcoin.pdf
28. Raddum, H., Semaev, I.: New Technique for Solving Sparse Equation Systems. In: ECRYPT STVL (2006), http://eprint.iacr.org/2006/475/
29. Sklavos, N., Koufopavlou, O.G.: On the hardware implementations of the SHA-2 (256, 384, 512) hash functions. ISCAS 5, 153–156 (2003)
30. Tillich, S., Feldhofer, M., Kirschbaum, M., Plos, T., Schmidt, J.-M., Alexander Szekely, A.: Uniform Evaluation of Hardware Implementations of the Round-Two SHA-3 Candidates. In: Second SHA-3 Conference (2010),
    http://csrc.nist.gov/groups/ST/hash/sha-3/Round2/
    Aug2010/documents/papers/TILLICH_sha3hw.pdf

Protocol for Detection of Counterfeit Transactions in Electronic Currency Exchange

Marek R. Ogiela and Piotr Sułkowski

AGH University of Science and Technology,
Cryptography and Cognitive Informatics Research Group,
30-059 Krakow, Al. Mickiewicza 30, Poland
mogiela@agh.edu.pl, piotr.sulkowski@o2.pl

Abstract. This paper reveals a possible attack on the well-known protocol for anonymous currency exchange by David Chaum et al. We show that there is a possibility to spend a single coin many times, so that the bank does not have absolute certainity about a real abuser. In such a case the bank can determine a small group of potential abusers, but cannot indicate a specific person. This potential situation has serious consequences and leads to the conclusion that the system should not be used for irreversible off-line transactions. We also present a modification which could prevent that kind of attacks and enable the protocol to be used for off-line transactions without regard to the reversability.

Keywords: electronic cash, anonymous transaction, protocols for exchanging electronic coins.

1 Introduction

Today, the electronic banking is very popular and it seems that it is going to replace the traditional paper cash soon. However, currently there is no easy way to perform a non-cash payment that could be used privately. All electronic payments are carried through banks or electronic card companies, which are able to trace any transaction with all its details. Although, it may have both positive and negative consequences, it could be desirable to enable users to make anonymous transactions. Such systems are usually called digital cash systems. One of the solutions, which recently gains popularity, consists in creating a distributed system without any central bank or authority. Such distributed system must be based on virtual currency, which is a very important side effect. Currently, there is such a system called Bitcoin [15]. It was created in 2009 and by now it is a fully functional world-wide system. Another option is to create a centralized system which uses some special protocols to ensure untraceability. Usually there is a bank generating digital banknotes and distributing them to its clients. Subsequently, the clients spend their digital cash in shops and later the shops communicate with the bank to exchange the collected digital notes for real money. This general scheme is sometimes slightly modified, but usually solutions are based on this approach. The main problem of such systems is how

Z. Kotulski et al. (Eds.): CSS 2014, CCIS 448, pp. 145–152, 2014.
© Springer-Verlag Berlin Heidelberg 2014

to guarantee anonymity to the users, restrain them from creating cheques on their own or copy and spend multiple times the same cheque. The first protocol to overcome those problems was David Chaum's et al. system described in [3,4]. It was developed more than 20 years ago and has been improved and modified many times, e.g. [1], [2], [5], [6], [8], [10], but it is still a reference example of a digital cash system [7], [10], [13], [14]. This publication is focused exclusively on this classic system. We present a flaw which could be used to spend one coin multiple times without leaving proof of the theft. The presented attack leaves a possibility of distinguishing a group of potential abusers. Nevertheless, the bank is not able to proove the theft to any of them. We also present a modification to the system which makes such attacks impossible.

2 Chaum's Protocol and Limitations of this System

The basic properties of this system are as follows:

1. A transaction can be concluded without the need to contact the bank at the time of its conclusion.
2. No need to use any special tamper-proof devices or cards.
3. Transactions are anonymous if the client behaves honestly.
4. The security of every party is guaranteed even if the remaining two parties act in collusion against it.

Apart from these properties, certain risks to the parties using this system may also arise. The main ones are: the same banknote being spent many times, counterfeit banknotes being made and the loss of the client's anonymity. Let us then consider a case in which the client tries to spend a banknote several times. In this case, the risk to the bank and the seller depends greatly on the strategy of action chosen. There are at least two different options:

(A) In exchange for every banknote correctly presented by the seller, the bank pays money out, even if the client has spent this banknote several times. The client is then obliged to pay for all transactions concluded.
(B) If it is detected that a banknote has been used several times, no funds are credited to the seller's account. The seller is only given the personal data of the dishonest client. It is then the seller who must reverse the transaction and possibly claim damages.

Adopting strategy B makes the system a soft one, so all the risk rests with the seller. If the seller incurs any costs of the transaction, it must charge them to the client itself. The limitations resulting from selecting strategy B are a reason to adopt strategy A. This solution implies that the bank is responsible for prosecuting dishonest clients. However, it is difficult to claim the amount due from clients. One can imagine a situation in which a person with an average income spends one banknote worth one dollar one million times. The bank has to pay a million dollars to sellers. However, it stands no realistic chance to recover this amount due from the client. Another problem is banknote theft. The thief can spend the stolen banknotes many times, each time charging the account of the client it has stolen them from. Consequently, strategy A gives rise to a greater risk of the bank and the client. Under the B strategy, the risk is mainly borne by the seller. True enough, strategy B restricts the functionality. If a system fulfils all the conditions for strategy A to be adopted, it can also operate according to strategy B. In the opposite case, it is necessary to introduce a mechanism for proving the sale. Let us thus consider whether the presented system is ready to operate correctly under the A strategy. Let us consider the following scenario. A client, intending to commit a fraud, spends a banknote exactly twice. The injured sellers can now secretly exchange the received information. Assuming that their challenges $Y1$ and $Y2$ differ in m bits, they can jointly generate as many as 2^m different combinations of transaction certificates. It is enough that they combine a part of one certificate with a part of the other. A new transaction certificate is thus produced. In this situation, the sellers have certificates of transactions which have never taken place. They can then approach the bank claiming that they have been cheated many times and the bank cannot establish how many times it was really the client cheating, and how many times the sellers. The bank cannot establish what amount the client has really spent, and therefore cannot demand compensation from the client. This situation makes the bank unable to accept the strategy of guaranteed disbursements in this system. The bank is forced to guarantee only to reveal the identity of dishonest clients. In the majority of frauds, it will probably be possible to charge double the amount of the transaction to the client, but it must be emphasised that if this method is the only one used, this can never be guaranteed. Hence the seller cannot rely on the regularity of the banknote itself until he cashes it with the bank. The above example thus shows that Chaum's et al. system is only capable of executing fully reversible transactions without a guarantee that damages will be received if a fraud is committed.

3   A Proposed Enhancement to the Protocol Supporting Multiple Transaction Detection

In order to enhance Chaum's et al. system so that irreversible offline transactions can be concluded, it is necessary to introduce the ability to prove all transactions concluded. This will make it possible to claim compensation if the same banknote is spent more than once. To this end, it is necessary to change the certificates issued by the clients in such a way that sellers cannot generate new ones based on any number of those already held. We therefore propose modification of the protocol in which clients sign all the challenges received from sellers and send them together with certificates. However, if they used their own key for signing, they would cease to be anonymous. It is therefore necessary to apply a one-time key which should be tied to the real key of the client somehow. One of the possible ways is to attach it to the banknote together with its certificate signed by the client (the structure of the banknote is presented in Fig. 1). In the original protocol, banknotes consist of pairs P_i. The modified protocol adds the one-time key to each pair, making it a triplet. The triplets are as follows:

$$T_i = (h(a_i, c_i), h(a_i \oplus (u \parallel C(K_i)), d_i), K_i) \,, \tag{1}$$

where:

a_i, c_i, d_i - random numbers chosen by the client

u – the unique ID of the client

K_i – public one-time RSA key generated by the client. This can be written e.g. as $(e \parallel n)$, where e is the public exponent of this key, while n is its module

C – the client's certificate employed to sign all K_i keys. This can be e.g. the number $h(K)^d$ mod m, where the numbers (d, m) constitute the private part of the RSA key published by the client (the so-called main key)

Before starting to create banknotes, the clients must register their main public keys with the bank [13]. It is best if clients use keys certified by a certain certification authority. The keys are registered only once for each client, at the time their account is created.

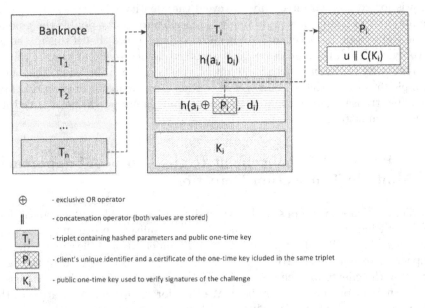

Fig. 1. Banknote in the modified protocol

The protocol of creating the banknote, in which the bank and the client are involved, is similar to the original version. The client sends to the bank $2*n$ obfuscated banknotes, from which the bank chooses one half and asks the client to remove the obfuscation from them. Having received all the necessary coefficients, the bank checks the regularity of the banknotes by comparing previously sent hashed banknotes with self-computed hashes of received coefficients. At this moment, the bank must assure itself that all certificates $C(K_i)$ contained in the sent banknotes are the correct certificates of keys K_i, i.e. they apply to the key K_i contained in the subsequent part of the banknote and they have been signed with the client's main key (which the bank holds in its database). If everything is correct, then the bank sends the signed banknote to the client. Thus the client, having removed the obfuscation, has the following number:

$$Z = \prod h(T_i)^d \, mod \; n, i \in L \;, \tag{2}$$

where:

d – the private exponent of the bank key
n – the bank signature module
L – a set of indices of banknotes selected for signing by the bank

The difference between the original protocol and the modified version consist in the fact that the banknote contains triplets with public keys instead of pairs without them. Additionally, in the original version the bank does not have to check the certificates $C(K_i)$. The idea of this entire improvement is that every transaction executed by the client should leave a unique trace that cannot be faked. To obtain this functionality of the protocol, the client signs the challenge sent to it by the seller using the K_i keys contained in the banknotes. The protocol for the banknote exchange between the client and the seller (presented in Fig. 2) thus looks as follows:

1. The client sends the banknote Z signed by the bank.
2. The client also sends the T_i triplets (i.e. the values $h(a_i, c_i), h(a_i \oplus (u \; \| \; C(K_i)), d_i)$ and K_i.
3. The seller checks whether banknote Z is the correct signature of the signed triplets.
4. The seller sends the challenge Y to the client.
5. The client provides the seller with the value of the challenge Y signed with all one-time keys K_i: $R = K_1(K_2 \ldots (K_n(Y) \ldots))$
   where:

   $K_i(x)$ – the signature of the value x with the use of the key K_i

6. The seller verifies the validity of the signature R.
7. The client provides the seller, respectively, with the values (a_i, c_i) or $(a_i \oplus (u \; \| \; C(K_i)), d_i)$ depending on the value of the $i - th$ bit of challenge Y (just as in the previous version of the protocol)
8. The seller checks whether the data sent corresponds to the hashes contained in triplets T_i. If everything is correct, the payment is accepted.

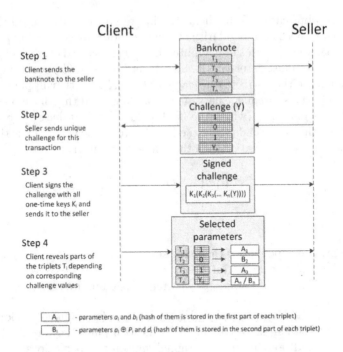

Fig. 2. The electronic coin exchange protocol between the client and the seller

In order to cash the banknote, at whatever moment, the seller presents the bank with the signed banknote Z, the sequence of triplets T_i, the generated challenge Y together with the signature R and all the values dependent on this challenge sent by the client. The bank is able to check the regularity of all data in the same way as the seller was able to when it exchanged the banknote with the client. Just as in the standard version of the protocol, after spending the banknote once, the client reveals only one half of each liability. At the same time, if the same banknote has been spent at least twice, the bank is highly likely to possess two complementary halves, but thanks to the modification it will learn not only the client's identity, but also at least one of the certificates $C(K_i)$. Thus the bank becomes able to prove to the client that it has spent a banknote more than once. This is because every transaction is signed by the client with all keys K_i. At the time of the fraud, the bank not only knows the identity of the client, but also holds at least one set containing the liability signed with a certain one-time key and the client's certificate authenticating this key. If the bank is able to provide the client with the signature R of a given challenge Y and to prove to it that the signature belongs to the client, this transaction can be considered proven. This is because no one other than the client can create the certificate for the key K_i used to sign the challenge. Neither can anyone fake this signature as the banknote only contains the public part of it.

If the client spends banknotes only once, then it is impossible to learn either its ID u, or any of the certificates $C(K_i)$. This certificate, together with the key

K_i, could also be used to identify the client. It is enough that the bank tries to verify this certificate by using all main keys of clients it holds in its database. One of them would probably be correct. This could be the basis for discovering the identity of the client, so certificates must be also kept secret until a fraud occurs. What is, however, overt is the key K_i itself. It is created randomly by the client and contains no information that could identify it.

After this solution is implemented, the bank is able to prove exactly how much the client has spent. Consequently (assuming that it is able to recover this receivable from the client by the way of effective collection), it can adopt the strategy of paying funds to all sellers who present correct transaction certificates. Thus the system makes offline transaction conclusion possible. What still remains is the problem of banknote theft. If a banknote ends up in the hands of an unauthorised person, it can be used to overdraw the owner's account without any limitation. To prevent this, once the client learns of the theft, it can report it to the bank so that the latter publishes a list of void banknotes. In addition, the bank itself, once it detects a double payment, can publicly report this banknote as stolen. On the other hand, if we assume that transactions are concluded without contacting the bank, we can never eliminate this problem completely. However, the same difficulty arises in the digital signature scheme itself. The problem can be eliminated if, every time before we start receiving a digital signature, we refer to a public database to check if the signature has not been stolen. However, if we decide to build a system which accepts signatures offline - without contacting a public database of stolen signatures – we can never be certain that the signature has not been stolen. If the risk of theft is considered to be too high, it is always possible to fall back on the strategy of concluding only irreversible transactions. Apart from capacity issues, the proposed modification does not weaken the original system in any way.

4   Conclusions

The system presented by David Chaum et al. in [4] is the first system capable of processing anonymous transactions offline and representing a ground-breaking discovery in the field of anonymous electronic payments. However, if the same banknote is spent at least twice by the client, the system becomes susceptible to attacks both by cheated sellers and the client itself. This weakness means it cannot be used to conclude irreversible transactions. The same problem also applies to other systems based on a similar protocol. The introduction of the modification proposed by the authors allows such attacks to be prevented and makes it possible to conclude hard transactions as well. At present there is no widely used electronic cash system based on the electronic cheque scheme, but there are no obstacles to building one. What is necessary is a certain surcharge of calculations for every transaction as well as the suitably greater storage resources which will allow data about used up banknotes to be stored for a long time. Solutions described in publication [6] allow the necessary resources to be significantly reduced. It seems that, sooner or later, electronic cash technology will gain in popularity and will start replacing traditional credit cards and bank transfers. This is very probable, as otherwise the banks would obtain huge amounts of confidential information about their customers. However, maintaining secrecy is crucial for the security and development of many companies, which will therefore be happy to use this new solution to mitigate the risk of losing data [11,12].

Acknowledgments. This work has been supported by the National Science Centre, Republic of Poland, under project number DEC-2013/09/B/HS4/00501.

References

1. Brands, S.: Untraceable Off-line Cash in Wallets with Observers. In: Stinson, D.R. (ed.) CRYPTO 1993. LNCS, vol. 773, pp. 302–318. Springer, Heidelberg (1994)
2. Brands, S.: Off-Line Electronic Cash Based on Secret-Key Certificates. In: Baeza-Yates, R., Poblete, P.V., Goles, E. (eds.) LATIN 1995. LNCS, vol. 911, pp. 131–166. Springer, Heidelberg (1995)
3. Chaum, D.: Blind Signatures for Untraceable Payments. In: Advances in Cryptology: Proceedings of Crypto 1982, pp. 199–203. Springer (1983)
4. Chaum, D., Fiat, A., Naor, M.: Untraceable Electronic Cash. In: Goldwasser, S. (ed.) CRYPTO 1988. LNCS, vol. 403, pp. 319–327. Springer, Heidelberg (1990)
5. Deng, R.H., Han, Y., Jeng, A.B., Ngair, T.: A new on-line cash check scheme. In: Proceedings of the 4th ACM Conference on Computer and Communications Security, pp. 111–116. ACM (1997)
6. Ferguson, N.: Single term off-line coins. In: Helleseth, T. (ed.) EUROCRYPT 1993. LNCS, vol. 765, pp. 318–328. Springer, Heidelberg (1994)
7. Goldwasser, S., Bellare, M.: Lecture Notes on Cryptography, Cambridge (2008)
8. Kim, S., Oh, H.: A new electronic check system with reusable refunds. International Journal of Information Security 1(3), 175–188 (2002)
9. Mao, W.: Blind Certification of Public Keys and Off-line Electronic Cash. Hawlett-Packard Laboratories (1996)
10. Menezes, A.J., van Oorschot, P.C., Vanstone, S.A.: Handbook of Applied Cryptography. CRC Press (1996)
11. Ogiela, M.R., Ogiela, U.: Linguistic Protocols for Secure Information Management and Sharing. Computers and Mathematics with Applications 63(2), 564–572 (2012)
12. Ogiela, M.R., Ogiela, U.: Secure Information Management using Linguistic Threshold Approach. Advanced Information and Knowledge Processing. Springer, London (2014), doi:10.1007/978-1-4471-5016-9, ISSN 1610-3947, ISBN: 978-1-4471-5015-2
13. Schneier, B.: Applied Cryptography: Protocols, Algorithms, and Source Code in C. Wiley (1996)
14. Schneier, B.: Secrets and Lies: Digital Security in a Networked World. Wiley (2004)
15. Website of Bitcoin foundation developing virtual currency with the same name, http://bitcoin.org

Practical Authentication Protocols for Protecting and Sharing Sensitive Information on Mobile Devices

Imed El Fray[1], Tomasz Hyla[1], Mirosław Kurkowski[2],
Witold Maćków[1], and Jerzy Pejaś[1]

[1] West Pomeranian University of Technology,
Faculty of Computer Science and Information Technology,
Szczecin, Poland
{ielfray,thyla,wmackow,jpejas}@zut.edu.pl

[2] University of Luxembourg, Computer Science and Communication Group,
6, rue Richard Coudenhove-Kalergi, 1359 Luxembourg, Luxembourg
miroslaw.kurkowski@uni.lu

Abstract. Mobility of users and information is an important feature of IT systems that must be considered during design of sensitive information protection mechanisms. This paper describes an architecture of MobInfoSec system for sharing documents with sensitive information using fine-grained access rules described by general access structures. However, the proper usage of general access structures requires trusted components and strong authentication protocols. They allow to establish secure communication channels between different system components. In the paper we propose a conference protocol based on Boyd's ideas with key transport and key establishment mechanisms. We show that the protocol achieves three goals: (a) the key and participants' mutual authentication, (b) the common secure communication channel, and (c) the personal secure communication channels between the protocol initializer and other protocol participants.

Keywords: mobile device, sensitive information, authentication protocols, conference protocol, secure communication channel.

1 Introduction

As more and more information within organisations is created, stored and shared electronically, the issue of protecting, sharing and archiving sensitive information has become a major concern. Shared information is often stored in the network and downloaded on mobile devices when they are needed. The information should be stored in an encrypted form at a fine-grained level to reduce the risks and vulnerabilities associated with information security, i.e., anonymity, privacy, information retrieval, loss, theft and interception. Such a solution is based on cryptographic access control mechanisms and is typically implemented in two stages [1,2]. At the first stage the information is encrypted (according to

Z. Kotulski et al. (Eds.): CSS 2014, CCIS 448, pp. 153–165, 2014.
© Springer-Verlag Berlin Heidelberg 2014

some pre-defined access control policy) and is made available on a public server. At the second stage the encrypted information can be collected by any entity. However, the information can be read only by an entity that meets the requirements specified in the access policy related to the encrypted information. Usually, the access policy requires a well-known group of participants who cooperatively try to decrypt a ciphertext. A group decryption process must be preceded by strong mutual authentication of all group members. The authentication process is initiated by an entity U_0 (called the chairman). The chairman is interested in deciphering the information downloaded from the network. If deciphering requires cooperation of $(n+1)$ entities $U_0, U_1, \ldots, U_n$ (participants of a group U), then authentication is not an easy task. In such a situation it is required to design authentication protocol that will be effective primarily in terms of running time. The natural solution to the problem is to use any two-party one-to-one authentication protocol (e.g., [3,4,5,6]). A chairman executes (sequentially or simultaneously) n times the one-to-one protocol with every other member from the group U. Successful completion of each protocol enables to authenticate every pair of users (U_0, U_i), $i = 1, \ldots, n$, and to establish n independent secure communication channels between them. This type of simple generalization of two-party protocols to the multi-party situation (especially for large group of participants) may be too expensive, in terms of both communications and computation, because each principal needs to receive and verify explicit authentication information from all other group members. Multi-party conference key agreement protocols are more advanced generalization of two-party protocols for establishing keys [1,6]. The protocols of this type are executed between entities belonging to a common group of entities (called the conference). However, the messages exchanged between the parties are authenticated only by the initiator of the protocol. On the one hand, this allows to reduce the time complexity of these protocols and enables to create a common secure communication channel, but on other hand, it does not ensure mutual authentication of an initiator with other group members.

1.1 Our Contributions

The first objective of this paper is to describe the general architecture of MobInfoSec system, which enables cryptographic protection of sensitive information in accordance with Originator Controlled (ORCON) access control rules [10,11]. The ORCON rules release a user from the obligation to monitor any information (especially against unauthorized copying). The information is removed when a user is no longer allowed to access it. The MobInfoSec needs the strong authentication between key components like secret protection modules. The definition of the MobInfoSec system, its properties and parameters allowed us to derive design goals for authentication protocol and achieve the second objective of this paper, i.e., the proposal of conference authentication protocol design for protecting and sharing sensitive information on mobile devices. The protocol summarizes the results from our previous work on authentication and key establishment protocols for different multi-party authentication models. We review the existing solutions and classify their suitability for protection of sensitive information in mobile devices. The result of this review is the proposal of multi-party key agreement protocol based on Boyd protocol idea [4,5,6,7]. The protocol allows the establishment of a common secure channel and enables mutual authentication of each pair of protocol participants (U_0, U_i), $i = 1, \ldots, n$. Additionally, personal secure communication channels are also established.

1.2   Paper Organisation

The remainder of this paper is organized as follows. In the next section we shortly describe the architecture of MobInfoSec system, its properties, components and their mutual relations. The same Section presents the identified trusted domains and authentications problem in MobInfoSec system. In Section 2.3 we derive design goals for authentication and key establishment protocols in MobInfoSec system and present comparison of selected protocols. Section 3 contains description of a new Boyd's based conference protocol and short discussion concerning its security. The paper ends with conclusions, including directions for our future investigations.

2   Background

2.1   MobInfoSec System

MobInfoSec is a distributed, modular, and configurable cryptographic access control system to sensitive information [1]. The system allows building confidence to software and hardware components of popular mobile devices available at the market. One of the most complex components that needs to be implemented properly to enable access control according to ORCON rules is a strong mutual authentication scheme between secret protection (SP) modules. In the MobInfoSec system the strong mutual authentication is required before any group decryption operation. Its main purpose is to create secure (trusted) communication channels between mobile devices (i.e., between SP modules inside mobile devices). MobInfoSec architecture (see Fig. 1 - the arrows use UML notation for labels) consists of several subsystems which are divided into three categories: subsystems working on server-side of the system (at service provider site), subsystems used by mobile users and external subsystems performing services used by MobInfoSec. The system consists of six logical subsystems connected with three subsystems in an external environment.

Server-side components. Policies and Assertions Management Subsystem (PAMS) contains several components that provide key features and can be divided into three categories. The first one is related to management of targeted access policies and their templates (generation, storage and distribution). The second group of functions is related to management of users and mobile devices.

The third category contains functions related to assertions (attributes) management. The subsystem only distributes the data to Standard Trusted Services (STS) and is not available directly for mobile devices. The STS is the source of that information via the trusted components providing the information from PAMS. Dispatcher Subsystem (DS) is used to generate targeted access policies and to encrypt documents with sensitive information in accordance with those policies. Generated policies are published in the repository located in STS. An encrypted document linked with a target access policy is published in External Subsystem in an untrusted document registry. **Mobile components.** User Subsystem (US) and Mobile Device Protection Subsystem (MDPS) are two logical subsystems that are located in Mobile Device. US is responsible for authentication and authorization of users and mobile devices, for distribution of access policies to mobile devices and it enforces access policy in the case of decryption. Additionally, there is located an application that presents the data subjected to access policy. The integrity of trusted applications sets is supervised by MDPS. MDPS through SP module provides specific cryptographic keys to the trusted code. The SP module is a source of trust (at various levels, depending on SP type). SP protects directly trusted US components implementing ORCON rules. **External components.** External PKI Services Subsystem provides services related to a public key infrastructure (PKI). Furthermore, External Model PKI Services Subsystem provides PKI services which are not available in External PKI and Cryptographic Services Subsystem and are necessary for the functioning of new algorithms and protocols developed especially for the MobInfoSec system. That subsystem is not a part of MobInfoSec system and belongs to its environment. External Systems subsystem contains untrusted mobile device that can be vulnerable for attempts tampering its integrity. The mobile device is a platform for placement of dispatcher or user subsystems. Another part of external systems is an untrusted document registry. The untrusted document registry contains encrypted documents. It might be public http or ftp server or service intended to store files in a cloud.

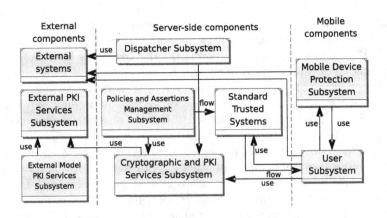

Fig. 1. MobInfoSec subsystems [1]

2.2   Trusted Domains and Authentications

MobInfoSec system can be treated as a set of distributed cooperating applications located in different network places (Fig. 2). Applications can be grouped according to the trust domain. A single domain is created around a trusted application or a group of trusted applications. Communication between applications in a single domain is secure, which may result, e.g., from the fact of deploying them in one location or the use of security technologies such as SSL. The problem that remains open is a communication between components located in different trust domains. The communication requires the creation of trusted paths and channels. The paths and channels created using strong cryptographic mechanisms allow applications from different trust domains to trust each other and mutually accept decisions.

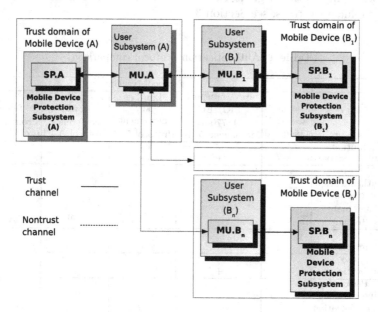

Fig. 2. Trust domains concept for different mobile devices

2.3   Basic Entity Authentication Protocols and a Key Establishment Protocols

Cryptographic authentication protocol depends primarily on the methods used to generate session keys and on the number of protocol participants (according to Boyd [7]). Generally MobInfoSec system requires secure communications between multiple entities. It is necessary to design protocols that establish keys for groups of principals to achieve such goal. In the MobInfoSec system the most important is a cryptographic authentication protocol implemented between SP components located in different trust domains. One of these domains (called a chairman) is the initiator of the protocol and should mutually authenticate with every other trust domain and establish secure communication channels.

Table 1 presents a few potentially useful protocols considered for MobInfoSec system and based on literature analysis [3,4], [6,7], [10]) compares their properties given in [4]. The most important are three groups of properties (in addition to confidentiality and integrity of keys): two or multi-party authentication, independent (personal) versus common communication channels and existence of a formal security proof. Protocols providing multi-party authentication are more effective (require fewer runs). However, they allow creating a common channel, which is not always beneficial from the specific application point of view. This is the case of MobInfoSec system, where communication channel are created for sending shadows to the initiator. The initiator is the only recipient of those messages and no other group member should have access to them. However, this problem can be solved, and it is possible to provide access to confidential information only to the originator of the protocol (at the expense of additional cryptographic operations, see Section 3).

Table 1. Authentication protocol comparison

No.	Property	Protocol (variant)				
		Transport RSA (EN 14890) [3]	Key transport ISO/IEC 11770-3 Mechanism 5 [10]	Lim-Lee key agreement Protocol 5 [6]	Boyd's conference protocol A [7]	Boyd's conference protocol B [4]
1.	Mutual authentication	+	+	+	−	−
2.	Multi-party authentication (one to many and many to one)	−	−	−	$+^{5)}$	$+^{5)}$
3.	Key integrity	+	+	+	+	+
4.	Key authentication	+	+	+	+	+
5.	Personal (independent) communication channels	$+^{1)}$	$+^{1)}$	$+^{1)}$	−	−
6.	Common communication channel	−	−	−	+	+
7.	Forward secrecy	−	−	−	−	−
8.	Backward secrecy	$N/A^{2)}$	N/A	N/A	−	−
9.	Liveness	$+^{3)}$	$+^{3)}$	+	+	+
10.	Key control	+	$+^{4)}$	+	+	+
11.	Key freshness	$+^{3)}$	$+^{3)}$	$+^{3)}$	$+^{4)}$	$+^{4)}$
12.	Key confirmation	+	+	+	$+^{5)}$	$+^{5)}$
13.	Formal security proof	+	$-^{6)}$	$-^{6)}$	+	+

Legend:

+ means that the protocol has indicated property, perhaps after meeting additional requirements presented in footnote

[1] It also applies to the case when the protocol is used to authenticate the initiator of the protocol with other members of the participants group

[2] N/A - not applicable

[3] Applies to all participants of the protocol

[4] Applies only to the initiator of the protocol

[5] If session key is used by all members of the group

[6] Lack of information about the existence of a formal security proof.

Considering the above facts and the existence of formal security proofs, for further work on authentication protocols in the MobInfoSec three protocols were adopted: RSA-based key transport protocol (according to EN 14890) and Boyd's conference protocols A and B. RSA-based key transport protocol is normally run by the two parties. Mutual authentication of protocol initiator with each of the n group members requires to initiate and perform n independent authentication protocols. Their successful completion allow to authenticate the protocols initiators with all the other participants and to establish n independent communication channels. Boyd's conference protocols in two variants (see Tab. 1) allow a chairman to establish a common communication channel with a certified key that can be established during running only one instance of the authentication protocol. Although it does not provide mutual authentication of the initiator with other participants in the protocol, this can be achieved after modifications introduced into the protocol presented in Section 3. Moreover, these modifications allow to achieve the independent communication channels, while there is still the common communication channel.

3   3 Conference Authentication Protocol Design

In this section the conference protocol SPs_Conference_Key_Agreement is presented, one of two designed especially for the MobInfoSec system. The main protocol purpose is mutual authentication of mobile devices, which are under control of a user A and users B_i, $i = 1, \ldots, n$, and establishment of secure communication channels. We assume that the user A is an initiator. In a typical use scenario of SPs_Conference_Key_Agreement a user A, (the owner of mobile device $UM.A$), needs to retrieve shadows of keys from devices $UM.B_i$, being under control of users B_i. Consequently, the restored key can be used to decrypt the document.

3.1 Notation and Assumptions

For the protocol description the following short names of components and notations are used (see also Fig. 2):

DS[key](msg)	A digital signature of a message <msg> created using a key <key>
E[key](msg)	Encryption of a message <msg> using a key <key>
h(msg)	A digest calculated for a message <msg> using hash function h
MAC[key](msg)	Message Authentication Code of <msg> built with <key>
MU.X	Authentication module under control of a user X installed in a mobile device
PrK.SP.X.AUT	A private authentication key installed in the SP belonging to an entity X
PuK.SP.X.AUT	A public authentication key installed in the SP belonging to an entity X
Q||Z	A concatenation of information Q and Z
SP.X	Secret Protection module installed in a user X mobile device
X	A protocol participant

We assume that for a given set of entities $P = \{A, B_1, \ldots, B_n\}$, where n ≥ 1, the entity A is the preferred entity responsible for initiating the protocol. The aim of the protocol is the mutual authentication with each entity $B_i, i = 1, \ldots, n$, and generation of a key material necessary to ensure the confidentiality and authenticity of information exchanged between the parties.

3.2 SPs_Conference_Key_Agreement Protocol Description

The SPs_Conference_Key_Agreement$(A, B_1, \ldots, B_n)$ protocol is based on the Boyd's conference protocol idea [4], [7]. Successful completion of the protocol authenticates directly only an entity A. Other entities authenticate themselves indirectly in the moment of usage of key generated based on an agreed key material. The key material is common for all entities that take part in the protocol. The SPs_Conference_Key_Agreement$(A, B_1, \ldots, B_n)$ protocol consists of five phases.

Phase I. Protocol participants exchange certificates between each other and activate necessary keys. After successful completion of that phase, SP.A has certificates C.SP.B_i.AUT and public keys PuK.SP.B_i.AUT of modules SP.$B_i(i = 1, \ldots, n)$, and each module SP.$B_i(i = 1, \ldots, n)$ contains the certificate C.SP.A.AUT and the public key PuK.SP.A.AUT of the module SP.A. Modules SP.A and SP.B_i $(i = 1, \ldots, n)$ have activated their keys needed during execution of cryptographic operations. Subsequent phases are performed as follows.

Phase II. Activation of the module SP.A and generation of the first component of common key material:

1. MU.A requests activation by SP.A of private key PrK.SP.A.AUT:

   MU.A → SP.A: `activate security key (PrK.SP.A.AUT)`

2. SP.A activates key PrK.SP.A.AUT and sends confirmation to MU.A:

   SP.A → MU.A: `conf.OK`

3. MU.A requests from SP.A to generate a random number and store it under its control:

   MU.A → SP.A: `get rand`

4. SP.A generate random number RND.SP.A and stores it in the memory:

   SP.A → MU.A: `conf.OK`

Phase III. (Generation of key material' components) For each pair of entities $(A, B_i), i = 1, \ldots, n$:

5. MU.A requests from $SP.B_i$ via $MU.B_i$ to generate a random number and to send it back together with ID.:

   MU.A → $MU.B_i$ → $SP.B_i$: `get challenge`

6. $SP.B_i$ generates challenge $RND.SP.B_i$ and together with its ID, $SN.SP.B_i$, sends it back to MU.A:

   $SP.B_i$ → $MU.B_i$ ↠ MU.A: $RND.SP.B_i$ || $SN.SP.B_i$

Phase IV. Signing and Decryption

7. MU.A sends authentication request to SP.A:

   MU.A → SP.A: `authenticate`$(RND.SP.B_1$ || $SN.SP.B_1$
   || $\ldots$ || $RND.SP.B_n$ || $SN.SP.B_n)$

8. SP.A generates random padding PRND.SP.A, prepares preToken.SP.A and signs it:

   DS[PrK.SP.A.AUT](preToken.SP.A)

   where:

   preToken.SP.A = textA.SP.A || PRND.SP.A

```
|| RND.SP.B₁ || SN.SP.B₁ || ...|| RND.SP.Bₙ
|| SN.SP.Bₙ || h(PRND.SP.A || RND.SP.A
|| RND.SP.B₁ || SN.SP.B₁ || ... || RND.SP.Bₙ
|| SN.SP.Bₙ) || textB.SP.A
```

and then for every $i = 1, \ldots, n$ generates additional random number exRND.SP.B_i and calculates a ciphertext in the form:

$$\text{E[PuK.SP.}B_i\text{.AUT](RND.SP.A || exRND.SP.}B_i\text{)};$$

next SP.A sends it together with its signature to each SP.B_i via MU.B_i:

```
SP.A → MU.A → MU.B_i → SP.B_i:
   E[PuK.SP.B_i.AUT] (RND.SP.A || exRND.SP.B_i)
   || DS[PrK.SP.A.AUT](preToken.SP.A)
```

9. Each SP.B_i (for $i = 1, \ldots, n$) decrypts E[PuK.SP.B_i.AUT] (RND.SP.A || exRND.SP.B_i) || DS[PrK.SP.A.AUT] (preToken.SP.A) and after that SP.B_i verifies SP.A signature (after the confirmation of compliance with a random challenge RND.SP.B_i sent previously) and returns back confirmation to MU.A:

$$\text{SP.}B_i \to \text{MU.}B_i \to \text{MU.A}\quad \text{SP.A: conf.OK}$$

Remark 1. When the protocol is completed - the module SP.A and each module SP.B_i (for $i = 1, \ldots, n$) have confidential key materials RND.SP.A and exRND.SP.$B_i(i = 1, \ldots, n)$. On this basis each party calculates:

(a) common key material:

$$\text{K.SP.A/SP.}B_{1..n} = \text{KDF (RND.SP.A || RND.SP.}B_1 \text{ || } \ldots \text{ || RND.SP.}B_n\text{)},$$

where KDF denotes a key derivation function (it is used to create session keys ensuring confidentiality and message integrity);

(b) personalised key material known only to a pair $(A, B_i), i = 1, \ldots, n$:

$$\text{inK.SP.A/SP.}B_i = \text{KDF (K.SP.A/SP.}B_{1..n}\text{||exRND.SP.}B_i\text{)}.$$

Phase V. Key material authentication and establishment of independent trusted channels. For each pair of entities $(A, B_i), i = 1, \ldots, n$:

10. MU.A sends authentication request to SP.B_i via MU.B_i:

$$\text{MU.A} \to \text{MU.}B_i \to \text{SP.}B_i:\quad \text{MACauthenticate(RND.SP.}B_i \text{ || SN.SP.}B_i\text{)}$$

11. SP.B_i calculates message authentication code and sends it back SP.A via MU.B_i:

```
SP.B_i → MU.B_i → MU.A → SP.A:
   MAC[inK.SP.A/SP.B_i](RND.SP.A || exRND.SP.B_i || RND.SP.B_i)
```

12. SP.A verifies MAC [inK.SP.A/SP.B$_i$] (RND.SP.A || exRND.SP.B$_i$ || RND.SP.B$_i$) and after successful verification of its compliance with received value sends it to SP.B$_i$:

$$SP.A \rightarrow MU.A \rightarrow MU.B_i \rightarrow SP.B_i: \ conf.OK$$

After the protocol completion module SP.A is authenticated mutually with every other modules SP.B$_i$($i = 1, \ldots, n$). It results from the step 8, in which module SP.A has used its private key to create a digital signature, which is then verified by each of modules SP.B$_i$ (step 9). Also, in step 9 each of entities SP.B$_i$ had to use its private key to decrypt a ciphertext received from SP.A. Thus each SP.B$_i$ might recover random numbers (RND.SP.A || exRND.SP.B$_i$) and calculate key material (K.SP.A/SP.B$_{1..n}$, inK.SP.A/SP.B$_i$). This material is used in step 11 by entity SP.B$_i$ to calculate message authentication code and then to successful verification by entity SP.A in the step 12; this ends authentication of entity SP.B$_i$ by SP.A. It is easy to notice, that key material K.SP.A/SP.B$_{1..n}$ allows to build common secure communication channel. Whereas material inK.SP.A/SP.B$_i$ is known only to a pair of entities (SP.A, SP.B$_i$) - it enables to create individual communication channels. This last property is particularly useful in the MobInfoSec system. In the system each of the entities SP.B$_i$ must send to SP.A a shadow or partially decrypted document confidentially.

3.3 Verification of Protocol's Security

In MobInfoSec system authentication protocol should work even under worst-case assumptions, namely messages may be eavesdropped or tampered by an attacker or dishonest or careless principals. The attacks can be conducted without attacking and breaking cryptography, but rather by attacking communication itself. These attacks exploit weaknesses in the protocol's design whereby protocols can be defeated by cleverly manipulating and replaying messages in the manner not anticipated by the designer [11]. Many formal methods for analysing cryptographic protocols and increasing the assurance that the protocol satisfies its security requirements exist. Some example of such methods and tools are CSP and FDR [12], OFMC [13] and the AVISPA tool [14], CryptoVerif [15], the crypto-module of the VerICS tool [16] and the PathFinder tool [17,18]. Three of these tools, i.e., AVISPA, VerICS and PathFinder, were used to investigate the main part (Steps 5-9) of proposed protocol (see Section 3.1). To model these steps we use HLPSL and ProToc languages. Next, we have examined correctness of the protocol using authentication and security properties. For all defined properties the proposed protocol is correct and secure. Computations were carried out on a computer equipped with the quad core processor Intel Pentium D (3000 MHz), 2 GB main memory, and the operating system Linux, and for each case took no more than 20 ms. More detailed description of the experiments and achieved results can be found in [19].

4   Conclusions

In this paper we have introduced a new multi-party conference authentication protocol based on ideas presented by C. Boyd [4], [7]. This protocol is a fundamental element of MobInfoSec system that enables access control according to ORCON rules to sensitive information stored and shared in encrypted form [2], [9]. The main objectives of this protocol is a mutual authentication of each pair of the protocol participants and building both common and personal secure communication channels between them. We model core security properties of proposed protocol in HSPL and ProToc languages and use the different tools, i.e., AVISPA, VerICS and PathFinder, to automate our security analysis. The protocol security analysis was conducted under the assumptions of perfect cryptography and that the protocol messages are exchanged over a network that is under the control of the Dolev-Yao intruder [20]. The extensive investigation has shown that our protocol does not contain flaws and is resistant against attacker following the Dolev-Yao model. The proposed protocol is a little more complex than Boyd's A or B protocol and: (a) it can be completed with $3n$ (n – number of protocol participants except an initiator) broadcast messages (without counting request messages), i.e., with n messages more than for Boyd's protocol, (b) the computation required for U_0 (the same as in Boyd's protocol) is one signature, n public key encryptions and (c) in opposite to Boyd's protocol, the n additional MAC calculations are required (one calculation per each entity $U_i, i = 1, \ldots, n$). However, main drawback of our protocol (like Boyd's protocol) is a lack of a forward secrecy, because the compromise of any principal's decryption key results in compromise of key materials (compare Step 9). Therefore, the future work will concentrate on extending our conference protocol to cover this drawback and to provide a forward secrecy.

Acknowledgments. This scientific research work is supported by NCBiR of Poland (grant No PBS1/B3/11/2012) in 2012-2015.

References

1. Hyla, T., Pejaś, J., El Fray, I., Maćków, W., Chocianowicz, W., Szulga, M.: Sensitive Information Protection on Mobile Devices Using General Access Structures. In: The Ninth International Conference on Systems, ICONS 2014, pp. 192–196. IARIA (2014)
2. Hyla, T., Pejaś, J.: A practical certificate and identity based encryption scheme and related security architecture. In: Saeed, K., Chaki, R., Cortesi, A., Wierzchoń, S. (eds.) CISIM 2013. LNCS, vol. 8104, pp. 190–205. Springer, Heidelberg (2013)
3. CEN, prEN 14890-1: Application Interface for smart cards used as Secure Signature Creation Devices - Part 1: Basic services (2012)
4. Boyd, C., Mathuria, A.: Protocols for Authentication and Key Establishment. Springer, Heidelberg (2003)
5. Dong, L., Chen, K.: Cryptographic Protocol Security Analysis Based on Trusted Freshness. Springer, Heidelberg (2012)

6. Lim, C.H., Lee, P.J.: Several practical protocols for authentication and key exchange. Information Processing Letters 53, 91–96 (1995)
7. Boyd, C., González Nieto, J.M.: Round-Optimal Contributory Conference Key Agreement. In: Desmedt, Y.G. (ed.) PKC 2003. LNCS, vol. 2567, pp. 161–174. Springer, Heidelberg (2002)
8. Chen, Y.-Y., Lee, R.B.: Hardware-Assisted Application-Level Access Control. In: Samarati, P., Yung, M., Martinelli, F., Ardagna, C.A. (eds.) ISC 2009. LNCS, vol. 5735, pp. 363–378. Springer, Heidelberg (2009)
9. Hyla, T., Pejaś, J.: Certificate-Based Encryption Scheme with General Access Structure. In: Cortesi, A., Chaki, N., Saeed, K., Wierzchoń, S. (eds.) CISIM 2012. LNCS, vol. 7564, pp. 41–55. Springer, Heidelberg (2012)
10. ISO/IEC 11770-3:2008 Information technology – Security techniques – Key management – Part 3: Mechanisms using asymmetric techniques (2008)
11. Matsuo, S., Miyazaki, K., Otsuka, A., Basin, D.: How to Evaluate the Security of Real-Life Cryptographic Protocols? In: Sion, R., Curtmola, R., Dietrich, S., Kiayias, A., Miret, J.M., Sako, K., Sebé, F. (eds.) FC 2010 Workshops. LNCS, vol. 6054, pp. 182–194. Springer, Heidelberg (2010)
12. Ryan, P.Y.A., Schneider, S.A., Goldsmith, M.H., Lowe, G., Roscoe, A.W.: The Modelling and Analysis of Security Protocols: the CSP Approach. Addison-Wesley (2001)
13. Basin, D.M., Mödersheim, S., Viganò, L.: OFMC: A symbolic model checker for security protocols. International Journal of Information Security 4(3), 181–208 (2005)
14. Armando, A., et al.: The AVISPA tool for the automated validation of internet security protocols and applications. In: Etessami, K., Rajamani, S.K. (eds.) CAV 2005. LNCS, vol. 3576, pp. 281–285. Springer, Heidelberg (2005)
15. Blanchet, B.: A computationally sound mechanized prover for security protocols. In: IEEE Symposium on Security and Privacy, Oakland, California, pp. 140–154 (2006)
16. Kurkowski, M., Penczek, W.: Verifying Security Protocols Modeled by Networks of Automata. Fundamenta Informaticae 79(3-4), 453–471 (2007)
17. Kurkowski, M., Siedlecka-Lamch, O., Szymoniak, S., Piech, H.: Parallel Bounded Model Checking of Security Protocols. In: Wyrzykowski, R., Dongarra, J., Karczewski, K., Waśniewski, J. (eds.) PPAM 2013, Part I. LNCS, vol. 8384, pp. 224–234. Springer, Heidelberg (2013)
18. Siedlecka-Lamch, O., et al.: A New Effective Approach for Modelling and Verification of Security Protocols. In: Proc. of CS&P 2012, pp. 191–202. Humboldt University Press, Berlin (2012)
19. Kurkowski, M.: Mobile device to protect classified information (MobInfoSec). Task 3: Protocols for authentication and information security. Part 2: Formal analysis of cryptographic authentication protocols. Technical Report, TR/ZUT WI KIO ZOI 0003.02/2014, West Pomeranian University of Technology in Szczecin, Poland (2014) (in Polish)
20. Dolev, D., Yao, A.: On the security of public-key protocols. IEEE Transactions on Information Theory 29, 198–208 (1983)

Secure Multihop Key Establishment Protocols for Wireless Sensor Networks

Ismail Mansour, Gérard Chalhoub, and Pascal Lafourcade

LIMOS, Clermont University, Campus des Cézeaux,
Aubière, France
gerard.chalhoub@udamail.fr

Abstract. Designing secure communication protocols is not an easy task. Cryptography is often necessary but does not always guarantee the security of protocols as several famous examples attest in the literature. Moreover, in the context of Wireless Sensor Networks (WSNs) the design is even more difficult due to the limited resources of sensor nodes that add extra constraints to take into account. During the life time of a secure WSN, one of the first crucial steps is the key establishment between two nodes. In this paper we propose four secure multihop key establishment protocols based on elliptic curve cryptography (ECC). For each protocol, we make a formal security proof using the automatic tool Scyther. Then, in order to evaluate their performances, we implemented them on testbeds using TelosB motes and TinyOS. Results allow us to estimate the overhead of our key establishment methods.

Keywords: authentication, key establishment, wireless sensor network, security, multihop, formal verification.

1 Introduction

Due to the technological advances, Wireless Sensor Networks (WSNs) are more and more used in diverse applications. In the first age of WSNs, the main concern was to efficiently transmit the data to the destination using wireless communications. Only few applications, like military WSN examples, required a high level of security [7]. In this context, it is important to design secure efficient communication mechanisms between nodes of the network, using cryptography. Moreover, with the expansion of the Internet of Things (IoT) more and more devices will be interconnected and monitoring critical human activities. For instance nowadays most of the smart phones have a GPS, a camera, and several sensors. In a close future our environment will be equipped with several sensors in order to collect data to inform the user. In this context the knowledge of this data can leak private information, one solution to avoid this is to use cryptography in order to preserve privacy of the users. One of the first steps in this situation is to design secure multihop key establishment protocols. This is the main motivation of this paper.

Z. Kotulski et al. (Eds.): CSS 2014, CCIS 448, pp. 166–177, 2014.
© Springer-Verlag Berlin Heidelberg 2014

1.1 Contributions

Our goal is to design several secure key establishment protocols for WSNs and to evaluate their performances on real nodes. Hence our contributions can be split in three points:

- Design of key establishment protocols based on ECC.
- Formal security analysis of the protocols.
- Evaluation on TelosB testbeds of the execution time of each solution.

All our protocols are based on Elliptic Curve Cryptography (ECC) with a key of 160 bits. We propose a first protocol called MKE_S. It allows nodes that already share a key with the sink to establish a new secret key. The idea is to use the sink as a kind of third trusted party to establish a new key. In addition, we propose an improvement of this protocol called $MKE_S - light$. In this version, the sink performs costly computation instead of the nodes, since in many situations the sink has no limited battery and more computation power than nodes of the WSN. We also give two other protocols that establish a secret key between two nodes without passing by the sink. The first one is called MKE_{NK}, it uses only the network key shared between all the authenticated nodes in the network. This authentication phase can be done for instance using one of the protocols proposed in [10]. The second protocol is called MKE_K, also it does not use the sink, but it uses the symmetric keys shared between neighbor nodes. In order to guarantee the authentication of nodes involved, this protocol only requires two flows of messages instead of three as it is the case for the protocol MKE_{NK}.

In order to prove the security of all these protocols, we used Scyther an automatic cryptographic protocol verification tool developed by Cas Cremers. It is easy to propose a flawed protocol, this tool helps to verify the correctness of the security protocol and make sure that it resists against several kinds of attacks. Each of our solutions uses a different approach to securely establish a new secret key, they vary according to the number of cryptographic operations involved and the trust level that we need to have in the network nodes.

Our last contribution is the implementation on real nodes of all our protocols. Our aim is to measure the execution time of each protocol, but also to compare them in order to be able to judge which one is the most suitable.

1.2 Related Work

Many contributions have been made in the key establishment and symmetric key distribution in WSNs. Some of them are based on a probabilistic predistribution that guarantees that any two nodes in the network are able to share a key with a certain probability, and others are deterministic but cause more storage overhead [1]. One of the most known symmetric key systems that were proposed for wireless sensor networks is SPINS (Security Protocols for Sensor Networks)

[13] which uses a simplified version of TESLA (Timed, Efficient, Streaming, Loss-tolerant Authentication) protocol [12]. In SPINS, the base station plays an essential role in the key establishment process. It is a lightweight protocol but suffers from scalability and high dependency on the base station.

Authors in [11] proposed a multi-hop key establishment between nodes called Micro-PKI. Their method is based on the pre-distribution of the public key of the base station. Using this public key, every node is able to create a secret key with any other node of the network. The authentication process in this proposal is only dependent on the public key of the base station, if a node has this key, it is considered authenticated. This makes the procurement of this public key very critical on which depends the whole security architecture.

In [3], authors proposed PIKE, peer intermediaries for key establishment, one of the most famous key establishment protocols that is not dependent on a central trusted node. According to PIKE, keys are pre-deployed in the nodes in such a way to guarantee that any two nodes in the network have at least one node in common with which each one of the two nodes has a secret key with it. Therefor, these two nodes are able to establish a secret key by using the trusted channel established with the common node. PIKE suffers from high memory storage to make sure that nodes are able to find at least one node in common to establish a new key.

CARPY and CARPY+ were proposed in [15]. They are based on the symmetric keys of Blom [2] with a perturbation function that makes more difficult for an attacker to guess the pairwise keys. In their paper they discuss the five criteria that were proposed in [16] and claim that CARPY+ satisfies all of them. These criteria are: *Resilience to the Adversary's Intervention* during the key establishment phase, Directed and Guaranteed Key Establishment for any couple of nodes in the network, *Resilience to Network Configurations* nodes should be able to establish keys in any kind of network topology, *Efficiency* of the key establishment process in terms of memory storage, communication overhead and complexity, *Resilience to Dynamic Node Deployment* which allows nodes to be added at any time to the network and enabling them to establish keys. The main weakness of this scheme is the lack of a rekeying process. The preshared matrices will only help to create one pairwise key for every couple of nodes.

Table 1 summarizes a comparison between the related work schemes and our proposition. The comparison is based on some repudiated criterias in WSN area. As the table shows, Yu et al. scheme [15] is the closest one to our schemes. Nevertheless, the authors use TelosB motes to evaluate energy consumption of basic operations used in their schemes and they provide a large scale simulation for thousands of nodes based on these measurements.

In this paper, we did not compare our time execution results with other protocols from the state of the art because implementations are hardware and system dependent. In addition, they can be optimized for certain platforms which makes the comparison unfair using different platforms and cryptographic primitives. Finally the main difference with other works is that we formally prove the security of all our protocols using the automatic verification tool Scyther [4].

Table 1. Comparison of related work schemes

Proposed scheme	Pre-distribution	Trusted Party	Cryptographic technique	Simulation	Implemen-tation	Verification
Perrig et al., 2000[12], 2002[13]	yes	Base station	symmetric	JAVA	none	manual
Chan et al., 2005[3]	yes	Base station	symmetric	yes	none	manual
Yu et al., 2009[15]	yes	none	symmetric	none	TelosB	manual
Munivel et al., 2010[11]	yes	Base station	symmetric/ asymmetric	manual	none	none
Our schemes	yes	Base station	symmetric/ asymmetric	none	TelosB	automatic

1.3   Outline

In the next section, we introduce the notations used and present four key establishment protocols. Then, in Section 3, we give the results of our implementation
on TelosB motes. Finally, we conclude in the last section.

2   Multi-hop Key Establishment Protocols

In our evaluation testbed, we used public keys based on Elliptic Curve Cryptog-
raphy (ECC), using parameters secp160r1 given by the Standards for Efficient
Cryptography Group [14]. Our implementation of ECC on TelosB is based on
TinyECC library [8]. More precisely we used the Elliptic Curve Diffie-Hellman
(ECDH) key agreement scheme [5]. For all symmetric encryption/decryption we
use an optimized implementation of AES with a key of 128 bits proposed by [9].

Note that we only use the public keys in order to establish symmetric keys
without doing any asymmetric encryption or decryption operations. Indeed, it
helps us establish a pairwise key without interaction between nodes thanks to
the predistribution of public keys before the deployment. Before deployment,
each node N knows the public key $pk(S)$ of the sink S and also its own pair of
private and public keys, denoted $(pk(N), sk(N))$ respectively. Based on ECC,
we have that $pk(N) = sk(N) \times G$, where G is a generator point of the elliptic
curve. Using this material, each node N can compute a shared key with the
sink S using a variation of the Diffie-Hellman key exchange without interaction
between the nodes, denoted $K_{DH}(N, S)$. These computations can be done by
the sink and by all nodes before deployment in order to preserve their energy.

- The sink knows its own secret key $sk(S)$ and the public key $pk(N)$ of a node
  N. The sink computes $K_{DH}(N, S) = sk(S) \times pk(N)$.
- Node N multiplies his secret key $sk(N)$ by the public key of the sink $pk(S)$
  to get $K_{DH}(N, S)$.

Both computations give the same shared key, since:

$$
\begin{aligned}
K_{DH}(N,S) &= sk(N) \times pk(S) \\
&= sk(N) \times (sk(S) \times G) \\
&= (sk(N) \times G) \times sk(S) \\
&= pk(N) \times sk(S)
\end{aligned}
\tag{1}
$$

Notations

In what follows, we use the following notations to describe exchanged messages in our protocols:

- I: a new node that initiates the protocol,
- R: a neighbour of node I,
- S: the sink of the network (also called base station),
- J_i: the i-th intermediate node between R and S,
- n_A: a nonce generated by node A,
- $pk(A)$: the public key of node A,
- $sk(A)$: the secret (private) key of node A,
- $K(I,S)$: the session key between I and S,
- NK: the symmetric network key between all nodes of the network,
- $K_{DH}(N,S)$: the shared symmetric key between N and S using the Diffie-Hellman key exchange without interaction described above,
- $\{x\}_k$: the encryption of message x with the symmetric or asymmetric key k.

In all the figures that describe our protocol, we denote a direct communication by an arrow between two nodes, and a communication passing by several possible intermediate nodes by a dotted arrow. We also explicit above each exchanged message the size in Bytes.

2.1   Protocols with Intervention of the Sink

Our aim is to establish a shared key between any two authenticated nodes I and R of the network (not necessary in range). We propose two protocols, called MKE_S and $MKE_S - light$. Protocol MKE_S, depicted in Figure 1, uses the secure channels created between the sink and each node to communicate the public keys of I and R. Notice that in our context the sink knows all the public keys of all nodes and a node only knows its public key and the public of the sink. The initiator node I builds a request containing the identity of node R and a nonce n_I. This request is encrypted with $K_{DH}(I,S)$ and sent to S. The sink S sends:

- to I, the identity of R, a nonce n_S, the public key of R encrypted with the shared symmetric key $K_{DH}(I,S)$,

- to R, the identity of I, the same nonce n_S, the nonce n_I received from I and the public key of I encrypted with the shared symmetric key $K_{DH}(S, R)$.

Once these two messages received by I and R, the two nodes are able to compute $K_{DH}(I, R)$ as follows:

- Node I computes $sk(I) \times pk(R) = sk(I) \times sk(R) \times G = K_{DH}(I, R)$.
- Node R computes $sk(R) \times pk(I) = sk(R) \times sk(I) \times G = K_{DH}(I, R)$.

To ensure mutual authentication of R and I, node R generates a nonce n_R, then uses $K_{DH}(I, R)$ to encrypt its own identity, the two received nonces from S plus its nonce n_R. This cipher is sent to I, without necessary passing by S. Finally, node I verifies that the received nonce from R is the same as the one sent by the sink. Then it confirms that it correctly received the message by sending to R its own identity and the two nonces n_S and n_R, encrypted with $K_{DH}(I, R)$.

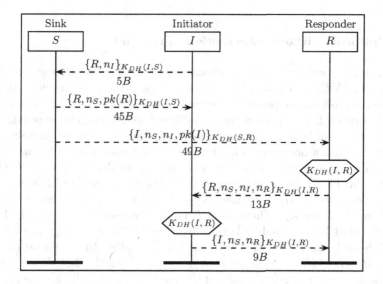

Fig. 1. MKE_S: Multihop Key Establishment using the sink S to deliver public keys. $K_{DH}(I, R)$ is computed by the initiator I and the responder R

Notice that the computation of the new key $K_{DH}(I, R)$ can be done by the sink in order to save some computations on nodes R and I. This version called $MKE_S - light$ is depicted in Figure 2.

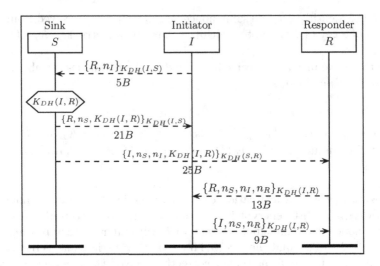

Fig. 2. $MKE_S - light$: Multihop Key Establishment using the sink S to computes and delivers $K_{DH}(I, R)$ to initiator and responder nodes

2.2   Protocols without Intervention of the Sink

In order to avoid exhausting nodes situated near the sink, we propose two protocols, called MKE_{NK} and MKE_K, that do not need the intervention of the sink in the key establishment process. The protocol MKE_{NK}, depicted in Figure 3, uses the network key NK allowing the initiator node I and the responder R to exchange their public key. The initiator node I builds a request containing his own identity and a nonce n_I. This request is encrypted with NK and sent to R. After decrypting this request, the responder R is able to extract $pk(I)$ and compute $K_{DH}(I, R)$. In order to ensure mutual authentication of R and I, node R generates a nonce n_R, then uses $K_{DH}(I, R)$ to encrypt the received nonce from I and its nonce n_R. Then, node R builds the response message including this cipher and his own public key $pk(R)$. The response message is encrypted using NK and sent to the initiator I. After decrypting the response message, node I extracts $pk(R)$ and computes $K_{DH}(I, R)$. Using this key, I decrypts the two nonces n_I and n_R. After verifying the nonce n_I, node I builds a reply message containing n_R, encrypted with $K_{DH}(I, R)$. Finally, node R verifies that the received nonce n_R from I is the same as the one it originally sent.

We note that the use of NK to exchange public keys between nodes I and R can be useful when the initiator I is in the neighborhood of R. Indeed, node I sends directly its request to node R without the need of intermediate nodes to forward its request. Since the network key NK is known by all nodes before deployment, the protocol MKE_{NK} may suffer from man-in-the-middle attack when an intruder is able to recover NK by capturing any node in the network for example. In what follows, we describe the scenario of such attack.

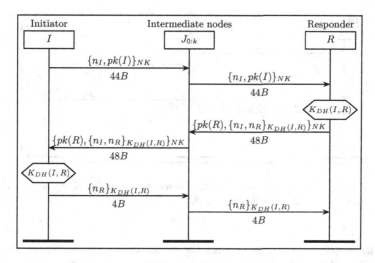

Fig. 3. MKE_K: Multihop Key Establishment using the network key NK. No encryption/decryption operations on intermediate nodes

An intruder, denoted E, captures a previously authenticated node N in the network and compromises the network key. Node E intercepts the request sent from I to R, decrypts the request and builds an intruder request instead by replacing the nonce n_I by its own nonce n_E and $pk(I)$ by $pk(E)$. Node E encrypts this new request using NK and sends it to R. Node R decrypts the request, extracts $pk(E)$ and computes $K_{DH}(R, E)$. The response message to E becomes $\{pk(R), \{n_E, n_R\}_{K_{DH}(E,R)}\}_{NK}$. Upon reception, node E decrypts the response message with NK, extract $pk(R)$ and computes $K_{DH}(R, E)$. Node E uses the key computed to decrypt the nonce n_R and sends it back to R encrypted with $K_{DH}(R, E)$. In order to finish his attack, node E builds a response message $\{pk(E), \{n_I, n_E\}_{K_{DH}(E,I)}\}_{NK}$ and sends it to node I. Using $pk(I)$, which was extracted from the request originally sent by I, node E is able to compute $K_{DH}(E, I)$. Upon reception, the initiator I decrypts the received response using NK, computes $K_{DH}(E, I)$ and replies with n_E encrypted with $K_{DH}(E, I)$.

In order to make the key establishment more resilient to node capture, we propose another protocol, called MKE_K that uses sessions keys previously established with common neighbors in order to establish new keys. The protocol MKE_K, depicted in Figure 4, uses the session keys established with common neighbors, denoted intermediate nodes $J1 : k$, in order to share a new key between an initiator I and a responder R. We assume that the trusted path from I to R is determined by a routing mechanism. Unlike the protocol MKE_{NK}, nodes $J1 : k$ are involved in the key establishment, they decrypt, modify and encrypt the exchanged messages between nodes I and R instead of just forwarding.

Indeed, each intermediate node $J_j, (j = 1, ..., k)$, extracts only the nonce from the request of the initiator I and replaces it by its own nonce n_j. Upon the reception of a response message sent by the responder R, node J_j recovers and

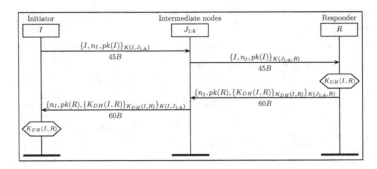

Fig. 4. MKE_K: Multihop Key Establishment using session keys. Encryption/decryption on every intermediate node

verifies its nonce n_j and replies with the nonce extracted previously from the request. The adding of nonces n_j at each hop helps to authenticate intermediate nodes. Note that $K_{DH}(I, R)$ is used as a common nonce between nodes I and R to ensure the mutual authentication between of I and R. Also, it should be noted that the protocol MKE_K can only be used if nodes I and R have at least one common neighbor.

3   Results

We prove the correctness of all our protocols automatically using Scyther a tool for the automatic verification of security protocols. Cas Cremers has developed an automatic tool called Scyther [4]. It is a free tool available on all operating systems (Linux, Mac and Windows). This tool can automatically find attacks on cryptographic protocols and prove their security for bounded and unbounded numbers of sessions. One main advantage of Scyther is that it provides an easy way to model security properties like secrecy and authentication. This tool abstract the cost of the communications and the execution times of each cryptographic operation. Scyther uses the Dolev-Yao intruder model [6]. In this model, the intruder controls the network and all communications pass through it. Which means that all packets can be captured by the intruder. Moreover the intruder has its own public and private pair of keys. Thus, it is able to play the role of any participant in the protocol. It can also encrypt messages with all public or symmetric keys that it knows and decrypts cipher-texts only if it knows the decryption key.

In Table 3, we present the execution time for our protocols using TelosB which are very limited in calculation resources and are used as a base for comparison between the different protocols and not for obtaining the best results in terms of performance. Notice that these results are done with the minimum required cryptographic operations necessary to realize each protocol. For example, the evaluation of MKE_S, $MKE_S - light$, and MKE_{NK} is done without intermediate nodes between node I and R. Indeed, the intermediate nodes are just forwarding the messages between I and R. In contrast, we evaluated MKE_K with one intermediate node between nodes I and R due to the necessity of one common neighbor node to use the session keys established with this neighbor.

Table 2. Execution times of all protocols

Protocol name	Time with S (ms)	Time without S (ms)	Gain	Standard deviation (ms)
MKE_S	6888.15	6625.94	4%	5.81
$MKE_S - light$	3679.30	365.85	90%	5.02
MKE_{NK}	6853.26	6853.26	0%	5.01
MKE_K	7434.95	7434.95	0%	3.44

Note that $MKE_S - light$ is the most efficient of all protocols. Indeed, the computation of new shared keys are done by nodes I and R in all protocols except $MKE_S - light$ where only the sink S is doing this computation. So $MKE_S - light$ is very suitable for protocols where the sink has more capacities than the sensor nodes. We note that the computation of new keys according to $ECDH$ without interaction is about 3.2 seconds. This time consumption has a clear effect on the execution time of protocols.

While the number of computation of new keys are equal in the MKE_S, MKE_{NK} and MKE_K, MKE_K differs from MKE_S and MKE_{NK} by the decryption/encryption operations done by intermediate nodes. Indeed, the difference is more than $400ms$ per each intermediate node.

In addition, MKE_S and MKE_{NK} have almost the same cryptographic operations which is why their execution times are very close. We can expect that the protocol MKE_S is more suitable when nodes I and R are next to the sink while the protocol MKE_{NK} is more suitable when these nodes are too far from the sink. So in a given topology, nodes should be able to execute the protocol that is less consuming according to their positions relative to the sink.

4   Conclusions

In this paper, we proposed different methods for establishing a secret key between two authenticated nodes in a WSN. We presented and validated two protocols that enables authenticated nodes to establish a common key in a multihop manner with the intervention of the sink or the base station of the WSN.

In order to avoid exhausting nodes that are located near the sink with the key establishment requests, we proposed two protocols that allow nodes to establish secret keys without the intervention of the sink MKE_{NK} and MKE_K. These latter protocols are based on the fact that nodes can use the network key to exchange key establishment messages or use previously established session keys on each hop.

Depending on the type of keys that are used and the intervention of the sink, the resiliency of the protocol against intruder attacks is different. The most vulnerable protocol is the one that uses the network key without the intervention of the sink MKE_{NK}, but it is the fastest one. The most secure protocols are MKE_S and $MKE_S - light$, but they exhaust nodes that are near the sink and might take longer routes to reach the sink compared to MKE_{NK} and MKE_K.

In our future work, we plan on evaluating the performance of each of these protocols with the presence of intermediate nodes between nodes that are establishing a new key, and between these nodes and the sink as well. Depending on the network topology, a trade-off might arise and we might need to make these protocols available at the same time and to be used according the relative positions of the involved nodes.

Acknowledgements. This research was conducted with the support of the Digital trust Chair from the University of Auvergne Foundation.

References

1. Bala, S., Sharma, G., Verma, A.: Classification of symmetric key management schemes for wireless sensor networks. International Journal of Security and Its Applications 7 (2013)
2. Blom, R.: An optimal class of symmetric key generation systems. In: Beth, T., Cot, N., Ingemarsson, I. (eds.) EUROCRYPT 1984. LNCS, vol. 209, pp. 335–338. Springer, Heidelberg (1985)
3. Chan, H., Perrig, A.: Pike: Peer intermediaries for key establishment in sensor networks. In: INFOCOM, pp. 524–535. IEEE Computer Society (2005)
4. Cremers, C.J.F.: The Scyther Tool: Verification, falsification, and analysis of security protocols. In: Gupta, A., Malik, S. (eds.) CAV 2008. LNCS, vol. 5123, pp. 414–418. Springer, Heidelberg (2008)
5. Diffie, W., Hellman, M.: New directions in cryptography. IEEE Transactions on Information Theory 22, 644–654 (1976)
6. Dolev, D., Yao, A.C.: On the security of public key protocols. In: Proceedings of the 22nd Annual Symposium on Foundations of Computer Science, SFCS 1981, pp. 350–357 (1981)
7. Hussain, M.A., Khan, P., Sup, K.K.: Wsn research activities for military application. In: Proceedings of the 11th International Conference on Advanced Communication Technology, vol. 1, pp. 271–274. IEEE Press (2009)
8. Liu, A., Ning, N.: Tinyecc: A configurable library for elliptic curve cryptography in wireless sensor networks. In: 7th International Conference on Information Processing in Sensor Networks, pp. 245–256 (April 2008)
9. Manica, N., Saloni, M., Toldo, P.: WSN - secure comunications with AES algoritms. University of Trento - Faculty of Computer Science (2008)
10. Mansour, I., Rusinek, D., Chalhoub, G., Lafourcade, P., Ksiezopolski, B.: Multihop node authentication mechanisms for wireless sensor networks. In: Guo, S., Lloret, J., Manzoni, P., Ruehrup, S. (eds.) ADHOC-NOW 2014. LNCS, vol. 8487, pp. 402–418. Springer, Heidelberg (2014)

11. Munivel, E., Ajit, G.: Efficient public key infrastructure implementation in wireless sensor networks. In: International Conference on Wireless Communication and Sensor Computing, pp. 1–6 (2010)
12. Perrig, A., Canetti, R., Tygar, J., Song, D.: Efficient authentication and signing of multicast streams over lossy channels. In: IEEE Symposium on Security and Privacy (April 2000)
13. Perrig, A., Szewczyk, R., Tygar, J., Wen, V., Culler, D.: SPINS: Security protocols for sensor networks. Wireless Networks (2002)
14. Certicom Research: Standards for efficient cryptography, sec 1: Elliptic curve cryptography (September 2000)
15. Yu, C., Lu, C., Kuo, S.: A simple non-interactive pairwise key establishment scheme in sensor networks. In: IEEE International Conference on Sensing, Communication, and Networking, SECON (2009)
16. Zhang, W., Tran, M., Zhu, S., Cao, G.: A random perturbation-based scheme for pairwise key establishment in sensor networks. In: ACM International Symposium on Mobile Ad Hoc Networking and Computing, MobiHoc (2007)

Comparison and Assessment of Security Modeling Approaches in Terms of the QoP-ML

Katarzyna Mazur[1] and Bogdan Ksiezopolski[1,2]

[1] Institute of Computer Science, Maria Curie-Sklodowska University,
pl. M. Curie-Sklodowskiej 5, 20-031 Lublin, Poland
katarzyna.mazur@umcs.pl
[2] Polish-Japanese Institute of Information Technology,
Koszykowa 86, 02-008 Warsaw, Poland
bogdan.ksiezopolski@acm.org

Abstract. Nowadays, security has become one of the most mandatory essences in the development and functioning of many software systems. For the reason of complexity of designing secure systems, distinct approaches that allow developers to focus on particular properties of the system of importance for their purpose are proposed. The majority of them are model-oriented since modeling helps show relationships between processes and can be used to predict the effects of changes in the land use. In the article we present and discuss PL/SQL, SecureUML and UMLsec in terms of the Quality of Protection modeling language (QoP-ML). We focus on their capabilities to model relevant information during various phases of security analysis. To assess and compare miscellaneous modeling systems we use a systematic methodology to point out their promiscuous aspects in context of the QoP-ML.

Keywords: security modeling, model-driven engineering, model-driven security, quality of protection.

1 Introduction

Security aspects have become an increasingly important in many engineering and scientific areas presently. The analysis of today security development process can be challenging for the reason of growing complexity of existing systems. Such intricacy can only be effectively represented by the use of strong abstraction mechanisms. As model is an abstract representation that helps highlight important connections in real world systems and processes, it can be also used in the development of more complex systems. Expressing the model with a formal framework provides the opportunity for making predictions about the modeled system, which can be later confirmed or disproved revealing truths about the abstracted problem. For this reason security modeling languages have evolved into the subject of research and experiments as ensuring security is indeed a basic requirement of miscellaneous IT systems. Security needs to be analysed, specified and implemented using the appropriate abstractions.

Z. Kotulski et al. (Eds.): CSS 2014, CCIS 448, pp. 178–192, 2014.

To address those problems several approaches were introduced. Among them one can enumerate PL/SQL, SecureUML and UMLsec. Contrary to SecureUML and UMLsec being extensions of the existing general purpose modeling languages, QoP-ML [8] as a dedicated, specialized solution sheds another light on the security modeling problem. Presenting a high level of abstraction, having the possibility of maintaining processes and communication steps consistently, QoP-ML provides a flexible approach for modeling complex systems and performance of multilevel security analysis. Additionally, in the QoP-ML the economic security analysis can be performed, in the literature being known as the adaptable security [6,7]. Since both SecureUML and UMLsec speak for an example of model driven security, in the light of the presented development methodologies, QoP-ML excellently fits in a the design known as Model-Driven Engineering. The Model-Driven Engineering (simply known as MDE) is meant to focus on the creation and utilization of the abstract representations of the knowledge that govern a particular domain, rather than on the computing, algorithmic or implementation concepts.

Nevertheless, the existence of various modeling systems leads to the conclusion that there is a demand for formal assessment and comparison of the available approaches. In [10] the authors proposed a methodology based on the SEQUAL framework which is capable of evaluating the quality of the security models prepared with diversified technologies. As the introduced method is a systematic approach which affords the assessment of the security development languages in the system modeling phase as well as on the implementation level, we would like to estimate the quality of the QoP model with the proposed framework.

In the article we intend to contribute to the assessment of the existing modeling approaches with the brand new, dedicated security modeling solution, namely QoP-ML. Such analysis should be performed not only in terms of the functionality, but also the usability as being the key aspect in the case of users' quality of experience. The main contribution of this paper is to compare modern, advanced modeling language, the QoP-ML with PL/SQL, SecureUML, and UMLsec. To support our theoretical analysis with the specific, practical example, we modeled a complex organizational structure and corresponding procedures that form the basis of role-based security policy, and assessed its quality with the systematic methodology. An additional contribution of the paper is the introduction of the extension of the methodology based on the SEQUAL framework.

2   Security Modeling Framework

In order to assess quality of distinct security modeling systems, systematic approaches need to be taken under consideration. Among miscellaneous methodologies, researchers in [10] chose the SEQUAL framework and formulated systematic, well organized steps on its basis.

The SEQUAL framework is a commonly used semiotics-based reference model for evaluating the quality of the models. It is a well developed, complex modeling approach which treats *physical, empirical, syntactical, semantic, perceived semantic, pragmatic, social* and *knowledge* qualities as its main targets. Being a set of essential modeling items, SEQUAL discusses the goals of modeling as well as means to achieve these goals, deals with aspects that can be expressed about the domain, aligns with the principles of the model and modeling language, and considers model creation as a correspondence between explicit knowledge of its interpreters.

Since the SEQUAL framework is a rich, complete and for this reason relatively complicated model, the authors in [10] utilized its abstract concepts and established a simpler set of systematic steps. In their study, researchers focused primarily on *semantics, pragmatics* and *syntax* qualities. They distinguished a group of qualitative properties along with their quantitative measures. As we used the proposed approach to evaluate the quality of the security model prepared with QoP-ML, below we introduce a brief overview of the presented methodology.

2.1   Semantic Quality

Semantic quality refers to the degree of the correspondence between the model and the domain that is modeled. Considering *semantic* quality, designers proposed five qualitative properties, namely *semantic completeness, semantic correctness, traceability, annotation* and *modifiability*.

Semantic completeness addresses the issue of including every meaningful aspect of designed system in the model. According to this property, *percentage of the domain coverage* measure is proposed. This measure is represented as the ratio of the number of concepts present in the model to the total number of concepts.

Regarding the *semantic correctness, percentage of security related statements* measure is introduced. *Percentage of security related statements* corresponds to the number of security modeling elements included in the model against the total number of modeling statements.

A measure known as *traceability* is calculated by counting the links that are traced to the model origin.

Being able to emphasize meaningful security aspects, *annotations* play an important role in the modeling process. Saying so, a *number of annotation elements* as the count of explanatory notes present in the model was proposed.

Assessing model *modifiability* is achievable through the evaluation of the *time spent to modify* measure, which refers to the time one needs to spend on customizing the security system.

2.2   Syntactic Quality

As *syntactic quality* expresses the relationship between the model and the modeling language, researchers suggested two relevant measures: *syntactic validity* and *syntactic completeness*.

To evaluate the *syntactic validity* of the model, one has to examine the *number of syntactically incomplete statements*. The above mentioned measure defines the degree of the grammatical correctness of the model. The lower the value, the better adjusted *the syntactic validity*.

Syntactic completeness defines if all available grammar structures of the language are included in the prepared model. Profound analysis of the modeling language syntax helps with estimation of the *number of syntactically incomplete statements*. The same as in the case of the *syntactic validity*, low value of the measure corresponds to the high *syntactic completeness*.

2.3 Pragmatic Quality

Considered as the level of usefulness and usability of the system, *pragmatic quality* focuses on the actors' interpretation of the model and their explicit knowledge about crucial aspects. Among quantitative measures proposed for this qualitative property, one can enumerate *time spent to understand, cross-referencing, organization* and *technology capable of executing the model*.

Understandability, or *time spent to understand*, defines how long it takes stakeholders to understand a prepared model. One can estimate this property with the amount of time needed to interpret modeled abstraction.

Cross-referencing and *organization* properties refer to the internal structure of the created model. The *number of cross-reference links* is helpful while evaluating the number of relationships between the model components. The high value of the *organization* measure indicates the fact that the model is well-organized and it is fairly straightforward to find significant information within it.

The presence of automated tools capable of executing the model reflects the value of the *executability* measure. Existence of non-manual tools being able to transform the model into running application is essential for modeling complex environments.

2.4 Methodology Extensions

Analyzing methodology introduced by researchers in [10] and discussed above, we observed a high demand for objective measures to assess the level of user's comprehension of the model in a systematic, standardized way. The properties presented by the authors focused mainly on empirical experiences and subjective opinions. Our approach is slightly distinct - we concentrated on estimating understandability in a technical context, emphasizing the role of automated tools in evaluating the level of comprehension. According to the presented framework, we proposed an additional measure for the *pragmatic* quality, named **technical understandability**.

Technical Understandability. When a user is capable of executing the model and is able to experience its changing nature, understands the syntax and semantics of the modeling system used for model creation, being familiar with its graphical representation at the same time, one can then assume the model is fairly *understood* (an important note: *understood*, but not *understandable* per se). *Technical understandability* consists of syntax, semantics and graphical features. Framework states that the user understands the model in a technical way, when she/he is able to validate relevant model elements with automated tools (making changes in the model, participants should verify correctness of modifications they made). The proposed measure can be considered in two aspects: firstly, one should define if the actor comprehends the model in general and investigate the level of comprehension in further analysis profoundly. If *technical understandability* is stated to be true, one should then examine its submeasures, namely: *syntax understandability, semantics understandabilities* as well as *graphical editability*; higher value means better understandability.

Syntax understandability refers to the validity of the grammatical constructs used in the model. To evaluate *syntax understandability* one has to check the correctness of the model elements using automated tools (analysing only syntax errors). The introduced submeasure is calculated as the ratio of the number of valid grammar constructs to the total number of syntax elements usage, times one hundred percent. Higher value (more than 70%) of this property means that it is quite straightforward to understand and learn the proposed syntax. (Example: the user made some modifications in a given model. After saving her/his work, she/he needs to verify, if all the changes are syntactically correct using automated tools. Such approach is a systematic, formalized way of testing the syntax validity and thus *syntax understandability*).

Semantics understandability Checking if all utilized grammar constructs were used in an appropriate context refers to the *semantics understandability*. Verification of the semantics comprehension must be performed automatically to provide meaningful results.

Graphical editability corresponds to the graphical representation of the model, its flexibility and ability to personalize model elements for better understanding. Thus, we identified a group of essential submeasures: *model layout customizability, fonts/colors/shapes customizability, customizability of the connections between model elements*. Submeasures are qualified highly if all (or almost all) of the mentioned graphical elements of the model are fully customizable, medium if more than 70% of the parts are personalizable, and low below 70%. As comprehension in general is a type of the empirical quality, *graphical editability* is a crucial mean to achieve understanding of the modeled abstraction.

3 Assessment of PL/SQL, SecureUML and UMLsec

3.1 PL/SQL Security Model

PL/SQL (Procedural Language/Structured Query Language) [2] being an Oracle Corporation procedural language extension for SQL, is an example of the programming language which developers may use for modeling. Since SQL by itself is a limited language, it cannot be used to implement models where conditional, iterative and sequential statements are required. To defeat these limitations PL/SQL as a common programming language that includes all the features of most other programming languages (such as loops and if/then/else statements) was introduced. On account of the establishment of the PL/SQL, modeling of the security system became feasible.

However, analysis of the results obtained by the researchers in [10] suggests that in general modeling security in PL/SQL can be problematic and insufficient. Considering the *semantic* quality as a compatibility between a model and its semantic domain, one can notice that not all the features that system should implement are included in the model. Furthermore, a low value of the measure called *percentage of security related statements* leads to the conclusion that separating data from the security concerns is not well supported by PL/SQL. Other facts that constitute against modeling security with the procedural language might be the lack of *annotation* elements and possibly long time one needs to spend to update the model. Modifying the existing PL/SQL model is a complex task since it requires a technical knowledge and full understanding of the syntax. Regarding the *syntactic* quality, which corresponds to the modeling language, security model as created with programmable language results in high *syntactic validity* and *syntactic completeness*. The ability to express the model with available grammar constructs and syntax is satisfactory. Examining the correspondence between a model and its interpretation defined in terms of understandability, organization, cross-referencing and executability, the biggest drawback of the PL/SQL security model is the *number of explanations* measure. The high value of this measure may indicate that the security model prepared with PL/SQL is not so obvious and easy to understand if one does not know the PL/SQL language sufficiently.

Due to the fact that security models may be used by users not familiar with PL/SQL (or any programming language) and in the case of its insufficient support for the modeling security aspects, PL/SQL might not be the best solution for creating complex security models where one needs to focus on the multilevel analysis so that the designed system will provide adequate level of protection.

3.2 SecureUML Model

SecureUML [9], [1], derived from the general purpose modeling language, namely UML, represents a model-driven security approach. SecureUML depicts security models as the UML diagrams extended with stereotypes, constraints and tagged values. The model prepared with SecureUML can be transformed into an executable application, although it needs to be translated into the PL/SQL code using automated tools in the first place and compiled after all. Such reasoning has an impact on the *executability* measure in *pragmatic* quality. Considering other *pragmatic* measures, one can notice that the security model prepared with SecureUML is characterized by great understanding and intuitiveness - anyone familiar with the UML modeling is able to modify it easily. It is worth mentioning that the SecureUML security model earns high scores also in a *number of elements for model organization* and a *number of cross-reference links*, meaning it has support of automated tools which makes the modeling process straightforward. Besides the *pragmatic* quality, SecureUML has great results in *semantic* quality at the same time. The model prepared with the UML dialect is semantically complete, possesses semantic correctness and remains fully modifiable. Nevertheless, the SecureUML approach has some drawbacks too. Its model suffers from *syntactic* invalidity, which states about the fact that not every grammatical expression used to prepare the model is part of the modeling language, which may be an awkward matter.

Although the SecureUML security model represents a significant role in security modeling, it has a serious flaw that refrains from utilizing it in intricate modeling projects.

3.3 UMLsec Model

With the usage of UML extension mechanisms, UMLSec [4] may serve as a powerful framework for development of high-quality security-critical systems. Being a lightweight UML dialect, UMLsec introduces elements required for a proper security modeling, such as stereotypes, along with their tags and constraints.

Taking into consideration its *semantic* quality, the authors proved [10] that *semantic completeness* of the security model prepared with UMLsec lies on the high level (about ∼86%). *Traceability*, *annotation* and *modifability* measures are similar as to the case of the SecureUML model. However, one should notice the value of the *semantic correctness* measure, which may point out that the model does not represent every security aspect to be developed appropriately. When it comes to the *syntactic* quality, the introduced methodology evaluated the UMLsec security model as syntactically valid and complete. Such assessment may be misleading and should be revised carefully by the reason that was performed without any automated tools. Last but not least quality measure, the *pragmatic* quality of security model created with UMLsec, is very much alike SecureUMLs. A noticable difference is the lack of automated tools capable of transforming the prepared model to the programming language code.

The UMLsec integrating security related information in the UML specifications allows to express security relevant aspects quite correctly. However, the main drawback of this approach is the inability of executing the UMLsecs model and a low value of the *semantic correctness* measure which corresponds to the presence of all required grammar constructs in the model.

4 Case Study - RBAC in QoP-ML

According to the *meeting scheduling system* example presented in [10], in our case study, we created an RBAC security model in quality of protection modeling language and evaluated it following the methodology introduced in [10]. We present our results as well as those gathered by the authors in [10] for comparison. The full syntax and semantics of the QoP-ML can be found in the article [8].

4.1 RBAC Security Model Prepared in QoP-ML

Modeling the RBAC model, we defined QoP-MLs functions, equations, channels, processes and hots. In this section we will present and discuss all the elements we prepared to create the security model.

In [10] the researchers proposed the RBAC model as an ideal example for modeling security systems. The above mentioned model distinguishes three types of user permissions: *User*, *SuperUser* and *Admin*.

Below we present the functions defined in the quality of protection modeling language which refer to the meeting scheduling system [10]. The declared operations represent the *User* role and its permissions.

```
functions                                fun Authorized(role);
{                                        fun GetMeetingID(meeting) ;
  fun SelectData(id);                    fun organize(startTime, endTime,
  fun InsertData(meeting);               location, ownerID);
  fun CheckCorrectness(meeting);         fun owns(userID, meetingID);
  fun UpdateData(meeting);               fun editable(meetingID);
  fun DeleteData(id);                    fun wait()[Time: seconds];
  fun GetRole();                       }
  fun GetUserID();
```

Along with *functions* we declared some *equational rules*.

```
equations                              eq owns(userID, meetingID) = true;
{                                      eq editable(meetingID) = true;
  eq CheckCorrectness(meeting) = true;  }
  eq Authorized(role) = true;
```

Table 1 summarizes the fundamental QoP-MLs *User* operations and presents their short descriptions.

Table 1. QoP-MLs functions for RBAC model

Function	Parameters	Description
fun SelectData(id);	id	selects information about the meeting with a given id
fun InsertData(meeting);	meeting	inserts information about the new meeting into the meeting resource pool, gives the meeting its unique id
fun CheckCorrectness(meeting);	meeting	checks if given the meeting information are correct
fun UpdateData(meeting);	meeting	updates information about the given meeting
fun DeleteData(id);	id	deletes information about the meeting with a given id
fun GetRole();	-	gets the role [user/superuser/admin] of the currently logged in user
fun GetUserID();	-	gets the id [user/superuser/admin] of the currently logged in user
fun Authorized(role);	role	checks if user with a given role is authorized to select/add meetings
fun GetMeetingID(meeting);	meeting	gets unique id of the given meeting
fun owns(userID, meetingID);	userID, meetingID	checks if a given user owns a given meeting id
fun organize(startTime, endTime, location, ownerID);	startTime, endTime, location, ownerID	creates a meeting with given parameters
fun editable(meetingID);	meetingID	checks if the meeting with a given ID can be edited
fun wait()[Time: seconds]	seconds	does nothing; waits for a given number of seconds

Since one needs communication between running processes, it is necessary to define the QoP-MLs channels.

```
channels
{
    channel ch1(*);
}
```

In our approach, processes express operations that can be performed by the *User*. modeling RBAC and considering *meeting scheduling system*, *User* is authorized to *select* and *insert* information about the meeting. If she/he owns the meeting, is able also to *update* or *delete* if necessary.

After defining processes, one can group them into *host* named *User* which expresses the *User* role in the RBAC model.

```
hosts
{
 host User(rr)(*){

  process Main(*){

   subprocess Select(*){
    role = GetRole();
    if(Authorized(role) == true){
     in(ch1:id);
     meeting = SelectData(id);
    }
   }

   subprocess Insert(*){
    role = GetRole();
    if(Authorized(role) == true){
     userID = GetUserID();
     in (ch1 : input);
     startTime = input[0];
     endTime = input[1];
     location = input[2];
     meeting = organize(startTime,
          endTime, location, userID);
     if (CheckCorrectness(meeting) ==
          true){
      InsertData(meeting);
     }
    }
   }

   subprocess Delete(*){
    role = GetRole();
    userID = GetUserID();
    if(Authorized(role) == true){
     in (ch1 : input);
     meetingID = input[0];
     if(owns (userID, meetingID) ==
          true){
      DeleteMeeting(meetingID);
     }
    }
   }
```

```
  }

  subprocess Update(*){
   role = GetRole();
   if(Authorized(role) == true){
    userID = GetUserID();
    in (ch1 : input1);
    meetingID = input1[0];
    if(owns (userID, meetingID) ==
         true){
     if(editable() == true){
      in (ch1 : input2);
      startTime = input2[0];
      endTime = input2[1];
      location = input2[2];
      newMeeting = organize (
           startTime, endTime,
           location, userID);
      if(CheckCorrectness(
           newMeeting) == true){
       UpdateData(newMeeting);
      }
     }
    }
   }
  }

 }

 host STDIN(rr)(*){
  process Main(*){
   subprocess GetID(){
    wait()[100];
    id = GetMeetingID();
    out(ch1:id);
   }
  }
 }
```

4.2   Assessment of the QoP-ML's Security Model

In this section we present the results of our evaluation of the QoP-ML security abstraction. We discuss *semantic*, *syntactic* and *pragmatic* qualities of the security model created with QoP-ML.

Table 3 summarizes the results of the *semantic* quality analysis. We examine every measure from the *semantic* quality set of measures step by step.

Percentage of the RBAC Domain Coverage. As QoP-ML is the extremely extensible modeling language, it is fairly straightforward to cover the RBAC domain entirely. Such flexibility influences the *percentage of the RBAC domain coverage* measure giving it the value of 100%. In the presented security model sample, we were capable of covering all out of seven RBAC concepts [Table 2].

Percentage of Security Related Statements. Besides the constructs associated directly with security aspects, we observed that our model consists of some actions related to the business logic (*SelectData, InsertData* and so on). Although separation between the data and security concerns is crucial in security modeling, in some cases business logic should be included into the model as well. However, in our model, each of the defined business actions to be executed require previously defined security methods. Analyzing simplest possible scenario (we defined functions for *User* role, where the user selects the data), we result in high value of the *semantic correctness* measure, meaning all of the actions were security related operations (directly or indirectly).

Number of Traced Links. We did not observe any security decisions explaining why such security solutions are included in the model. For this reason we donated a *number of traced links* measure the value of 0.

Number of Annotation Elements. As QoP-ML is more alike the programming language, it provides a set of valuable features, which are not directly available in other modeling languages. Saying so, QoP-ML allows developers to place comments (which can be considered as some kind of annotations) everywhere in the model making it fully annotated.

Time Spent to Modify. In our research, we identified the measure called *time spent to modify* as 10 minutes long for a fluent designer, who knows at least one general programming language (considering stakeholders, this time may be even longer since the value of this measure mainly depends on developer's skills).

Table 2. QoP-MLs correspondence to the RBAC domain

RBAC concept	QoP-MLs RBAC domain coverage
users can be assigned to roles	if user is assigned to the specific role, he/she has permissions given to this specific role, functions like `Authorized` have the ability of authorizing the user
permissions are assigned to roles	if user is assigned to a given role, she/he has permissions defined for the specific role, functions like `Authorized` have the ability of authorizing the user
users acquire permissions	when user is given a role, she/he acquires permissions too
the same user can be assigned to many roles	in our example model, users are distinguished by their unique ids - it is fairly straightforward to manage roles and users in such case
single role can have many users	same as above
single permission can be assigned to many roles	modeling security with QoP-ML one has enormous flexibility - declaring functions and equational rules, one can decide which permissions assign to which roles
single role can be assigned to many permissions	same as above

Table 3. Semantic quality of compared security models

Qualitative property	Measure	QoP-ML security model	PL/SQL security model	SecureUML security model	UMLsec security model
Semantic completeness	Percentage of the RBAC domain coverage	100%	42.86%	71.43%(100%)	85.71%
Semantic correctness	Percentage of security related statements	100%	7.69%	100%	33%
Traceability	Number of traced links	0	0	0	0
Annotation	Number of annotation elements	fully annotated	0	5	1
Modifiability	Time spent to modify	about 10 minutes (or not known)	not known	5 − 10 minutes	5 − 10 minutes

We assessed the *syntactic* quality of the QoP-MLs security model through *syntactic completeness* and *syntactic validity* measures [Table 4].

Syntactic Completeness and Validity. Being much alike the general programming language in its essence, QoP-ML gains high scores in the *syntactic* quality evaluation. After profound investigations of the language syntax, we state that the security model prepared with QoP-ML is syntactically valid and complete. All the grammar constructs and structures used in the modeling process are the part of the language resulting in a low value of the *syntactic completeness* measure (which is the desirable value of this measure).

Table 4. Syntactic quality of compared security models

Qualitative property	Measure	QoP-ML security model	PL/SQL security model	SecureUML security model	UMLsec security model
Syntactic completeness	Number of syntactically incomplete statements	0	0	0	0
Syntactic validity	Number of syntactically invalid statements	0	0	1	0

Aside from *semantic* and *syntactic* qualities, we evaluated a set of *pragmatic* measures in terms of the QoP-MLs security model.

Number of Explanations. *Understandability* in its intent, is similar to the *time spent to modify* measure from the *semantic* group of measures. It focuses on the aspects that can be measured with subjective opinions. As *pragmatic* quality expresses the relationship between the model and its recipients, it is quite problematic to measure and evaluate the model on such basis, since the model may be viewed by the security engineers as well as the stakeholders. Although, in our sense, QoP-MLs model is quite *understable* since it is prepared in the consistent and logical language.

Number of Elements for Model Organization. The model created with QoP-MLs is well *organized*. It is divided into logical modules so one is able to find needed information and note crucial logical relationships among associated facts easily. Within the *organizational* elements one can enumerate *functions*, *equations, processes, hosts, channels, versions* and many more, not included in the article.

Number of Cross-Reference Links. *Number of cross-reference links* measure expresses the internal structure of the created model. Even though QoP-ML's model does not contain direct reference links, it is cross-referenced by the means of its structure. The QoP-ML design allows individual modules to cooperate with each other: *hosts* contain *processes, processes* are made of *subprocesses* which can execute *functions* with the help of defined *equations*.

Tools to Execute the Model. Regarding the QoP-ML's *executability*, it is achievable to execute the prepared model. Quality of protection modeling language has a powerful tool named AQoPA which is an automated quality of protection tool [12] capable of running models created in QoP-ML.

Table 5. Pragmatic quality of compared security models

Qualitative property	Measure	QoP-ML security model	PL/SQL security model	SecureUML security model	UMLsec security model
Understandability	Number of explanations	5 − 10 minutes	more than 45 minutes	10 − 15 minutes	10 − 15 minutes
Organization	Number of elements for model organization	5	2	4	4
Cross referencing	Number of cross-reference links	plenty	1	3	3
Executability	Tools to execute the model	Yes (AQoPA)	Yes	Yes	No

Table 6. Evaluation of the extended pragmatic measures

Qualitative property	Measure	QoP-ML security model	PL/SQL security model	SecureUML security model	UMLsec security model
Technical understandability	Syntax understandability	93%	70%	95%	97%
	Semantics understandability	98%	70%	80%	85%
	Graphical editability	No	No	Yes	Yes

Besides evaluating the *pragmatic* measures introduced in [10] we estimated properties proposed by us in this work. We analyzed *syntax understandability, semantics understandability* and *graphical editability* with the respect to the models prepared in QoP-ML, PL/SQL, UMLsec and SecureUML.

Technical Understandability scores high for UMLsec, SecureUML as well as for QoP-ML and PL/SQL. Although, considering QoP-ML and PL/SQL models we were not capable of evaluating the *graphical editability* property. However, the lack of *graphical editability* results from the nature of these languages and cannot and should not be considered as a limitation or a drawback of given modeling languages, since this measure is simply not applicable to the general programming languages like QoP-ML or PL/SQL. Thus, as stated in our methodology extension, we can estimate *model layout customizability, fonts/colors/shapes customizability* and *customizability of the connections between model elements* only for the UMLsec and SecureUML security models.

We evaluated *syntax understandability* to be 93% for the model created with QoP-ML meaning that having 100 QoP-ML's statements prepared by the developer, who knows fluently at least one general programming language, only 7 of them were defined as invalid by AQoPA. Compared to the PL/SQLs model, QoP-ML's is characterized by high intuitiveness. As it could be assumed, SecureUML and UMLsec as graphical modeling languages represent the best *understandability*.

As the developer is already familiar with basic concepts, grammar structures and fundamental principles of modeling, in QoP-ML it is fairly straightforward to understand its *semantics*. Comparing *semantic comprehension* of miscellaneous security models, QoP-ML's is estimated as *best-semantically-understood*.

Values of *model layout customizability, fonts/colors/shapes customizability, customizability of the connections between model elements* highly depend on tools one used for the analysis and creation of the considered model. In our study, we followed the approach presented in [10] to estimate these measures. As tools used by the researchers are very powerful applications, all properties of *graphical editability* were evaluated high for SecureUML and UMLSec models.

4.3   Comparison of Security Models in Terms of QoP-ML

Table 7 contains all the results we gathered comparing various security models. As the authors in [10], to determine varied measures, we followed the presented methodology. Comparing the QoP-ML's and PL/SQL models one can notice that seven remaining qualitative properties, namely *percentage of the RBAC domain coverage, percentage of security related statements, number of annotation elements, time spent to modify, number of explanations, number of elements for model organization, number of cross-reference links* are assessed to be more suitable for the QoP-ML's model. Equal values were evaluated for *number of traced links, number of syntactically incomplete statements, number of syntactically invalid statements, tools to execute the model* measures. The survey showed that regarding the QoP-MLs' and SecureUML's models, one created in QoP-ML gains higher scores. The same condition can be observed when one compares the QoP-ML's and UMLsecs models.

The model prepared at the implementation stage with PL/SQL by the authors in [10] turned out to be less powerful than that created with QoP-ML. Analyzing the quality of these models one should notice that the PL/SQL's model is more challenging in modifying than QoP-ML's, does not have a satisfactory number of security-related elements, and is insufficiently annotated.

Comparing the models designed at the system development stage with the QoP-ML models, it is worth mentioning that QoP-ML's model has a great advantage over UMLsec's. A model created with QoP-ML can be executed with AQoPA, while UMLsec does not offer any automated tools capable of executing the model. Regarding SecureUML's model we observed a serious drawback

Table 7. Comparison of PL/SQL, SecueUML, UMLsec and QoP-ML security models

Model A created in	Model B created in	Model A is better in	Two models score equal in	Model B is better in
QoP-ML	PL/SQL	*percentage of the RBAC domain coverage, percentage of security related statements, number of annotation elements, time spent to modify, number of explanations, number of elements for model organization, number of cross-reference links, syntax understandability, semantics understandability*	*number of traced links, number of syntactically incomplete statements, number of syntactically invalid statements, tools to execute the model, graphical understandability*	-
QoP-ML	SecureUML	*percentage of the RBAC domain coverage, percentage of security related statements, number of annotation elements, number of syntactically invalid statements, number of cross-reference links, semantics understandability*	*number of traced links, number of syntactically incomplete statements, number of explanations, tools to execute the model, time spent to modify*	*syntax understandability, graphical understandability*
QoP-ML	UMLsec	*percentage of the RBAC domain coverage, percentage of security related statements, number of annotation elements, number of elements for model organization, number of cross-reference links,, tools to execute the model, semantics understandability*	*time spent to modify, number of syntactically incomplete statements, number of syntactically invalid statements, number of explanations,*	*syntax understandability, graphical understandability*

- researchers stated that it may contain *syntactically invalid statements*, which is not possible with QoP-ML modeling.

5 Conclusions

In the article we evaluated the security model created in QoP-ML and compared it with other available security modeling systems. In our approach we utilized the methodology introduced in [10] which has its roots in the SEQUAL framework. Following systematic steps we performed the quality analysis of the RBAC model prepared with the quality of protection modeling language. In our case study, we compared miscellaneous models, namely PL/SQL's, SecureUML's, UMLsec's to our QoP-ML model.

It is worth noticing that the methodology proposed by the authors in [10] (and the results obtained with it) should be reviewed carefully. During our study, we observed that some of the proposed measures can be based on inner experience rather than a fact, since their value depends mostly on subjective opinions. Taking this into consideration, we proposed an extension to the *pragmatic* quality along with its qualitative property and quantitative measures. Our analysis showed the flexibility of the quality of protection modeling language and confirmed the fact that the multilevel analysis is crucial in modeling security systems. Although at first it may be a bit harder to understand the model created with QoP-ML than that prepared with the usage of graphical approaches, the power of the language is undeniable. The most powerful aspect of the language is the possibility of performing multilevel security analysis in terms of performance and energy consumption evaluation. Such an analysis is especially important for the devices with limited resources like Wireless Sensor Networks [11,5].

Acknowledgments. This work is supported by Polish National Science Centre grant 2012/05/B/ST6/03364.

References

1. Basin, D., Doser, J., Lodderstedt, T.: Model Driven Security: from UML Models to Access Control Infrastructure. ACM Transactions on Software Engineering and Methodology (TOSEM) 15(1), 39–91 (2006)
2. Feuerstein, S., Pribly, B.: Oracle PL/SQL Programming, 4th edn. O'Reilly Media Inc. (2005)
3. Gasevic, D., Djuric, D., Devedzic, V.: Model Driven Engineering and Ontology Development. Springer, Heidelberg (2006)
4. Jurjens, J.: Secure Systems Development with UML. Springer, Heidelberg (2005)
5. Ksiezopolski, B., Kotulski, Z.: On scalable security model for sensor networks protocols. In: 22nd CIB-W78 Conference Information Technology in Construction, Dresden, pp. 463–469 (2005)
6. Ksiezopolski, B., Kotulski, Z.: Adaptable security mechanism for the dynamic environments. Computers & Security 26, 246–255 (2007)
7. Ksiezopolski, B., Kotulski, Z., Szalachowski, P.: On QoP method for ensuring availability of the goal of cryptographic protocols in the real-time systems. In: Conference: European Teletraffic Seminar (2011)
8. Ksiezopolski, B.: QoP-ML: Quality of protection modeling language for cryptographic protocols. Computers & Security 31(4), 569–596 (2012)
9. Lodderstedt, T., Basin, D., Doser, J.: SecureUML: A UML-Based Modeling Language for Model-Driven Security. In: Jézéquel, J.-M., Hussmann, H., Cook, S. (eds.) UML 2002. LNCS, vol. 2460, pp. 426–441. Springer, Heidelberg (2002)
10. Matulevičius, R., Lakk, H., Lepmets, M.: An Approach to Assess and Compare Quality of Security Models. ComSIS 8(2), Special Issue (2011)
11. Szalachowski, P., Ksiezopolski, B., Kotulski, Z.: On authentication method impact upon data sampling delay in wireless sensor networks. In: Kwiecień, A., Gaj, P., Stera, P. (eds.) CN 2010. CCIS, vol. 79, pp. 280–289. Springer, Heidelberg (2010)
12. The official web page of the QoP-ML project, http://www.qopml.org

Context-Aware Secure Routing Protocol for Real-Time Services

Grzegorz Oryńczak[1] and Zbigniew Kotulski[2]

[1] Jagellonian University,
Department of Physics, Astronomy and Applied Computer Science,
Reymonta 4, 30-059 Cracow, Poland
Grzegorz.Orynczak@uj.edu.pl
[2] Warsaw University of Technology, Institute of Telecommunications,
Nowowiejska 15/19, 00-665 Warsaw, Poland
zkotulsk@tele.pw.edu.pl

Abstract. The purpose of this paper is to propose a context-aware secure routing protocol suitable for real-time services. Since such a protocol undergoes a number of independent constraints connected with: dynamic changes of the environment, security assumptions, network limitations and end-users personal requirements, the context factors need specific treatment to be real support for an optimal route selection. The proposed framework systemizes the roles of all actors in establishing optimal and secure network connection for real-time services. The most suitable routing scheme is selected dynamically from the available portfolio, basing on actual context factors. Optimally, in the case of absence of any routing scheme satisfying a specific criterion given by context, a new scheme can be created on-demand, using the multi-constrained optimal path selection technique. The framework supports also additional optimization techniques (like fast packet retransmission, redundant routing etc.). Also the necessary security mechanisms have been implemented. Besides standard hard-security mechanisms, like private key encryption, also soft security techniques (i.e. reputation management) for detecting and blocking malicious nodes are used.

Keywords: context aware routing, real-time communication, routing security, quality of service.

1 Introduction

Modern real-time services are strongly affected by external circumstances. Firstly, they take place in dynamic environment where the conditions of work are result from activities of independent network operators, service providers and end-users pursuing their own interests. Next, a service itself undergoes different factors, like business constraints, social interactions, including hacker attacks, and user's personal preferences. A remedy to many problems in realizing secure and effective information services in dynamic environment is the context-aware approach.

Z. Kotulski et al. (Eds.): CSS 2014, CCIS 448, pp. 193–207, 2014.
© Springer-Verlag Berlin Heidelberg 2014

This method makes an attempt to classify and manage the supplementary information (called context, see [1]) to improve security and service quality decisions in the time the decision is made, and thus, to guarantee its correct functioning in some future perspective. The problem to solve is how to include effectively the contextual information into the service description increasing its quality and not indisposing operational real-time management.

In literature there are many specific context-aware solutions for concrete secure services (for recent critical analysis of the state-of-the-art see [2,3]), attempts of generalizations for building context-management framework for some classes of secure services (see e.g. [4]) and building general context-management frameworks for a wide spectrum of secure information services, see e.g., [5,6,7].

As we have already mentioned, the purpose of this paper is to propose a context-aware secure routing protocol suitable real-time services. Since such a protocol undergoes a number of independent constraints connected with: dynamic changes of the environment, assumptions concerning security, network limitations, and end-users personal requirements, the context factors need specific treatment to be real support for an optimal route selection. In the next section we propose a dedicated framework which systemizes the roles of all actors in establishing optimal secure network connection for real-time services.

2   Dedicated Context Management Framework

For the purpose of optimizing the routing protocol for real-time services we assumed a very simple model of the context management framework. It allows, except for optimization of a routing protocol, implementation of all required security services and additional application of mechanisms supporting quality of transmission which in real-time services is a crucial factor. It is usually considered either as the Quality of Service, or as the Quality of Experience, see [8,9]. The framework is shown in Figure 1; it consists of six layers, some of them applied optionally. The layers are:

- Context Establishment: it discovers context sources, measures context factors and delivers contextual information for routing and security applications;
- Context Classification: it validates context factors and builds contextual recommendations (images) for security services and routing protocols;
- Routing Protocol Selection: basing on the contextual recommendations it selects a routing protocol from some portfolio assumed (optionally, it constructs the routing protocol);
- Routing Optimization: parameters of the routing protocol are selected and appropriate protection mechanisms applied;
- Supporting Mechanisms Application: additional mechanisms supporting routing are applied (e.g., packages resending) and Quality of Protection mechanisms applied;
- Service Validation: the real-time service is validated from the point of view of the end-user, the service provider, and the network operator. If requested, the mode of operation is changed.

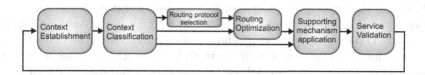

Fig. 1. Management Framework for the context-aware secure routing protocol for real-time services

The framework can work in three modes:

- Configuration mode: all layers are in action. The system is configured of significantly reconfigured;
- Unstable mode: the Routing Protocol Selection phase is omitted. The system is being protected and tuned;
- Stable mode: Routing Protocol Selection and Routing Optimization phased are omitted. The system works using its desired settings.

Each mechanism used by the Framework has been described in detail in the next chapters.

3   Context Establishment and Context Classification

Context establishment mechanism (CEM) is responsible for discovering the context sources and gathering context data. Our framework uses four main context sources:

1. User profile presented at the network registering stage. Each user, joining the network, automatically generates and sends information about used services (real-time stream types), type of the power source, remaining battery capacity, power management scheme, supported encryption mechanisms, social aspects, etc. If available, additional information, like location, mobility and preferences, can be presented. This profile can be updated at any time;
2. The data given by the service provider. Service providers are also obliged to present their profiles. Besides the aspect similar to those described in the user profile, service providers can present the additional information concerning available resources, economic aspects, types of preferred client, etc.;
3. The data provided by the reputation system. The presented framework uses the reputation system to evaluate behavior of each connected nodes. The reputation system is described in more details in Sect. 5;
4. Network analyzing mechanism. Information about network topology, links bandwidth and its reliability is generated on-line. Each node in the network (excluding energy bounded ones) periodically tests its direct link quality. The parameters like delay, jitter, packet loss ratio, and bit error rate are determined and sent to the Network Analyzing Mechanism, where network topology is updated. Based on long term observations, indices of link and node reliability are created.

After the detection process, gathered data are validated, redundant information merged and contextual space (CS), utilizing all unique context aspects (given as CA) is created. Next, depending on its nature, context aspects are classified into different classes related respectively to: network information, security scheme, social and business model, etc. In the case of incomplete information, CEM tries to determine missing data using the inherence methods (e.g. based on the type of real-time service, it is possible to determine link parameters like bandwidth, maximal acceptable transmission delay, etc.). Context aspects that cannot be assigned to a specific class are ignored.

Context itself can be classified according to several criteria (see, for example, [10]): it can be internal or external and it can be connected with entity, activity or situation. In these classes context can be considered with place, time, neighbourhood, etc. For the purpose of our paper we define three classes of context:

- The user context (UC): user expectations and recommendations, economic and social constraints, trust and reputation valuation, required protection expectation, etc.;
- The network context (NC): includes the network state, reputation of nodes and links, tests results, threats and vulnerabilities, etc.;
- The service-provider context (SC): business constraints of the service provider, reputation and trust recommendations, etc.

In the basic framework configuration, for each user $u \in U$, we distinguish the following list of factors:

- Security factor, describing the required and supported security mechanism: $S : U \rightarrow \{trans\_sec, signaling\_sec, authentication, authorization\}$;
- Network requirements related to the service used by the user: $NR : U \rightarrow \{best\_effort, max\_delay, max\_packet\_loss, max\_jitter, reliability\}$;
- Business model: $BM : U \rightarrow \{free\_acount, normal\_user, premium\_user\}$;
- Energy scheme: $ES : U \rightarrow \{energy\_aware, net\_powered\}$;
- Social aspects: $SA : U \rightarrow R \times R_{rec} \times T$, where R is a reputation score, R_{rec} recommendation reputation, and T is a trust rate.

Therefore, each user can be described with a given set of factors:

$$UC(u) = \{NR(u), S(u), BM(u), ES(u), SA(u)\}. \qquad (1)$$

The number of context classes can be also extended during the framework configuration mode, additional classes and classification rules can be added.

In the last step, to determine the contextual recommendations and requirements, particular context factors are automatically mapped into integers of range [0,4] using predefined mapping tables.

For example, in the case of packet loss, Table 1 can be used. Then, the labelled factors are divided into two groups: requirements and recommendations. Network and Service Provider context factors, requirements and recommendations are created in a similar manner.

Table 1. Example of the mapping table for packet losses

Packet loss ratio (plr)	Score
<0.001%	4
0.01% ≥ plr > 0.001%	3
0.1% ≥ plr > 0.01%	2
1% ≥ plr > 0.1%	1
>1%	0

4 Routing Protocol Selection

We present two methods of determining routing policy based on available context information. In the first method, at the configuration mode, we are build a portfolio of available routing protocols from which we can later choose the most suitable one for the given context factors. The second method, on the contrary, is able to build new routing policies on demand, accordingly to the needs defined by the context. The presented context-based framework can utilize any of those methods, however the best performance is achieved in case of the hybrid scenario. Firstly, the framework tries to select the best possible routing from the available portfolio and in the case of absence of any suitable one, a new routing scheme is constructed on demand, employing the second mechanism.

4.1 Routing Protocols Portfolio

At the configuration mode, a new routing protocol can be added to the framework. Thus, the framework can comprise many popular protocols suitable for different routing scenarios. From the logical point of view, the routing protocols can be divided into overlapping groups, based on the construction aspects:

1. Quality degradation preventing mechanisms. Real-time services are very sensitive to any degradations of link quality. Therefore, the techniques for detecting the degradation and rerouting should be supported. The routing method involving software agents to constantly control real-time transmission quality was presented in [11], while the fast path switching techniques were proposed in [12].
2. Quality-of-service (QoS). Because of the best-effort packet delivery nature of the Internet, most of the common routing protocols (RIP, OSPF, BGP) cannot guarantee the required link quality. However, within the increasing popularity of real-time services, much work has been done in implementing new QoS aware protocols, or designing the extensions to the existing ones. Services like IntServ, which allow reserving a required bandwidth on the entire path, have been presented. Overview of routing algorithms supporting QoS can be found in [13,14]
3. Power efficiency. The vast majority of popular real-time routing mechanism has no implemented power-saving mechanism. Although, a few algorithms, designed especially for battery powered nodes, like sensor networks,

have been proposed. They implement advanced sleep management techniques and/or adaptive transmission power scheme. The example of real-time power-aware routing is described in [15].

4. Security. A wide range of attack aimed at routing protocols can be performed (see Chapter 5). Different routing protocols can offer, respectively, non-security mechanism, security against eavesdropping (data encryption with or without authentication), or additional security against malicious nodes [16].

5. Path detecting method. We can distinguish between two main path detecting modes. Proactive routing – based on constant controlling the state of the network and updating the routing data. To check topicallity of each link, the regular keep alive/hello packets are sent and in the case of any changes, bringing up-to date the route is broadcasted to other network nodes. Opposite to proactive approach, in reactive routing, the new routes are discovered on demand which is more suitable for the power-aware nodes. Additionally, in specific situations, the hybrid methods can be used [17].

Besides the above listed ones, there are other parameters (optimization techniques, retransmission modes, etc.) that specific routing scheme can take into account and that can be important in a given context.

Every new protocol added to the framework has to be (manually) evaluated against each used context factors (CF). Therefore, the subsets of routing protocols suitable for secure transmission, real-time traffic, prioritized queuing, energy efficiency, etc. are constructed. For a given list to routing protocols (R) and that of context factor CF, a classification function σ is used to evaluate each protocol against a given context factor:

$$\sigma : R \times CF \to \{4, 3, 2, 1, 0\} , \qquad (2)$$

with the values corresponding to $\{very\ good, good, average, poorly, very\ poorly\}$ indicators. Additionally, to be successively applied, each protocol has to provide a set of requirements (if any), given as:

$$req := \{(cf, v) : cf \in CF\} , \qquad (3)$$

where v is a minimal value that given Network, User or Service Provider context factor (cf) has to fulfill.

Now, the Evaluated Routing Protocol Portfolio $(ERPP)$ can be defined as:

$$ERPP := \left\{ (r, \pi, req) : r \in R \wedge \pi = \left\{ \bigcup_{cf \in CF} (cf, \sigma(r, cf)) \right\} \right\} . \qquad (4)$$

We assume that on the same network infrastructure, simultaneously, many different types of real-time transmissions can be carried out. Therefore, different routing protocols can be selected for different groups of users and service providers. For each class of users, the most suitable routing protocol is chosen by using the ranking function rf defined as below:

Definition 1. *Ranking function. For a given class of users U' with their context given as $UC' \subseteq UC$, let:*

- *$SC' \subseteq SC$ be a Service-provider Context, defined for services correlated with U';*
- *CF be a list of context factors in respect of which routing protocols were evaluated;*
- *NC be a Network Context, describing actual network state;*
- *$USNr$ be a set of requirements specified by UC', SC', and NC;*
- *R being a list of all routing protocols from the portfolio;*
- *$ERPP$ Evaluated Routing Protocol Portfolio defined as (4);*
- *Routing protocol requirements (for each protocol, obtained from $ERPP$) labeled as req;*
- *$PP \in [0,1]^3$ be priority policy, specifying impotency weights for Users, Service Provider and Network Operator respectively.*

We define Ranking Function rf, as:

$$rf : UC' \times SC' \times CF \times NC \times ERPP \times R \times PP \to \mathbb{R} \cup \{null\}. \qquad (5)$$

The *rf* function works as follow:

1. Taking into account current network state (NC) and specific requirements for each routing protocol (req), a subset of possible to use routing algorithms is determined from the portfolio;
2. Each protocol determined in step 1. is evaluated by comparing the factors given in $ERPP$ to those donated by the context recommendations.

The basic example of *rf* can be given as:

$$rf(UC', SC', CF, NC, ERPP, r, PP) =$$

$$= \prod_{x \in req} p(x, UC' \cup SC' \cup NC) \prod_{y \in USNr} s(y, r, ERPP) \left(\alpha \sum_{i \in UC' \cap CF} q(\sigma(r,i), \tilde{i}) + \right.$$

$$\left. + \beta \sum_{j \in SC' \cap CF} q(\sigma(r,j), \tilde{j}) + \gamma \sum_{k \in NC \cap CF} q(\sigma(r,k), \tilde{k}) \right), \qquad (6)$$

where $\alpha, \beta, \gamma \in PP$, $\sigma(r,i)$ is the value of factor $i \in CF$ for protocol r obtained from $ERPP$ (as described in (2)) and $\tilde{i}$, $\tilde{j}$, and $\tilde{k}$ are the values of factors from UC', SC', and NC, respectively (after evaluation). Additionally we use two simple checking functions:

$$p : req \times \{UC' \cup SC' \cup NC\} \to \{1, null\} \qquad (7)$$

for checking if all requirements for protocol r are satisfied, and function

$$s : USNr \times r \times ERPP \to \{1, null\} \qquad (8)$$

for checking requirements described in User, Service and Network context. Finally, q function is used to evaluate each context factor from the routing protocol in comparison to the context recommendations. To strengthen the impact of the unmatched factors on the ranking function, the additional multiplication by 2 has been used:

$$q(a, b) = \begin{cases} a - b & \text{if } a \geq b \\ 2(a - b) & \text{if } a < b \end{cases} . \tag{9}$$

Depending on the adopted policy, routing can be e.g. user oriented (α=1, β=0, γ=0), of use other priority policy. Finally, the protocol chosen to be used is the one which maximizes the function rf over the whole space/portfolio of the routing protocols.

In the case of failure (that is, the absence of any suitable routing protocol in the portfolio), the on-demand generic routing method, described below, can be used.

Routing Selection Case Study. Because of its flexibility, the framework described in the present work can be adopted to very wide range of services and network types. To show the example configuration, a very simple case study was performed. At the beginning, six types of routing algorithms have been added to the framework:

- A – simple distance-vector based routing protocol;
- B – shortest path first (SPF) algorithm [18];
- C – QRON [19] - like B but with the additional node balance support;
- D – 1-800-OVERLAYS [20] – VoIP oriented routing protocol;
- E – routing based on higher traffic prioritization and bandwidth reservation – limited only for premium users (business oriented);
- F – routing similar to B, with the added security supports for high security level (only trusted nodes are used) and with (if required) anonymization support (Onion like).

Each of those routing algorithms has been manually evaluated (with the values from 0 to 4) over a list of context factors given in Table 2. Only one requirement

Table 2. Results of routing protocols evaluation

Context factor / Routing algorithm	A	B	C	D	E	F
Business oriented	0	0	0	0	4	0
QoS support (jitter, delay, packet loss)	1,1,1	2,2,2	2,2,2	3,2,1	4,4,4	1,2,2
Coexistence (fairness)	4	4	4	4	2	2
Node balancing support	2	3	4	3	3	2
Overhead size (bigger better)	3	2	2	1	2	2
Security (trust, reputation, anonymization)	1	2	2	2	3	4

has been set – algorithm "E", because of the additional traffic prioritization, has lower level of coexistence with other algorithms, so it can be used only for premium users. We assume 5 types of different users, with their context information given in Table 3. Also only one requirement has been set: security level 4 for secure VoIP connection.

Table 3. Different users and their context (mapped to the values 0-4)

Context User	Security requirements	Business model	QoS requirements
VoIP client normal account	2	0	3,2,1
VoIP client premium account	2	4	3,2,1
VoIP client secure connection	4	4	3,2,1
Video on Demand	1	0	2,2,2
Telemetry	3	0	1,2,4

We also assumed minimal values of context recommendation for the network operator as: 0 for business model and 2 for coexistence, node balancing, and protocol overhead size.

Finally, each of the routing algorithms has been evaluated accordingly to the users' requirements with the function (4) (as a priority policy we assumed the following values: 0.8 for the user, 0.2 for the network operator, and 0 for the service provider). The evaluation results are given in Tab 4. The selected protocols (with the biggest score) were highlighted. If two or more algorithms obtained the same score, final one is selected randomly from those with the best score. As can be observed, ranking function, based on the context information, has selected reasonable algorithms for each user class.

4.2 On-demand Generic Routing

Generic routing mechanism allows to create new routing schemas, based on the requirement specified in the context information. Firstly, using contextual recommendations about the energy scheme, a route discovering method is selected (proactive or reactive). Next, the aspects like support for packets prioritization (if context describes unequal user treatment or different business models), security scheme and optimization mechanism are selected (according to Sect. 5). Secondly, the routing scheme is determined by applying one of the two mechanisms described below.

Multi-constrained Optimization. In general, we can distinguish between two classes of parameters related with an individual link within the routing path. The first group contains the parameters that propagate in the additive way within the path. Therefore, the value of those parameters for the end-to-end path can be easily calculated as $c(p) = \sum_{l \in p} c_l$. Common parameters of

Table 4. Results of the routing algorithm evaluation for the given types of user classes

	A	B	C	D	E	F
VoIP normal	−5.6	−0.2	0	**0.2**	null	−0.8
VoIP premium	−5.6	−0.2	0	0.2	**6.4**	−0.8
VoIP secure	null	null	null	null	null	−2.4
Video on Demand	−4.2	1.4	**1.6**	0.2	null	0.8
Telemetry	−7.4	−1.8	**−1.6**	−3.0	null	**−1.6**

those types are, for example, delay, jitter, used energy or cost of other consumed resources. For instance, in the case of delay, having the mean delay $\mu_{del,l}$ and its standard distribution (jitter) $\sigma_{del,l}$ for each link l from path p, and assuming that it follows the normal distribution, the probability that end-to-end delay will exceed a given boundary can be calculated using the error function (erf) as follows:

$$P_{del\_exc} = \frac{1}{2}\left(1 - \mathrm{erf}\left(\frac{d_{ete}^{max} - \sum_{l \in p}\mu_{del,l}}{\sqrt{2}\sum_{l \in p}\mu_{del,l}}\right)\right), \qquad (10)$$

where d_{ete}^{max} is the maximum acceptable delay. This probability, often in combination with other parameters, can be then taken as one of the optimization criteria for the best path search algorithm.

Additionally, we also classify to our additive group the parameters that propagate in a multiplicative way. The reason for this is that they can be easily transferred into a sum using logarithm function. For example, an end-to-end packet loss ratio can be presented as: $e^{\sum_{l \in p}\ln(lr_l)}$, where lr_l is a packet loss ratio related to link l. On the other hand, there is also a second group of parameters, that does not follow the additive (or multiplicative) behavior, and therefore it constitutes non-additive parameters group. Those parameters are usually related to the global constraints on the path, like the minimal bandwidth, minimal supported security level or reputation of the intermediate nodes. However, from the optimization point of view, those non-additive parameters do not affect significantly the computational complexity of the path finding problem. Due to the fact, that those constraints translate to the problem of finding the path bottleneck, therefore they can be fulfilled by reducing the solution space (network structure) given by a graph $G = (E, V)$ to its subgraph $G' = (E', V')$ where $E' = \{e \in E : \forall_{i=[1...k]} c_i^e \geq L_i^{NA}\}$, L_i^{NA} for $i = 1...k$ are non-additive constrains (given by UC or SC) and c_i^e is an actual value of the parameter constrained by L_i on link given by e (from the network context NC).

On the other hand, the additive constraints form a problem, which is much harder to solve. Formerly, assuming transmission cost for each $l \in p$ link as s_l, and taking into account addictive constrains, optimal the path problem is defined as: minimization of the path cost function $S(p) = \sum_{l \in p} s_l$, while meeting all $i = 1...n$ additive constraints: $\sum_{l \in p} c_i^l \leq L_i^A$.

This optimization problem, known as a multi-constrained optimal path (MC-OP) problem, sometimes defined also as Restricted Shortest Path (RSP), is often used for finding QoS routing paths, but also applies to a wide range of other fields (like supply chain or road traffic management). However, finding the exact MCOP solution in acceptable time is possible only for small size of networks, as it was shown to be NP-complete problem [21]. Other similar cases from this class, like multi-constrained problem MCP, which finds only the feasible path, without optimization, is also known to be NP-complete. In case of small networks, the exact solution can be found using brute-force method or exact algorithms [22].

In the case of larger networks, or when the faster search time is required (for example to perform fast rerouting in the case of link failure) a wide range of approximate and heuristic algorithms can be used to solve MCOP. A detailed survey of the exact and proximate MCOP solution algorithms can be found in [22,23].

Multi-criteria Optimal Function. If additional control over the priority of optimization goals is needed, an optimization route cost function, which incorporates additional weights for each criterion, can be constructed. The following conditions on the route cost function (τ) must be fulfilled:

a) All necessary aspects related to contexts, path quality and security, as well as optimization aspects should be taken into account;
b) Each given criterion $c_{[1...n]}$ related to the context requirements (NC, UC or SC) has to be fulfilled, in other case, the function should take a value of zero (or infinity, depending on the configuration) even if all other criteria are take the maximal value:

$$\tau_p(c_1, ..., c_n) > 0 \Rightarrow \forall_{i \in [1,n]} f_p(c_i) > 0 , \tag{11}$$

where $f_p(c_i)$ is a function giving value of c_i factor for path p. It prevents from selecting the unfeasible routes, e.g. in case when the path has a good connection quality but is unsecure.

The b) implies that the function should take the form of a product rather than a sum of partial objectives. Additionally, to allow the disabling of irrelevant parameters (with cost set to zero), the individual weights may be included as exponents. Therefore, the optimization function can be written as:

$$\tau_p(c_1, ..., c_n) = \prod_{i=[1...n]} g_p(c_i)^{w_i} , \tag{12}$$

where g_p gives the exact value of c_i factor related with path p, or bonds more factors into additional optimization criterions (like probability of exceeding maximum delay given in (6)). As one can notice, defining a suitable normalized g_p function is crucial for obtaining good results. Because of the fact that τ_p is similar to MCOP problem, it is also a NC-complete. However, for the small networks, the exact optimization is possible. The examples of using a similar function for optimal routing in the wireless sensor networks can be found in [24].

5 Routing Optimization

To improve the quality of the transmission, utilization of the network resources or rerouting time, some additional optimization techniques can be used. First of all, assuming the support from the network, a centralized server can be used to collect link quality data, calculate feasible routes and send them in a secure way to other nodes. This approach allows to significantly reduce signaling data inside the network, gain faster network convergence and react faster to link failures/quality drops. Although normally centralized architectures have lower reliability levels due to the single point of failure problem, the self-healing technique [25] can be used to detect server failure, choose a new one in the process of decentralized voting and restore the necessary data.

Context information can also be used to minimize infrastructure overload. Especially, when UC and SC provided location data, users and service providers should be, if possible, paired within same Autonomous System (AS). Additionally, the optimization methods of the path length, like Shortest-Widest-Path selection [18], can be used.

Our framework supports also two mechanisms for compensating packet losses during the routing:

a) Fast retransmission mechanism (FRM) [20] proposed for P2P networks can be used to recreate packets lost during the transmission. As opposite to relatively slow retransmission known from TCP, FRM retransmission process can be significantly accelerated using the direct retransmission during routing. This mechanism works by equipping each node with a small buffer where recently relayed packets are stored. During routing, each relaying node checks the sequence number of actually routed packet, and in the case of inconsistences, request the missing packet from the directly connected neighbour.

b) Forward Error Correction (FEC) techniques can also be used to send redundant data and minimize impact of packet losses [26].

6 Routing Security

There are many types of attacks that can be conducted in order to intercept transmission or destabilize network functionality. Basically one can distinguish between:

- Passive attacks, when the attacker tries to eavesdrop the transmission without performing a harmful action;
- Active attacks, when the attacker performs various actions aimed at modification of the transmission routes, dropping packets or generating high unfeasible routing signalization (to perform DoS attack).

Wider description of the common attacks on the routing mechanisms can be found in [27]. In the case of the presented routing framework, we propose two methods that can be used to minimalize the thread associated with the presence of malicious nodes. The first mechanism utilizes the standard cryptographic methods. Therefore, all signalization data is signed using private key of the sender. Additionally, if presently used routing mechanism supports the central route management, only the central server (as described is Sect. 5) should be used for sending update info about the new routes.

On the other hand, the second mechanism utilizes the soft-security mechanism, i.e. reputation. After each transaction, directly involved nodes evaluate each othe'sr behavior. The centralized reputation system is used to collect and process the sent data. The data are aggregated using the Beta reputation scheme [28] with the additional recommendation reputation [29], describing the ability of each node to fairly evaluate others. Alternatively, if additional information about nodes trustworthiness is available, the other reputation mechanism (like Eigentrust) can be used.

The collected reputation data are used in the paths selecting mechanism, therefore the nodes labelled as dishonest can be excluded from the newly determined route. Also signaling data sent from dishonest nodes is ignored.

7 Service Validation

The presented framework provides the real-time service validation mechanisms. Each entity involved in communication (service provider, end user, and network operator) can validate the system from its point of view. The framework supports the two types of validation:

a) Automatic – the information about infrastructure efficiency (objective quality and reliability measures) as well as the ratings about entities involved in communication (reputation scores) are sent automatically by user-agents.
b) Manual – the users of the infrastructure can provide social feedback about behavior of the service. Especially, each malicious action that cannot be detected automatically, should be reported.

The reputation system is used to collect and filter out unfair votes. Then, depending on the used business model, majority, premium users or service, the providers can enforce changes in the routing used routing protocol. Especially, the different supported mechanisms can be automatically switched (like FRM and FEC).

8 Conclusions

Adapting the context-aware approach to the real-time data routing problem can bring many benefits to all entities involved in transmission. For the users, consideration of their individual context in the routing selection mechanism means better connection quality, ensured desired security level, efficient resource management (bandwidth, battery life) and possibly a wider range of supported services. From the Service Provider point of view, including the context in routing brings better optimization of infrastructure (i.e. by location-aware routing) and enlargement of the group of potential recipients. Finally, more efficient network utilization for Network Operator is obtained.

Management Framework for the context-aware secure routing protocol for real-time services, proposed in this paper, systemizes the roles of all actors in establishing optimal and secure network connection. By introducing Evaluate Routing Protocols Portfolio the standard well-known routing protocols still may be used. Furthermore, the optimization mechanism is provided, which can additionally improve transmission quality (e.g. by using fast packet retransmission). In turn, introducing the security mechanism gives additional protection against malicious peers (by using the reputation system and Service Validation stage). Finally, the Framework is easy to implement, utilizes a small amount of resources and can be easily adapted to existing infrastructures, especially those based on P2P overlay networks.

The future research will include more detailed aspect of the Framework configuration, as well as the wider range of support mechanisms. The real-life test cases (preformed on the P2P overlay network) will also be introduced.

Acknowledgments. This work is supported by the National Science Centre under Contract No. UMO-2011/01/N/ST6/07387.

References

1. MacDonald, N.: The Future of Information Security is Context-Aware and Adaptive. Gartner RAS Core Research Note G00200385 (2010)
2. Baldauf, M., Dustdar, S., Rosenberg, F.: A survey on context-aware systems. Int. J. Ad Hoc and Ubiquitous Computing 2(4) (2007)
3. Jovanovikj, V., Gabrijelcic, D., Klobucar, T.: A conceptual model of security context. Int. J. Inf. Secur. (2014), doi:10.1007/s10207-014-0229-x
4. Hayashi, E., Das, S., Shahriyar, A., Owusu, E., Han, J., Hong, J., Oakley, I., Perrig, A., Zhang, J.: CASA: A Framework for Context-Aware Scalable Authentication. In: SOUPS 2013: Proceedings of the Ninth Symposium on Usable Privacy and Secrecy, Newcastle, UK (2013)
5. Michelberger, B., Mutschler, B., Reichert, M.: A Context Framework for Process-Oriented Information Logistics. In: Abramowicz, W., Kriksciuniene, D., Sakalauskas, V. (eds.) BIS 2012. LNBIP, vol. 117, pp. 260–271. Springer, Heidelberg (2012)
6. Li, W., Joshi, A., Finn, T.: CAST: A Context-Aware Security and Trust Framework for Mobile Ad-hoc Networks Using Polices. Distributed and Parallel Databases 31(2), 353–376 (2013)
7. Kotulski, Z., Sepczuk, M., Sitek, A., Tunia, M.A.: Adaptable context management framework for secure network services – to be published (2014)
8. Fiedler, M., Hossfeld, T., Tran-Gia, P.: A generic quantitative relationship between quality of experience and quality of service. IEEE Network 24(2), 36–41 (2010)
9. Ciszkowski, T., Mazurczyk, W., Kotulski, Z., Hossfeld, T., Fiedler, M., Collange, D.: Towards Quality of Experience-based Reputation Models for Future Web Service Provisioning. Telecommunication Systems 51(4), 283–295 (2012)
10. Wrona, K., Gomez, L.: Context-aware security and secure context-awareness in ubiquitous computing environments. Annales UMCS Informatica AI4, 332–348 (2006)

11. Oryńczak, G., Kotulski, Z.: Agent based infrastructure for real-time applications. Annales UMCS, Informatica 11(4), 33–47 (2011)
12. Tao, S., Xu, K., Estepa, A., Gao, T.F.L., Guerin, R., Kurose, J., Towsley, D., Zhang, Z.-L.: Improving VoIP quality through path switching. In: 24th Annual Joint Conference of the IEEE Computer and Communications Societies, INFOCOM 2005. Proceedings IEEE, vol. 4. IEEE (2005)
13. Chen, X., Wang, C., Xuan, D., Li, Z., Min, Y., Zhao, W.: Survey on QoS Management of VoIP. In: International Conference on Computer Networks and Mobile Computing (ICCNMC 2003), IEEE (2003)
14. Aurrecoechea, C., Campbell, A.T., Hauw, L.: A survey of QoS architectures. Multimedia Systems 6(3), 138–151 (1998)
15. Chipara, O., He, Z., Xing, G., Chen, Q., Wang, X., Lu, C., Stankovic, J., Abdelzaher, T.: Real-time power-aware routing in sensor networks. In: Proceeding of the 14th IEEE International Workshop on Quality of Service (IWQoS). IEEE (2006)
16. Zapata, M.G., Asokan, N.: Securing ad hoc routing protocols. In: Proceedings of the 1st ACM Workshop on Wireless Security. ACM (2002)
17. Haas, Z.J., Pearlman, M.R., Samar, P.: The zone routing protocol (ZRP) for Ad-hoc networks. In: Proceedings of the 55th Internet Engineering Task Force (2002)
18. Ma, Q., Steenkiste, P.: On path selection for traffic with bandwidth guarantees. In: Proceedings of the 1997 International Conference on Network, ICNP 1997, p. 191. IEEE Computer Society, Washington, DC (1997)
19. Li, Z., Mohapatra, P.: QRON: QoS-aware routing in overlay networks. IEEE Journal on Selected Areas in Communications 22(1), 29–40 (2004)
20. Amir, Y., Danilov, C., Goose, S., Hedqvist, D., Terzis, A.: An overlay architecture for high-quality VoIP streams. IEEE Transactions on Multimedia 8(6), 1250–1262 (2006)
21. Garey, M.R., Johnson, D.S.: Computers and Intractability: A Guide to the Theory of NP-Completeness. Freeman, San Francisco (1979)
22. Garroppo, R.G., Giordano, S., Tavanti, L.: A survey on multi-constrained optimal path computation: Exact and approximate algorithms. Computer Networks 54(17), 3081–3107 (2010)
23. Kuipers, F., Van Mieghem, P., Korkmaz, T., Krunz, M.: An overview of constraint-based path selection algorithms for QoS routing. IEEE Communications Magazine 40(12), 50–55 (2002)
24. Wenning, B.L., Pesch, D., Timm-Giel, A., Görg, C.: Environmental monitoring aware routing in wireless sensor networks. Wireless and Mobile Networking 284, 5–16 (2008)
25. Oryńczak, G., Kotulski, Z.: Notary-based self-healing mechanism for centralized peer-to-peer infrastructures. Annales UMCS, Informatica 12(4), 97–112 (2012)
26. Nafaa, A., Taleb, T., Murphy, L.: Forward error correction strategies for media streaming over wireless networks. IEEE Communications Magazine 46(1), 72 (2008)
27. Abusalah, L., Khokhar, A., Guizani, M.: A survey of secure mobile ad hoc routing protocols. IEEE Communications Surveys & Tutorials 10(4), 78–93 (2008)
28. Jøsang, A., Roslan, I.: The beta reputation system. In: Proceedings of the 15th Bled Electronic Commerce Conference (2002)
29. Liu, J., Issarny, V.: Enhanced Reputation Mechanism for Mobile Ad Hoc Networks. In: Jensen, C., Poslad, S., Dimitrakos, T. (eds.) iTrust 2004. LNCS, vol. 2995, pp. 48–62. Springer, Heidelberg (2004)

Author Index